Education under Islam

Education Under Islam

S.Z. Rahman

Reference Press

4831/24, Ansari Road
Darya Ganj
New Delhi-110 002
Phone: 51563444
Fax: 51563334
E-mail: info@essessreference.com
url: http://www.essessreference.com

First Published 2005

ISBN: 81-88583-82-0

Rs.750/-

Published by:
Reference Press
4831/24, Ansari Road, Darya Ganj,
New Delhi-110 002.
Phone: 51563444
Fax: 51563334
E-mail: info@essessreference.com
url: http://www.essessreference.com

Printed in India at:
Mehra Offset Press, New Delhi

Contents

Preface

Islam makes it mandatory for its followers to seek knowledge and travel to distant lands, in search of it. Holy Quran says that God has given us knowledge and skill to grab it and impart it to others also. Quranic commands are enthusiastic to provide the people, with such knowledge, so that he could be able to make distinction between good and evil and could emerge out successfully, shaping his life in a better way. Islam showers on its followers, varied ideas and knowledge in terms of education. It teaches them a substantial lesson, regarding morality of masses. Islam has a modern outlook for education. It lays emphasis on enriching a child with education

For this purpose, Islam holds parents, teachers, rulers and the government, equally liable to take the responsibility to provide useful and better education to the children. Islam talks about a specific budget and allocation of funds for education and also calls for a perfect assessment system. In Islam for imparting education, the role of parents and teachers has been defined, with a belief that a child learns his first lesson from his mother only.

It is deliberately expected that this work will certainly help the readers to know in detail about the education system under Islam. The suggestions for improvement of all sorts in this regard are cordially solicited.

Author

1

Historical Backdrop

The Quran throws interesting light on the nature of man "Verily we have created many? Ahsan-i-Taqwim"' (according to the best of the plan). The term 'Taqwim 'has the same derivation as that of 'Qayyim' the adjective used for the true faith. 'Verily this is 'Din-al-Qayyim' (the straight faith). Hence according to the Quran the essence of the true faith and that of human nature is derived from the same foundations.

Various Stages of Education

The Quran also reveals the stages of the development and perfection of human nature as it passed through the hands of the Creator. 'Fa sawwaka' (he has equipoised you). 'Fa Adalaka' 'he made you equable or tempered you.' Elsewhere 'wa alladzi Qaddara (and He who has set you according to a measure).

And then last of all 'Fa hada' (Verily He has shown the right path).

All these stages lead ultimately to the final climax of perfection 'Ahsan Taqwim.'

God has imparted to man knowledge of Evil and Good (*Fujuraha wa Taqwaha*) and after subjecting him to these various stages God has ultimately given him the Freedom of Choice to select between Good and Evil "Verily one who purifies his Nafs is redeemed and one who soils it is condemned." (*Qad Aflaha man Zakkaha wa Qad Khaba man dassaha.*)

Original Shape

According to a well known Tradition of the Prophet all children are born according to nature (Fitrat) and it is the parents who turn them into a Jew, a Christian or a Magian. They are born whole just as one quadruped brings forth another quadruped in whole; then he asked, "Do you find them ever crop-earred?" On another occasion he added, "They are born like the camel. Do you find them crop earred unless you cut them off yourself?"

In the light of the above Tradition all children are born according to Nature, but how are we going to interpret the term nature in this context? It is not merely the physical nature of Rousseau which is governed by the laws of physical life. The Muslim thinkers recognise the baser aspects of the nature of Man. But the above Tradition must be interpreted, according to Abu Hurrayrah, the authority in this case, according to the Quranic verse that runs as follows: "The nature (Fitrat) after which God has created beings would not change; this (Fitrat) is true religion." This meaning is supported by another verse from the Quran which gives the text of the Primal Covenant which Man made with his Creator. When Lord put the question. "Am I your Lord?" All of them replied, "Yes."

The Roots

Hence there lies buried in man the seed of ultimate Good from eternity. In the words of Ghazzali, it is as natural for man to know the Divine as his acceptance of the simple mathematical truth that two is bigger than one. He might not have heard this statement from another previously or affirmed it with his own tongue before; yet his inner self is brimming over with its recognition and acceptance. The function of the Prophet is to awaken his people to its realisation in thought and action."

Role in Society

The above Tradition is concerned with the thought aspect of the process while another throws light on the practical aspect of human development. The term Fitrat is used in a different way elsewhere with a social and practical bearing. In some of the Traditions contained in the Chapters on Purification (Taharat) occurs the text, "Ten things belong to Fitrat, hair cutting, nail cutting etc." These Traditions describe five to ten things pertaining to the cleanliness of the body and social usages sanctioned and approved through centuries old practice. Fitrat implies not only the innate capacity of recognising the Ultimate Good but also realising it through socialised efforts under the guidance of a Prophet. True education is therefore not possible in isolation; the process continues from one age to another in a social atmosphere and in a social context.

The positive aspect of the social influence is symbolised by the Prophet who presents the ultimate values of life in a concrete and palpable form while the negative aspect is represented by the 'Ear cropping' business of society referred in the above Tradition. The society can make as well mar human nature; it may burnish the original steel till it becomes dazzling bright and mirrors the entire universe in it may soil its surface and deface it beyond all recognition.

Non-aligned Character : Such a conception of human nature implies that man if left to his own resources, even in an environment isolated from social influences, could discover through trial and error and intuition those ultimate values of moral life which form the foundation of Islamic thought and practice. The Tradition appears to have influenced philosophic thought in later periods and the Romance of Hayy bin Ziqan is most probably inspired directly by the Quran and the Traditions. The hero of the romance is left stranded on an isolated island, in circumstances strongly reminiscent of Rousseau's Emile who is segregated in a country-house on purpose under the supervision of a tutor and is directed by the forces of nature to discover for himself the highest laws of ethics, metaphysics and sociology. Nature functions as a Mentor in the case of Hayy the hero of Ibn Tufayl's romance while nature under the eliminative and selective direction of the tutor is the moulding force in Rousseau's Emile. The nature of Ibn Tufail and the process of Negative Education in the case of Rousseau is replaced by something more positive and constructive in the Islamic teachings which may be styled Positive Education as it does not reject outright the rich heritage of humanity which has come to us from times immemorial.

Gold and Silver : The modern psychologist may interpret the term Fitrat occurring in the Traditions according to his own ideas. He may read into them the fundamental principle of Individual Psychology that every child is gifted with instincts, innate tendencies and temperamental qualities peculiar to himself and the primary function of education is to discover them and make the most of them in building up the child's personality. A more comprehensive study of the Traditions bears out the Prophet's refreshing optimism about human nature and his heartening faith in the good that lay in man. In one of his sayings he compares men to mines of gold and silver uncut diamonds waiting only for a skilful polisher to release their glorious radiations into the four quarters of the globe.

Nature of the Child : As for the children he had supreme faith in them because of the possibility of development and the promise of improvement in coming years; his view of their nature was also determined by his charitable disposition and great affection for them.

Faith in Childhood : The Prophet had a tremendous faith in the strength that lay in innocence and the children in his opinion could tempt the devil to dangerous extremes with perfect immunity. According to a Tradition received on the authority of Abu-al-Darda', the Prophet threatened to pillory the Evil One to a column in the mosque and leave him to the tender mercies of the children of Medina, so that they may sport with him as a plaything at day break, certainly a fair present for the 'little angels' to ride as a hobby horse and twist his tail ever so merrily. He relaxed the rigour of injunctions on purification in the case of a person whose clothes had been soiled by the urination of baby; he would sprinkle water over the spot after such a domestic accident and offer his prayers without much ado.'

In the face of these facts and religious observances, we can affirm that in his opinion a child was not the seedbed of evil or a fountain head of pollution. The same faith in the inherent Good of the child is met with in the sayings of his Companions also. Abdullah b. 'Umar when they came across a tiny little girl who was singing ever so merrily; thereupon Ibn 'Umar said, "If ever the Evil One would leave any one in peace, it would be this girl."

A problem which is allied with the above discussion is about the end of the children of the unbelievers who die young. In more than one Tradition from different sources, the Prophet appears to have maintained an eloquent silence over the query and his reply has been invariably as follows, "Only God knows what he (child) would have turned out later on," which is interpreted in the sense that he has been saved for the present although nobody except God knew what was in store for him if he had attained the age of maturity. In fact, he along with his Companions had a great charity of heart for children which was often expressed in beautiful language when they came to know of the death of a child. Once Aishah heard about the demise of a child and gave way to her grief in the following words, "Blessed is the child because he would be a bird among the birds of Heaven. He did no sin neither did he attain to the age of discretion."

It would be interesting to study the conception of child mind according to St. Mark and the thinkers of the patristic period and the Middle Ages in comparison with above. The doctrine of the Fall, the Original Sin of Adam, implying the innate Evil that lies in human nature was formulated by St. Paul and supported by others. According to St. Augustine, even unbaptised infants incurred damnation—so complete is the depravity introduced in the nature of man by Adam's Fall.

The idea of the Original Sin in man cast a sinister shadow over the schools of Medieval Europe where a Biblical sanction was placed on corporal punishment. The monasteries transformed themselves into so many prison-houses for young souls, gloomy cells wherefrom day to day the 'little Satan hiding somewhere inside the child was exercised with the help of the birchrod. The Middle Ages have passed but the tradition of corporal punishment hallowed by centuries long practice has persisted with a malignant tenacity in the school world.

What is in brief the chief distinction between the thinkers of the patristic period and the Prophet on the vital problem of education and the nature of man?

In one case the child is believed to have his birth in sin whose shadows chase him throughout his life; in the other, the child is perfectly immune from the Evil One, so fortified is he in the strength which lay in innocence, nay he could play the dare devil with the Evil One; he could tweak his nose and twist his tail ever so merrily and by a single joyful note of his song, he could drive away any number of Evil Ones.

Such a supreme confidence in Human Good in the earliest years found a practical and eloquent expression in one of the Traditions where he enjoins upon the Faithful to honour their progeny (Akrama is the term used by the Prophet), meaning thereby that we should learn to respect the personality of the child, have a delicate regard for his feelings and provide proper avenues for the exercise of his innate capacities and aptitudes.

2

Roots of Education

Traditions have a unique importance as a branch of study in the history of Islamic education. It has the distinction of being the first branch of learning to be taught in the mosque circles in Islam. The subject was instrumental in initiating a variety of methods for the technique of teaching which included both the oral and the textbook lesson. Starting with the oral lesson, it developed finally into the textbook method, a transition which was an important landmark in the history of methodology and which profoundly influenced the technique of teaching in other subjects also.

Not a Preserve of the Elite : Again the Traditions was one of those branches which were not the preserve of the intellectual elite. When taught orally, its classes were attended by the masses and sometimes these gatherings exceeded a hundred thousand souls. This huge congregation was taught with the help of a large number of Mustamali or lecture assistants and Muid. Through such huge audiences this branch of learning acquired a popular appeal denied to other subjects.

Degrees and Diplomas : It is interesting to learn that the method of teaching traditions was directly responsible for the introduction of the ceremony of convocation and the conferment of a variety of degrees and diplomas (Ijazah) in Islamic Education.

The various kinds of Diplomas awarded for proficiency in Traditions have been listed up by the Books on Ilm al-Hadith Ibn

Salah and Abu Bakr Khatib-al-Baghdadi have devoted whole chapters to them in their works entitled Muqaddimah and Kifaya.

These diplomas varied according to the nature of the method adopted by the teacher in imparting knowledge. The system helped in developing a rich variety of approach in the technique of teaching and their adaptation to the needs and standards of individual pupils.

Abu Bakr Baghdadi lists up a number of diplomas under this heading.

Kinds of Ijazah : The highest Ijazah according to him is the Manawalah. In this case the teacher hands over to the pupil a book written in his own hand and says "This is my sama from so and so and you are permitted to relate it on my authority." The second variety is inferior to Manawalah. In this case a book (Sahifah) is transcribed by the teacher with the condition that the pupil is permitted to relate whatever he has learnt correctly from the traditions. In the third kind of Ijazah, the teacher sends his permission in writing.

Then there is the Ijazah by Mukatibah. He gives five kinds of Ijazah in all.

Religious Sanction for the Ijazah : It is interesting to learn that Abu Bakr al-Baghdadi traces the religious sanction for the Ijazah from a tradition of the Prophet on Mughazi which he had delivered in writing to Abdullah bin Jalish when he sent him along with a party to the suburbs of Nakhlah and instructed him not to break the seal before he had travelled two days journey.

In another case the Prophet had sent the sura of Barat as inscribed in a book and sent it through Ali to Mecca who opened it there and read it out to the people. In that way the written word received the same authority as that of the spoken word. The written order was as obligatory as the oral order.

These examples set the vogue of textbook lessons where instead of depending entirely on the oral words of the teacher they had recourse to the textbook. It gave not only a stability to knowledge but also to the traditions of imparting knowledge.

Traditions Enrich the Curriculum : This subject enriched the curriculum by introducing a number of subsidiary branches like

Usual-al-Hadith, the science of Higher criticism (Jarh wa Tadib) and Asam-al-Rajal (Biography).

It would be out of place to discuss at length the tremendous work that the scholars have done in connection with the preservation of the text and their critical and scientific appraisal on the basis of internal and external evidence. The study has given rise to the growth of a multifarious variety of branches dealing with classifications of Hadith, The Asnads, Urn al-Rawayat (science of external evidence), Ilm al-Darayah (science of internal evidence). Ilm al-Nasikh-wal-Mansukh (abrogation) Ilm al-Mawdhuat (Fabrications), Ilm Tashif al-Asma (corrupting the names of the narrators), etc.

Out of the sciences, that developed out of the study of Traditions, namely Ilm Asma al-Rijal had a profound influence in giving an impetus to the growth of biographical and historical literature in the Islamic world.

Five Hundred Thousand Biographies : According to Dr. Sprenger; the well known orientalist who had edited Asabah of Ibn Hajar, there is hardly any nation in the past or in the present which created such a magnificent science as Asma-al-Rajal that has preserved the biographies of five hundred thousand narrators.

Some of the most voluminous histories like Tarikh al-Baghdadi by Khatib Baghdadi is a direct outcome of the study. The labour and effort brought to bear upon the subject is stupendous and stands unrivalled in the history of authorship.

Certain titles and degrees conferred on the scholars of the subject reveal the magnificent scope of achievement in this subject.

Titles for the Traditionist : According to the current terminology of Ilm al-Hadith, a person who has learnt one hundred thousand Traditions by heart, is called Hakim and one who has memorised three hundred thousand traditions was styled as Hujjat. A savant who knew all the narrated Traditions, with their text, chain of narrators, their criticism both for and against and its chronological data was called Hakim.

Rigorous Standards of Higher Criticism : In spite of aphorismic literature and considerable circulation of spurious traditions, there is no doubt that the annals of historical scholarship have seldom witnessed such rigorous standards of critical study and standardisation of the authenticity of historical facts.

Usually the historian states facts on his personal authority or at best mentions an authority who relates the event on hearsay. The stupendous task of mentioning not only the name of a single narrator but a whole chain of them, along with sufficient evidence to testify that each one of them satisfied certain criteria of reliability is an approach which was established in the academic world only through a study of the Traditions of the Prophet. The system of Asnad in its very essence was a genuine attempt to preserve and maintain the authenticity of the Traditions of the Prophet.

An Experiment in Source Method : Although primarily meant for the faithful preservation of the text of the Traditions, it was accepted as a scientific method for ensuring the authenticity of historical facts in other branches of learning also. The chain of narrators became a feature in the sphere of Political History, Fiqh, Exegesis, Literature and Grammar and was followed with a considerable degree of consistency in the field of secular education.

Presents a Picture of the Period : As a record of historical facts, the Traditions provide a rich source material for the presentation of the true picture of the social, cultural and economic conditions of the period. They lend that deeply human colour to the historical description that is conspicuous by its absence in books of history. It gave rise to biographical literature in the form of Asma al Rajal and this valuable branch of study concerned itself not with the life of the courts and kings but those of men who belonged to the masses and who lived their lives in the seething welter of humanity which surged and heaved in the market place and in the countryside.

Studying a Vertical Section of Society : And through the chain of traditions, a single narration could provide to a discerning pupil, a vertical section of the society through the ages, right from the time of the Prophet to the contemporary period. The study provided sidelights on the character and personality of the narrators belonging to different periods and gave some idea of the cross sectional view of the historical events as well.

Heuristic Method in History : For one who is interested in the exercise of heuristic method, in the field of historical knowledge.

Traditions provide an enormously rich field of interest. They present to the student of history research problems as regards the chain of Asnad, character and personalities of individual narrators, their chronological data and sequence, their preferences and prejudices, the political, social and other beliefs of their periods, their reactions to those beliefs of their periods, their reactions to those beliefs and a thousand other collateral problems.

There is no doubt that this critical and scientific approach to the scrutiny of historical material paved the way to that mental and moral discipline which produced great historians like Ibn Maskwayh, Ibn Khaldun and Al-Bayruni.

Traditions and the Quran : Traditions not only explain and amplify the Quranic text but they also supplement in many cases the injunctions laid down in the Quran.

The books of Traditions invariably contain a chapter on Exegesis (Tafsir) which provides the human background for the text and throws light on the particular occasion for the revelation of a Quranic verse and every good teacher knows how these minor details, these soft human touches, the historical, social and human associations of the piece illumine the meaning and impress it on the mind of the pupil in its proper human setting.

Perpetuates the Moral Attitude : Not only does it pave the way for a clearer comprehension of the text but it also enriches the mind and perpetuates the moral attitude that the verse intends to cultivate.

For instance the rugged grandeur, the fiery, awesome eloquence and the denunciatory style of some of the Suras in chapter 30th of the Quran cannot be fully appreciated until one has the picture of the small persecuted group of Muslims in Mecca and the heroic struggle that they had to put up against heavy odds.

Ammar of the Traditions : And when one reads the simple verse of the Quran "except those who have been forced to do so," one can hardly picture to his mind. Poor Ammar coming with tears rolling down his shaggy beard and the Prophet wiping them with a kind wave of the hand and saying "Never mind, you were forced to say so." Ammar, the son of a slave was subjected to extreme punishment by the Quraish who seemed to be past masters in third degree methods and had forced him to repeat words expressing the denunciation of the Prophet, after them.

And who could read the great sorrow which sat like the pall of death over Kaab bin Malik, the poet who had not joined the Tabuk campaign from the verses of the Quran. His deep sense of desolation, the great wilderness of the soul in which he was lost, his ecstatic joy on the reprieve, as described in the Traditions, all present a richly emotional background for the events which are narrated with economy of word and description in the Quran. These and hundreds of other details are provided by the traditional literature. As regards Ahkam or religious injunctions, the Traditions not only amplify and supplement, they also clarify and explain.

The Black Thread and the White : The similes and the metaphors used by the Quran were sometimes interpreted in a ridiculously objective manner by the Arab of the desert and such misunderstandings could be removed only by their further amplifications as supplied by Traditional literature.

This aspect may be illustrated by an interesting episode of the lifetime of the Prophet. When the divine commandment for fasting was revealed for the first time and the hours of the fast were appointed by the following verse of the Holy Quran: "When appears to you clearly the white thread out of the black one", Adi, the son of the famous Hatim, a Companion, took the verse in a literal sense and kept two threads, one black and another white, in order to be more exact about the time for keeping fast.

When he mentioned it to the Prophet in the morning, the latter told him that the Quranic text implies the light of the morning by white and the darkness of the night by black.

Traditions Supplement the Quran : The Traditions not only explain but supplement in a large number of cases, the text of the Quran. For instance, the chapters on ablutions, prayers, fastings, Hajj and others provide several essential details which are not available in the Quran. In other cases like Zakat, business transactions and other matters the detailed injunctions can be found in the Traditions only. The Prophet's instructions on Zakat were contained in the numerous epistles he had despatched to his officers like Maadh bin Jabal, the Qadi of Yemen, and Abu Bakr bin Hazm of Bahrayn. They are found also in letters of authority which he bestowed on the tribal chiefs like Wail bin Al Hajar the Prince of Hadhramut. It contains details of taxes on goats, camels, vegetables, etc.

There were cases in early Islam when a religious decree was issued exclusively on the basis of a tradition of the Prophet.

Divine Wisdom

Such is the case of the share of the grandmother on the father's side in the legacy, left by the grandson.

When a grandmother sought Abu Bakr's decision on her share Abu Bakr replied that he did not know of any decree on the subject in the Quran and that he did not know whether the Prophet gave any ruling concerning the subject.

Then Mughirah stood up and said that the Prophet had ordered one sixth share for the grandmother. Abu Bakr called for further evidence and Muhammad bin Muslim supported the statement of Mughirah. Thereupon he issued orders accordingly.

Personal Verification of Traditions : The verification in person of a particular tradition had become a common practice even in the days of the first cycle of the Prophet's descendants and his companions would take upon themselves long and arduous journeys in order to acquire the certification of a tradition.

A companion went all the way to Egypt to verify a tradition from Fudhalah bin Ubaid the governor of the province.

Jabir bin Abdullah, another well known Companion, took one month's long journey to obtain the certification of a tradition on Qisas (blood money) from Abdullah bin Unays Juhanni in Egypt. According to Abu al-Abbyah, we used to listen to the Rawayat of the Companions at Basra and we would travel all the way to Medina for their verification from the Companions themselves.

Verification Takes up a Legal Form: With Abu Bakr and Umar, verification took a regular legal form and any tradition narrated by a person had to be confirmed by a number of witnesses. Abu Bakr had called for witnesses as regards the tradition on the share of the grandmother.

Umar took even a more serious view of the whole affair. When Abu Musa al Ashaari called on him and withdrew after seeking permission for admission for three times he asked him the reason whereupon Abu Musa quoted a Hadith. Umar caught hold of him very nearly as one would secure a criminal and brought him to the mosque. He was released only when some companions including Abu Dhar Ghaffari confirmed the tradition, Umar explained that he did not desire to accuse him but he wanted to be extremely cautious for purposes of verification.

Umar Decides on the Basis of a Tradition : When Umar declared his intention of extending the area of the Prophet's mosque, he bought off all the houses adjacent to it with the exception of the Houses of the Prophet's wives and that of Abbas who refused point-blank to sell the property. The matter was referred to Ubayy bin Kaab who decided in favour of Abbas and he quoted in this context a tradition of the Prophet in which he had related how David desired to plan the Holy temple in the form of square and seriously contemplated to take over the house of a person that was included in the marked area by force. But he was ordained by God not to do so.

When Umar heard the Tradition, he caught hold of his undergarment and brought him to the Prophet's mosque where three of the companions present on the occasion confirmed the narration of Ubay. The witnesses included Abu Dhar. It is needless to add that Abbas gave away his house as a free gift after this altercation.

Narrators under Trial : The same narrator was tested again after the lapse of a fairly long interval of one year or more and a careful comparison made between the two versions. This method of testing the reliability of individual narrators had been set in vogue right from the earliest days.

Aishah was extremely careful in such matters and whenever a Tradition was related in her presence she would ask the narrator to repeat it after a pretty long interval in order to find out whether there were any variations.

Once she asked Abdullah bin Amr bin Abi-al-Ath to repeat a Tradition after one year and he rendered the words exactly. Aishah expressed high approach of such a faithful rendering.

How Abu Hurrayrah was Examined : One of the Amirs sent for Abu Hurrayrah and asked him to narrate a certain Tradition. Meanwhile he had secreted a scribe who took down all that Abu Hurrayrah narrated. He was asked again to narrate the same traditions after one year and when the text was compared with the previous one, there were no additions, no abbreviations, no Qadm, nor Akhar (change in order).

One of the Caliphs put Imam Zahri to a similar test. He asked Zahri to dictate four hundred Traditions to one of his sons and after some time it was reported to him that the book had been lost. Zahri sent for a scribe and once more dictated the same traditions. When the two manuscripts were compared there was not the difference of a single letter.

Higher Criticism on Historical Basis : The systematic and scientific study of biographical literature with special reference to the Traditions (Asma-al-Rijal) helped considerably in a critical assessment of the Traditions because a comparative study of the time and date of two narrators could easily reveal whether the fact of narration was physically possible in the chronological sense.

When a Dead Man was Made to Rise : The more objective compilers who had a keener consciousness of chronology would often reject traditions on this ground.

Imam Muslim instances in his Muqaddimah (Foreword) the case of a narrator who told that Abdullah bin Masud had participated in the battle of Siffin. But Abu Nairn to whom this tradition was being related turned upon the narrator and said, "Did Ibn Masud arise from his grave to join the battle."

In fact, Ibn Masud had died in 32 or 33 A.H., during the period of Uthman (R.A.A.), while the Battle of Siffin had been fought in the days of Ali (R.A.A.).

When a person related a tradition to Imam Abdullah Hakim which he had heard from a narrator in a particular year, Hakim who was teaching his class turned to his pupils and said, "Here is a prodigy. He has heard this tradition from a person seven years after his death".

Anachronism under Fire : The period and the life events of the narrators who were associated with a particular tradition were brought under the searching fire of scrutiny and cases of anachronism were discovered through tests of chronology.

Once Umar bin Musa bin Wajih narrated something on the authority of one Khalid bin Madan. He was asked when he met Khalid. He told that he saw him in 158 A.H., during the campaign of Armenia. Thereupon he was told that he should not tell lies because Khalid died In 154 A.H., and at the top of it, he never joined the Armenian campaign.

Jews Fake a Document : A historic example of this kind of criticism is the faked document alleged to have been granted to the Jews of Khyber by which they had been exempted from the *Jizya* (Poll tax) and forced labour. Fortunately the great Traditionist Abu Bakr Khatib al-Baghdadi was still alive in those days. The document was rejected on grounds that were essentially chronological.

One of the witnesses mentioned in the document was Saad bin Maadh who had died immediately after the Battle of the Ditch and this happened fairly long before the Expedition to Khyber. Again the Agreement was alleged to have been written by Muawiyyah bin Abi Sufiyan who had not entered the fold of Islam at that time.

Points at Issue : It would be interesting to study the points raised by Mulla Ali Qari on this fabricated document in greater details:

1. It is witnessed by Saad bin Muadh who died immediately after the Battle of the Ditch.
2. It was alleged to be in the hand of Muawiyyah who embraced Islam subsequent to the Khyber campaign. He became a Muslim in the year of the fall of Mecca.
3. The Jizya was levied after the Battle of Tabuk, an event much later than the Fall of Khyber.
4. The document mentioned remission from forced labour, a practice unknown in the days of the Prophet.
5. The people of Khyber could not be granted a remission of the Jizya because of their hostility to Islam.
6. Their hostile attitude towards Islam is proved by their expulsion from Arabia.

And not only the text of a tradition but the character and reputation of individual members of the chain of Asnaad did not escape the searchlight of scrutiny.

X-raying the Narrator's Personality : They would make a thorough investigation into the character and personality of a person before accepting a narration from him, "When we intended to acquire a tradition from a person, we enquired so much about him that people began to wonder whether we were going to arrange for his marriage ceremony". The compilers of standard collections took great pains in ascertaining the reliability of individual narrators and Imam Bukhari took a good deal of care in this respect. In his great wanderings which he made for compiling his work he would begin with a thorough enquiry about the reliability of the person from whom he desired to acquire a Tradition and did not make a request for narration until he had satisfied himself about the integrity of his character and his dealings in his daily life. He would refuse to rely on a person if he found him remissive even in the most insignificant details of daily duties.

The method of verification was followed with amazing single mindedness by scholars in the later period.

It is interesting to discover the tremendous pains which these researchers took in verifying traditions. A person went to Madain, Wasit, Basrah, and Abadan for confirming a single Tradition and found out ultimately that it was a concoction made by a saintly person who desired to popularise the reading of the Quran. This faked tradition pertained to the excellences of the reading of Quran.

A Public Test for Imam Bukhari : Sometimes the verification took the form of a public test. According to Khatib Baghdadi, Imam Bukhari was given a public test at Baghdad. One hundred Traditions were selected for this purpose. The Asnad of the traditions were mixed up and ten persons were selected to narrate ten traditions out of them in the presence of Bukhari. To each of these narrators he replied, "I do not know", and when they had finished, he took the traditions one by one, and narrated the Asnad in the correct order.

There is evidence to show that the historical validity of the narrators came under the searching of scrutiny quite early. According to Hassan bin Thabit, we did not find anything more useful against concoction than history. I usually enquire about the period of his (narrator's) date of birth and this helps us in distinguishing the true from the false.

It is said that when Hassan bin Rabi' visited Baghdad he was much sought after by the students of Tradition, and he received a visit from Imam Ahmad bin Hanbal.

The first question that he put to him was "When did Abdullah bin Mubarak die?" And when he was asked why had he put the question, he told that he desired to find out whether the man was a fabricator of Traditions.

A Common Charge : A common charge levelled against Traditions is that they emphasize only the reliability of the Asnad or the narrators, and discuss merits and demerits of individual narrators but they conveniently ignore the text of the tradition and would credit the most absurd statements provided they are made on the authority of Asnads which are reliable. According to Lammens, unilateral criticism confines itself to setting the degree of credibility of the attestors and the possibility of their meeting. Beyond this, it leaves in suspense the very essence of the debate namely the judgement to be passed on the value of the tradition, that is to say the matn.'

According to another critic, Hadith was not criticised from the point of view of what was inherently reasonable and to be regarded as worthy of credence, but for a consideration of the reputation which the guarantors of the tradition bore." But he recognises its restraining influence over a purely subjective approach." However, the doctrine may have had a restraining influence on purely subjective criticism, for quite early it had been extended to cover the sphere of Hadith and what the community agreed upon was above serious questioning.

Rawayat and Darayat : One must concede that the scholars of traditions have been mainly occupied by the Problem of Rawayat but there is hardly any justification for the charge that they had ruled Darayat altogether out of court. Books on Mawdhuat (spurious traditions) list up the criteria for the acceptance or rejection of the matn (text) of a tradition on the principles of Darayat.

Criterion of Reason: Ibn Jawzi sums up his views on the subject as follows:

"Whenever you come across a tradition which runs counter to reason on established axiom, you should reject it as spurious. There is no need of discussing the reliability of its asnad. It should be rejected if it is repugnant to feeling and observation or contradictory to the Quran, the Repeated (Mutawatir) traditions, or Ijma". It is untenable if it lays down a disproportionately heavy penalty for minor lapses or awards too great a merit for small actions as is the usual custom with the Qass (the class of story tellers). It should be rejected also if it is against reason and is irrational. (laghw).

Rational Basis of Higher Criticism : A critical analysis of these principles would reveal the importance that the doctors of Hadith attached to higher criticism as based on reason and critical judgement, common experience and observation, its language and style and its agreement with the Quran and traditions of recognised reliability. For instance according to Bukhari, Adam was sixty yards in stature. Ibn Hajar the commentator of Bukhari remarks that a study of the archaeological remains of the ruins of ancient people like Thamud reveal that they were not of extraordinary dimensions.

Traditions which ran counter to every day experience or common observation were also rejected as spurious. According to Mulla Ali Qari all Traditions forecasting coming events with exact dates should be rejected. Traditions that state the age of earth to be seven thousand years have been also rejected on the same ground.

Traditions are rejected on the basis of their language and style as well.

The Criterion of Language and Style : A person who has made an intensive study of the traditions and is impregnated with its linguistic discipline is able to discriminate the spurious tradition from the genuine, after an analysis of its linguistic form and structure, one of the most obvious criterion in such cases being the occurrence of the uncommon, outlandish words or those which are alien to the genius of its style. For instance, Suyuti rejected the well known tradition in which the Faithful is exhorted to seek knowledge even if it is to be met with in China. He had rejected it most probably on account of the use of such a rare and uncommon word as as-Sin (China).

The authorities on traditions hold that the study of the subject provides an intuitive discipline of its own which helps a student of the subject to discriminate a genuine tradition from the false.

When Hafiz Ibn Qayyim was asked whether a person could discover a false tradition without referring to the Asnad he told that it could be only that person who had identified himself with the subject and had imbibed so much of the moral teachings, the habits, the likes and dislikes of the Prophet as if he had associated with the Companions in the Prophet's assembly.

Traditions have their Light and Shade : According to Khatib, tradition has an illumination like unto the refulgence of the moon by which it can be accepted and it has the Darkness like the darkness of the night by which it is rejected.

The authenticity of the text of the Quran was incontrovertible and the scholars of traditions rejected all traditions that went against the letter or the spirit of the Quran, as spurious.

The criterion of judging the authenticity of traditions seems to be fairly advanced in the earliest days.

When somebody related to Aishah the tradition that the dead are penalised if they are lamented over in a loud voice, she rejected it as unauthentic because it was contrary to the verse of the Quran, "No carrier of burden will carry another's burden."

Again Umar rejected the contention of Fatima bint Qays that the divorcee had no right to receive maintenance allowance (Nafqd) and residential facilities on that. In fact the Prophet had made an exception in her case and the instance could in no way be generalised.

The Writing of Hadith : The writing of Hadith raises a number of controversial issues which have a special bearing on the problem of the reliability of traditional literature and whether traditions were preserved in the oral or in the written form or in both. When were they put in black and white? To what extent were they compiled in a cognisable form in the earliest period? How far these early writings helped in the preservation of this class of literature?

The Arabs relied generally on oral traditions, its chief cause being not only an inordinate love of this form of tradition or their stupendous memories but the scarcity of writing material and of persons who could write.

The Skill of Writing not Unknown : But they were not oblivious to the advantages of a written document. According to Dhul Rumma, "Write down my poetry for the written word is more pleasing to me than memory..... a book does not forget, nor does it substitute one for another."

And the skill of writing was not unknown in a commercial centre like Mecca. It was more common among the Jews and Christians who preserved their religious lore in writing. The Quran makes frequent reference to this topic.

The Holy Book

The first verse revealed to the Prophet declared, "The Lord taught man through the Pen," and on another occasion, the Lord has said, "Nun, and by the Pen and what they write."

Again phrases like, "The Lord wrote", "Your Lord wrote (ordained)" recur with considerable frequency in the Quran. Words like "The day of reckoning", "The two honoured scribes appointed for all." "The epistle of Solomon to the Queen of Saba and terms like 'suhf', 'asfar' 'kutub' all indicate how common was the knowledge of the terminology for writing and its material among the audience of the Quran".

The Prophet Encourages the Skill : And although the Prophet had no knowledge of the skill of reading and writing he was very keen in propagating their knowledge among his people. The captives of Badar were promised freedom if they taught the skill of writing to the people of the Suffa. He employed scribes who frequently wrote letters and orders which he sent to the people of Arabia and outside. The office of the scribe was held by a number of Companions who knew languages other than Arabic.

Paucity of Writing Material : The paucity of writing material in Arabia must have held up the compilation of the traditions in a regular book form. The Egyptian papyrus though not unknown in Arabia, must have been prohibitive in its price. There is a single stray case in which Ali appears to have possessed a rolled parchment which might have been papyrus. Otherwise the common material on which the Prophet sent his epistles or written orders to the tribes was skin parchment. In one case a recalcitrant tribal chief used the material of the Prophet's letter for repairing his leathern bucket. Bones of the shoulder blade or tablets made of ivory or other material were also used for this purpose. Under such conditions it was not easy to publish collections of the Traditions during the lifetime of the Prophet. It was made possible only when paper made from cotton became more abundantly available during the second century of al-Hijra.

Rough and Ready Material : All kind of material was used for writing purposes in those days and a person who chanced to listen to a Tradition when he had no writing material nearby had to be quick and resourceful and would make a note of it on any object he could lay his hand upon. Said bin Jubair who learnt Traditions from Abdullah ibn Umar and Ibn Abbas during a journey to Mecca would write them on the front portion of his seat on the camel during night time and when they camped in the morning, he would fair them out in his notebook. In case he ran short of paper when taking down the traditions he would use the surface of his leathern socks or slippers for taking notes.

There are cases when Traditions had been taken down on the palm of hand or on the surface of a wall and faired out later on. Skin parchment and bones were often used for writing purposes in those days.

Persons in affluent circumstances, would use tablets of a more costly and durable material. Aban bin Uthman was seen once taking down dictation from Anas on ivory tablets.

But this scarcity of material does not imply that no efforts were made to preserve the Traditions in a written form during the lifetime of the Prophet.

The Safeguards

The Companions of the Prophet took care in preserving the text of the Traditions from the earliest times. They felt very keenly the religious and social obligation of acquiring knowledge of religious injunctions from the Prophet and made special effort in preserving and propagating that knowledge. For this purpose they insisted on first hand information. Umar I lived in the Awali or the higher reaches of Medina and he could not attend the Prophet's assembly every day. He would come on alternate days and share the duty of listening to the Traditions with a neighbour of his, Ataban bin Malik who attended on the days in between. They compared notes later on.

Abdullah bin Abbas would stay at the house of Maymunah, the wife of the Prophet who was his aunt on the mother side. He would render small services to the Prophet and would bring for the Prophet water for ablutions. In this way he acquired an intimate knowledge of the Prophet's prayers at night.

The Preservation

But Abu Hurrayrah, the prolific narrator was the most indefatigable of all. He had joined the people of Suffa who lived in the mosque in order to be always near the Prophet and he underwent the direct form of privations in his pursuit of knowledge. According to him, while the Muhajirin attended to their business and the Ansars to agriculture he stuck fast to the Prophet. He would sometimes have a fling at Aishah who criticised his narrations and told how her household pursuits and her womanly interests did not allow her enough time for the pursuit of knowledge. He would not only stay in the mosque but follow the Prophet when he visited the bazar or the house of Fatima who lived at a distance in the Bazar of Bani Qaynuqah. He would follow him like a shadow to the outskirts of Medina and picked up every word which came from his lips.

It will be interesting to study in some details the life of the students of Traditions in the early period. Their great desire for learning is evidenced in the life and activities of Abdullah ibn Abbas, a cousin of the Prophet who had a high social status on account of his kinship with Prophet. Yet he would wander from door to door in Medina in search of Traditions. During the lifetime of the Prophet he would remain in the company of the Prophet during daytime and would make a point to stay at night at the House of Maymuna, a wife of the Prophet who was a maternal aunt of Ibn Abbas. In this way he kept a record of the night prayers and other activities of the Prophet.

As a field worker for the collection of Traditions he would wait on people's doors during their leisure hours specially when they retired for their siesta. He would sit outside waiting for the person to wake up and all the time he was being buffetted by the scorching simoom of the noon. He would spread his covering sheet on earth and sit patiently waiting for the opportune moment.

The people of Medina considered it a sacrilege that a person of his status and dignity should wait on them. They told him that he should have sent for them but he would answer 'I have a more urgent need for waiting on you.'

He would not only try to preserve the oral word but also make an effort to put it in black and white. Once he was seen questioning Abu Rafi, a freed slave of the Prophet, about some religious practices of the Prophet and taking notes on tablets.

Functional Aspects

It would be interesting to study the ways and means adopted by the early Muslims for acquiring the knowledge of the Prophet's Traditions. The nature of work was essentially that of the field survey. The main body of persons who devoted themselves to the preservation of the lore of traditions more than others were the Ansar because they had the attitude and leisure to attend to this business.

Ubadah bin Wahid bin Ubadah bin Samat narrates how once he and his father went out to collect the knowledge of traditions from the Ansar. They went on a searching tour and met one Companion of the Prophet after another.

First of all they visited Abu al-Yasr a Companion who was accompanied by a slave who was carrying a load of written documents.

Strategic Efforts

What is remarkable in their educational methods is the activity principle which these teachers of tradition emphasized in the course of their teaching.

The distinctive note of their method of teaching was its close correlation with life situations. The teacher actually behaved, acted or expressed himself in a particular way and he would support his action by quoting the relevant tradition of the Prophet.

In the Tradition of Abu al-Yasr, the teacher along with his slave was seen wearing two garments, the upper and the lower which were a sharp contrast in colour. Thereupon he was asked why he did not select for his use two garments of the same colour. Thereby he and his slave could both have a suit of two clothes, matching closely in colour.

Thereupon Abu al-Yasr quoted a tradition exhorting the Faithful to accord equality of treatment to the slaves. He told how this tradition explained his queer behaviour in wearing two garments of different colours. He wanted to follow the tradition to the very letter and hence he and his slave had divided the pair of garments between themselves so that both of them were dressed identically. Next they visited a debtor of Abu Yasr who fought shy of him and was reluctant to meet them. Thereupon al-Yasr remitted the debt in the name of the Lord. Here also he quoted the relevant tradition of the Prophet on the excellence of treating a debtor in a generous manner.

Then these two students of Traditions went to see another Ansari Jabir bin Abdullah in a mosque. He narrated to them a tradition which enjoined how the mosque should be kept scrupulously clean. He told how a person spitting while at his prayers spits into the face of the Lord and as he quoted the Tradition he came across some marks of spitting in the mosque. He removed them by scrubbing it with his stick and rubbing scent over the spot.

In this way these early teachers of Traditions correlated their teaching to the actual life-situations and demonstrated them by personal practice and exercise.

The Roots

Recent researches have revealed that written records of the Traditions began to be prepared in the lifetime of the Prophet and Imam Zahri of the early Ummayide period. Imam Malik bin Anas, the compiler of Muwattah and later compilers like Bukhari and Muslim all followed a tradition that had been established to some extent in the days of the Prophet.

All the important compilations on Traditions contain a chapter on the Permission to write Traditions. The main objective of the Prophet being their faithful preservation.

Keeping Records : He had told Abdullah ibn Umar to 'imprison' (Qayyid) knowledge by which he implied that it should be preserved through writing. And when an Ansari complained that he could not learn Traditions by heart, the Prophet signed with his hand, indicating that he should seek help from the art of writing.

He had also asked Jabir bin Abdullah and Ibn Abbas to practise writing.

There is quite a considerable amount of Traditional literature which had been recorded under the direct instructions of the Prophet. They were various religious injunctions on Zakat, Ahkam al-Hudud etc.

Written Instructions : Written instructions were often sent by the Prophet to the Qadis (judges) or Amils (Governors) in various parts of the Peninsula. Maadh bin Jabal in Yemen and Amr bin Hazm in Bahrayn received such instructions on Zakat, Dit, Faraiz and Sunnah.

He had sent a special document to the people of Yemen on divorce, manumission of slaves etc.

According to Abdullah bin Umar, a kitab al-Sadaqah (Book of charities) had been prepared under the orders of the Prophet and he intended to send it to various *Amils* (Governors) but it could not be despatched in his lifetime. These written directions were sent later on by Abu Bakr. A copy of these instructions which contained schedule of rates of taxation on various commodities had been preserved in the family of Abu Bakr bin Amr bin Hazm. It covered two pages.

Traditions were sometimes ordered to be put in black and white for better comprehension also. For example, the address given on the entry into Mecca was written down on the request of Abu Shah, a companion who appears to be of non-Arab origin.

Written instructions were often sent to the tribal areas. A Tradition on the use of the skin of dead animal as sent to the tribe of Juhniyyah.

The tribal and other chiefs who visited Medina sometimes received written injunctions which they carried back to their people. Wail bin Hajar, one of the princes received such a paper of authority by the Prophet.

There have been instances when the Companions put certain Traditions in black and white with the tacit approval of the Prophet. Such was the case of Abdullah bin Amr bin Abi al-Ath.

This collection of Traditions which was titled Sadiqah was highly prized by Abdullah bin Amr and he used to say in his old age, "Nothing makes me suffer life except Sadiqah."

The book passed on to Shuayb, the grandson of Abdullah bin Amr who used to narrate Traditions on its authority.

But this was not an isolated example.

According to Maabad bin Halal, whenever we asked something on Traditions from Anas bin Malik, he would take out some folios and would say that they contained those Traditions which he had written down and which had received the certification of the Prophet.

It was not uncommon to find Companions sitting in his presence and taking down his words. According to Abdullah bin Amr, "We were seated near the Prophet and writing when he was asked which town would be conquered first out of Constantinople and Rumiyyah. He replied that the city of Harqal would be conquered first."

Other Companions who had preserved the Traditions of the Prophet in writing were Samrah bin Jundab, Jabir bin Abdullah, Saad bin Ubadah, Ibn Abbas, and Abu Hurrayrah.

These records of the Prophet's Traditions in his lifetime were kept in the form of a book as in case of al-Sadiqah of Abdullah bin Amr bin abi-al Ath. The collection was one of the two most cherished possessions of the author, the other being a property which had been made into an endowment. Sometimes those records were kept in loose sheets as in the case of Abu Hurrayrah. It is said that Ali used to keep some records in his scabbard perhaps for ready reference and once he took them out and showed them to the audience on request.

According to Muslim, a large portion of the legal decrees (Fatwa) of Ali were once brought to Ibn Abbas.

According to Zahri, 'It is said that Abu Bakr had collected 500 Traditions which he destroyed because he was afraid that some of them might be not authentic.

Solicitous Recorder : Abdullah bin Amr bin abi al Ath had compiled his book Sadiqah after receiving a permission from the Prophet to preserve Traditions in writing. The book contained Traditions which he had directly listened from the Prophet without any intervening authority between him and the Prophet.

It appears that Abdullah was so solicitous that he put everything that came out of the mouth of the Prophet in black and white. He was advised by some of the Quraish not to put down everything because it was possible that the Prophet might be emotionally exercised on some occasion and it might not be desirable to record his words under such conditions. Thereupon he left off the recording of Traditions. He was questioned by the Prophet on the suspension of his activities and when he explained the reason, the Prophet enjoined upon him to write and while pointing towards his mouth said, "Nothing but truth emanates from it." The collection passed on to his grandson Shuayb after his death who used to narrate traditions on its authority.

It appears that in spite of his great reliance on his wonderful memory Abu Hurrayrah also kept a record of traditions. According to Hassan bin Umar when he narrated a Tradition in the presence of Abu Hurrayrah, the latter refused to credit it. Then Hassan claimed that he had learnt the Tradition on the authority of Abu Hurrayrah himself. Thereupon Abu Hurrayrah told that in that case he must have kept a record of the Tradition somewhere and he took Hassan to his house. There he saw a number of writings containing Traditions and after searching for some time the said Tradition was found in one of them.

According to Babir bin Nubayk he would often borrow records of Traditions from Abu Hurrayrah, copy them out and then read them out again to Abu Hurrayrah. But writing was not the strong point of Abu Hurrayrah and he would concede precedence to Abdullah bin Amr bin abi al-Aas in this respect. His superiority lay chiefly in the fact that he had preserved Traditions in writing.

Recording: a Common Practice

In fact the majority of those Companions who had distinguished themselves as teachers and savants would maintain records of religious literature specially Traditions.

According to Ibn Saad Abdullah ibn Abbas used to take down the Traditions in black and white. Once he was seen recording certain Traditions from Abu Rafi, a freed slave of the Prophet. It seems that the copies of his collection of Traditions had been published because in his later years when his eyesight was fast fading and he could not read, a group from Taif came to him with copies of his manuscript. They expected that Ibn Abbas would read out the writing to them and certify them. This would add greater authenticity to the narration. But Ibn Abbas excused himself on account of his physical infirmity and asked them to make a recitation and declared that his personal recitation or the recitation by another person in his presence and his approval of the same have the same value with respect to the authenticity of Traditions.

According to Darmi, people would come to Ibn Abbas for copying out his records of Traditions. Once Said bin Jubair, the pious savant who was murdered by Hajajj bin Yusuf later on was seen copying out Traditions in the presence of Ibn Abbas.

His most active period as a student and compiler of Traditions began immediately after the death of the Prophet. He was stimulated to launch on this field work when he asked an Ansari to send for some Companions of the Prophet so that he might relate Traditions to them (in order to propagate their knowledge). But the man told him that he himself stood in greater need of their help because they had a greater stock of Traditions with them. Thereupon he took upon himself the great work of going from door to door in his search of Traditional literature.

Ultimately he acquired such a reputation as a scholar that people would muster strong round him in order to receive knowledge. It was on such an occasion that the same Ansari whom he had consulted in the beginning declared that this young man, implying Ibn Abbas had proved more far sighted than himself.

Other Companions who insisted on the writing of knowledge included Anas bin Malik who had counselled his progeny to imprison (Qayyidu) knowledge through writing.

Abdul Rahman the son of Abdullah bin Masud took out once a manuscript which he claimed on oath to have been written in the hand of his father.

Guillaume on the Subject : Professor Guillaume concedes that some traditions of the Prophet had been preserved in writing during the life time of the Prophet but in his opinion there is no possibility of their having been incorporated in the form of regular collections. In his own words: "The extraordinary importance attached to every utterance naturally led his followers who were able to write to record his words in order to repeat them to those who clamoured to know what he had said....But it cannot be proved that any single tradition or group of traditions now extant were copied from the memoranda of the Companions.

Although there is not much evidence to prove that the writings of the Companions had been incorporated on a large scale but recent researches are gradually unearthing evidence which proves that some of them were included in standard collections. For instance, the narrations of Abu Hurrayrah as preserved by Humam bin Manbah have been included at length in the Musnad of Imam Hanbal. It is possible that future work may discover more incorporations of this kind. Standard collections were made rather late. But the work of compilation had begun early. Under the Ummayids this great task was continued by the succeeding generation with equal zeal and energy. One of the most outstanding figure among them was that of al-Zahri.

According to Sidou, Ibn Shahab al-Zahri was the first scholar who attempted a collection of Traditions. Zahri may carry the palm as the most voluminous compiler but he can hardly claim to hold the place of a pioneer in this field. He was a Tabii and belonged to the second generation of narrators. He was preceded by the first group which comprised those Companions who had acquired knowledge directly from the Prophet. It is said that the writings of al-Zahri were preserved in the treasury of the Ummayids and once when they were moved out, they had to be carried on pack animals. As a Tabii he has certainly the distinction of being perhaps the first person to acquire *rawayat* (relation) from the Companions.

3

Evolution and Development

Knowledge imparted by God is a revelation for humanity which cannot be attained through efforts of scientific method or discovered by the processes of pure Reason. The greatest thinker of modern philosophy who opened a new era in the history of critical thought devoted a life time of intensive contemplative struggle to the problem in his work on the Critique of Pure Reason and arrived at conclusions startingly similar to the fundamental postulates of religion as regards knowledge. According to Kant, "Reason by all its contemporary principles never teaches us anything more than objects of all possible experience and even of these nothing more than can be comprised in experience." Again "what the objects are by themselves would never become known to us even through the clearest knowledge of that which alone is given us, the Phenomena."

Light from Almighty

Knowledge imparted by God is 'Ilm-i-Ladunna with which He blessed Khizr, knowledge which lay in God and was imparted by Him to the prophets, knowledge which never came to the fortune of any other person previously. Abraham told his father how he was the recipient of a kind of knowledge from above which he had never received. David, Solomon and other prophets of old were all endowed with this richly heritage of divine knowledge from above.

Wisdom from within

But besides this education of the spirit from above and the Divine lore which regaled the personality of the Prophet as a goblet overbrimming with milk, an apostle is endowed also with the faculty of discrimination, the power of reasoning and differentiating Good from Evil. The prophets were gifted with an intuitive knowledge from above but they were also blessed with powers and capacities which lay within.

The Prophet was obviously referring to such knowledge when he related the following experience. He describes as if he was asleep and was given a goblet of milk which he took abundantly till he felt that he was overbrimming with it to the very tips of his fingers; the rest of it he gave to 'Umar. When asked to explain, he told that the milk symbolised knowledge. But according to the Quran, the Elect of God, the Prophets were not only gifted with knowledge that lay in God (Ilm i-Ladunna), they were also provided with Hukm, interpreted as kingdom of Earth by some and the Kingdom of Heaven by others. It may imply also the sense of discrimination in the moral sphere and the capacity to distinguish Good from Evil.

This capacity the Prophets share to a certain extent with the rest of humanity. Every child is born with such innate tendencies and powers which are in harmony with the spirit of Islam and there lies buried in him, this spark of the Divine light which illumines and differentiates for him good from evil, and this capacity is capable of considerable improvement. But any plan of moral education is hardly practicable without a basis for secular knowledge which provides the means and the wherewithal while the former determines the aims and objectives of the process. Hence the Prophet was keenly alive to the significance of secular knowledge which would function as the stage where the social and the moral tendencies in men could be exercised to play their roles in the Drama of Life.

Secular Knowledge

We come across a Tradition which recognises the significance of secular knowledge and styles it as one among other kinds of knowledge. "Knowledge is of two kinds:

Ilm-al-Adyan and *Ilm- al-Abdan*, i.e., the Knowledge of Religions and the Knowledge of Bodies" While on another occasion, he used it with more comprehensive implication of its nature and its use in social context. In this connection, the Prophet made a pointed reference to the material benefit which follows as a necessary corollary to the learning of knowledge, "Wisdom increases the worth of the good and raises a Mameluke to the royal rank of Kings." When Ali declared that knowledge was the lost heritage of a Muslim and he should retrieve it even from the hands of the unbelievers, he had most probably the secular knowledge uppermost in his mind.

One day the Prophet entered the mosque and came upon a group who had gathered round a person. On enquiry he was told that he was an allama (a learned fellow). "And what is an 'Allama?" asked the Prophet in return. They told him that he was renowned for his knowledge of genealogy, languages, poetry and other topics covering debatable ground. Upon this the Prophet told that it was a kind of Knowledge which brought no profit and the ignorance of which might not be reckoned as a loss.

According to some it does not signify that the Prophet decreed a summary rejection of all these branches of learning; rather it implies that a knowledge of these subjects brings no benefit if it is not accompanied by a knowledge of the Quranic Text, the Traditions and Fiqh.

In fact religion does not impose limitations on the nature and scope of a particular branch of learning but it claims the right to determine its aims and ideals when it is utilized for social purposes.

As an organism can be properly called alive only if it maintains a condition of dynamic adjustment with the environment, mind also needs a living contact with experience, always responsive like a sensitive diaphragm to the outside impressions, moulding them into thought patterns of ever changing, ever developing forms; such a process is the life source of moral and intellectual existence; it relapses into a quiescent state of existence if it fails to perform the function so essential to its nature.

Fath Mawsali gives three days as the minimum period for which an individual may keep himself aloof from knowledge with immunity to his intellectual or moral existence. If a diseased person is refused food, drink or medicine he won't continue to live and similarly if knowledge and wisdom is withheld from the mind, it will die.

Traditional Concept

It was such a dynamic conception of experience which found expression in the following words of Ali:- "There is a kind of knowledge which may lie skin deep and another which may penetrate the limbs and organs and set vibrating the entire personality a dynamic force which tingles the moral fibre of the individual through and through."

According to another saying, the process of education is a microcosm of the life process and it provides all those opportunities for doing good which are available in everyday life—In fact it is not a preparation for life, but a life in itself, to be judged and appreciated by values determined by the process and its reference to the social context.

"Seek knowledge because learning it for the sake of the Lord is piety; its search is prayer; its repetition and memorising amount to rosary counting, its debates a crusade; its teaching (imparting it to the ignorant) is charity and its bestowal on persons who deserve it draws one closer to God. It is thy conciliator in wilderness, a companion on the travels, a friend in loneliness, a discriminating guide for Good and Evil, a weapon against the enemies and an adornment among friends. "Knowledge is the landmark which discriminates the lawful from the unlawful and they are the minarets planted on the path to Heaven"...Further on it continues; "Thoughtful activity in learning tantamounts to fasting while its instruction amounts to praying."

Knowledge Described in Figurative Language : It would be interesting to make a careful study of the instructive figures of speech and graceful similes with which knowledge is compared in the Traditions and early literature. This would reveal not only the deep moral and emotional attachment which the Muslims always associate with the process of learning but throws light on some aspects of the educative process as well. It is likened to a cloud which would turn the scales in favour of the teacher on the

Doomsday; it gives a fresh lease of life to the towns like the bountiful rains from heaven and like the quality of mercy it blesseth him that gives and him that takes it.

According to some, knowledge is the life-buoy which would keep you afloat when your boat springs a leak and begins to sink, implying thereby the tremendous force of sustenance and strength which knowledge and thought provide for one whom the treacherous vagaries of fortune have thrown of the plank of life.

God Almighty who imparted knowledge and who bestowed upon man the Book and the Pen is bountiful in his mercy to the seeker after knowledge even though he has gone astray.

According to 'Umar, God has a sheet of love in which he enfolds a person who is engaged in the pursuit of learning and even though he persists in his career of infamy. God in his beneficence holds its folds tightly on him and does not unmask him for public exposure.

In one of his sayings, Ali refers to those safeguards which knowledge provides against moral degeneration or intellectual lassitude. "Knowledge is better than wealth because you have to guard wealth but are guarded by the knowledge;...the amasser of wealth passes away but the savants live to eternity."

Universal Education

Islam is essentially a Message and it is incumbent on the Faithful to convey its blessings to others. The obligation, though appertaining to religious knowledge in the beginning, must have influenced profoundly the tradition of secular education which was fostered in the cradle of religious institutions and sanctified by religious savants. Ibn al-Bar, in his first chapter on the Stages of Knowledge, gives, according to the best of authorities, the various stages of knowledge as sitting quietly, listening, under standing, comprehension, memorising, acting and finally publishing and propagating knowledge. On the authority of Zayd bin Thabit the Prophet has blessed with everlasting freshness a person who remembered a saying of his and transmitted it to others. In fact he expected every Faithful to be a missionary of the message of Islam and the obligation was imposed with equal emphasis on all the members of the Islamic Society.

Once in an address he denounced in general terms those tribes who did not impart to their neighbours an understanding of religion or otherwise educate and advise them. The audience grew inquisitive about the defaulters, such rare cases drawing general disapprobation of the Islamic Society. They insisted on the disclosure of the name of that particular tribe. They were allowed a period of one year for instructing their neighbours in religion, educating and advising them. It is interesting to note that the Tradition includes both the aspects of knowledge, specific instruction in religious lore and education in a broader sense.

Delegations of Teachers : The Prophet would often delegate a choice band of his Companions for towns people and Ibn-um-Maktum and Musib bin 'Umair were specially selected to impart Quranic lore to the People of Medina. After his migration to Medina, he appointed Said Ibn-ul-As for teaching the people of Medina the art of writing and he was selected for this purpose because he was a renowned penman. The informal education of the population widely scattered among tribes and nomadic families was arranged either by delegating teachers to the people or by inviting the Tribal leaders or chieftains to Medina where they obtained an opportunity of staying in the company of the Prophet and his Companions and breathing for a while in an atmosphere, charged with social and spiritual fervour, all the time being moulded and transformed through the impact of personal influence and social contacts.

Perennial Source : "The educative process is vital for the continuity of the life of a community." According to Salman. "and if the preceding generation passes away before the succeeding is educated, it would certainly spell disaster for the life of the whole community." It was why the Prophet counted knowledge which a person has imparted and propagated as Sadaqa-Jariah (a perennial work of charity).

According to Abu Hurrayrah, one of the deeds whose reward continues after the demise of a person is the knowledge which he had imparted and propagated. In fact knowledge in its process of communication is strongly reminiscent of the torch bearers who ran the relay races at the Olympics, one torch being ignited by the other and continuing in its turn the glorious career of illumination and enlightenment. The comparison of the teacher to the light-houses on land emphasizes the social function of the teacher in society.

Fertile, Fallow and Barren : A Tradition narrated on the authority of Abu Musa al-Ashari reveals vividly the social aspect of the educative process in a suggestive simile. According to the Prophet:

> "God has delegated me to my people with knowledge and admonition and verily this knowledge may be likened to the rainfall on a piece of land which is partially fertile, absorbed moisture and put forth grass and green fodder; a part of it was low land and the water collected there and God turned it to profitable account for the purpose of drinking and irrigation for the people while the third part was all barren; it neither produced grass nor preserved water." The rich and alluvial soil of the first kind symbolises the case of a person who developed his individuality and devoted his talents to the service of the group in an enthusiastic spirit of cooperation. The second is the example of a man who enriched his individuality but was not responsive to the call of group service while the third is the instance of a man who is a morally bankrupt, individually and socially.

The Hell-fire : There are a large number of Traditions which enjoin the Faithful to take an active share in publicising the Truth. The hiding of knowledge has been condemned and one who learns knowledge and does not impart it to others is compared to a man who is crazy after collecting a treasure but who does not make any proper use of it; capitalism in fact is discouraged in Islam on all counts, economic, intellectual or moral. "Do you know," he asked one of his Companions, "who is the most generous of the generous?" and he told that it was God and after Him, the Prophet himself was the most generous out of the progeny of Adam, and after him the most generous was the Man of Learning who published his knowledge far and wide. One of the sages said to his brother, "My brother the secreting of knowledge is perdition and the secreting of virtue is salvation."

According to a Tradition, one who will act secretively in the case of knowledge will be brought on Doomsday with a bridle of the fire of Hell in his mouth—a form of poetic justice for one who kept his mouth closed from publishing the word of truth in this world.

Seeker of Knowledge : The Prophet (PBUH) had blessed a person who propagated his word:

> "May God bless the person who has heard a word from me, has memorised and preserved it and has rendered it as he had heard it from me."

In fact the Prophet visualised a time when people would accost his Companions from all parts of the world. During his own great teaching work he had faced problems which he had tackled with a profound sense of forbearance generosity and large-heartedness. His great desire was that his Companions should carry on his educational mission and cultivate the professional qualities of their great master.

The establishment of an intimate contact between the teacher and the taught is the first essential of good education and the Prophet had enjoined on his Companions to make a courteous gesture and welcome the pupil with a 'Marhaba'. The Tradition has been related by Abu Hurrayrah and Abu Said al-Khudri both of whom belong to the group of Mukaththirin (the copious narrators).

According to Imam Hassan Basri, a number of persons went to see Abu Hurrayrah who was ill. Abu Hurrayrah drew up his feet on that occasion. This was a gesture to honour the visitor and provide more room for him and he related:

> "Once we went to see the Prophet. He behaved in the like manner as you saw me doing. The Prophet had remarked "Men will come to thee in search of knowledge. You should accost them with a Marhaba, a Tahiyyah and teach them."

According to Abu Said al-Khudri he said, "People will flock to you from the four quarters of the globe; you should treat them well."

Technique of Propagation : It would be interesting to make a study of the methods which the Prophet adopted for the propagation of his Great Message.

It appears that the Kaaba was the chief centre of religious life at Mecca and its proximity to the spring of Zam Zam made it a convenient meeting place for the people. During the Mecca period it was the main rendezvous for prayers and having a quiet talk with his Companions. Abu Dhar Ghaffari had the first opportunity of meeting the Prophet and Abu Bakr when he first came to Mecca, in the Kaaba and he was conducted in secret to the residence of the Prophet from the same spot.

In the beginning the message of Islam was propagated in secret. The dangerously explosive atmosphere in which he carried on his work in the early days lends a gloomy and sombre background to the story of the conversion of Abu Dhar Ghaffari as described in Sahih Muslim.

The message began to be professed and preached publicly after the conversion of powerful adherents like Umar. The Prophet lost no opportunity for bringing home the message wherever he found the opportunity to do so. He would frequent the marketplace or the streets, the hill-side or the valley if he could fulfil the great task assigned to him by God.

Sometimes he would try to go out and contact people outside Mecca. He and his loyal attendant Bilal were severely manhandled when they visited Taif for this purpose. At Mecca the chief opportunity for contacting the tribes belonging to various parts of Arabia was the time of the pilgrimage.

Preaching to the Pilgrims : There was usually a huge congregation of pilgrims on the eve of the Hajj even during the Jahiliyyah and men would muster strong from distant parts of Arabia for the performance of the ritual ceremonies. The four months of the year (Shahr al-Haram) provided special facilities for movement according to a widely accepted inter-tribal covenant. The Prophet would go from one camping ground to another and would try to bring home the message of Islam to the pilgrims. His main difficulty was the hostile attitude of the tribe of Quraish who enjoyed considerable prestige among the Arabs specially because they were entrusted with the important office of keeping the keys of the Kaaba, distributing the water of Zam Zam, and other functions, and when he visited the camping stations of the tribes they would scoff at the Prophet who was not recognised by his own people.

It was on such an occasion that a party of the tribe of Aws and Khazraj accepted Islam and prepared the way for the great migration to Medina. It was also during the period of pilgrimage that he had preached his message to the Yemenite tribe of Kindah. But they did not accept Islam at that time.

Personal Education

In the early years, one of the chief methods by which the message was broadcast in the Peninsula was through individual converts who would return to their people for the propagation of the message. One of these was the poet Tufayl bin Amr of Daws a tribe of Yemen. But the personal influence of Tufayl took a long time in converting his people to the new faith and it was finally in 7 A. H. that the whole tribe embraced Islam, Abu Hurrayrah who belonged to this tribe also came into the fold of Islam in that year.

In the beginning Tufayl bin Amr met with unusual difficulties in his task of proselytizing so much so that once he came to the Prophet and requested him to invoke a curse on his people which the latter refused to do. On the other hand he prayed that God may show them the Right Path.

Abu Dhar Ghaffari was also one of those individual pioneers who came alone and professed the new faith with all the boldness and strength of character that had distinguished him throughout his career. He was introduced into the presence of the Prophet by Ali under conditions which seemed to be extremely inflammable but the very next day Abu Dhar Ghaffari made an open declaration of his faith in the market place.

He was severely manhandled by the Quraish on that occasion. He went back to his people and one half of his tribe embraced Islam. The other half were converted after the migration of the Prophet to Medina. The tribe of Aslam who lived in their neighbourhood also accepted Islam under their influence.

Periods of Activity : The progress of the missionary activities can be divided into well marked periods. During the early stage, the first converts had to work among a hostile community with powerful elements counteracting their influence. The work bad to be carried on under the deep shadow of lurking dangers and persecution at the hands of powerful factions which were hostile to their religious activities.

With the conversion of Umar and other persons, there was a slight feeling of relief in an otherwise tense and extremely oppressive atmosphere.

The migration to Medina extended the sphere of his activity but still the powerful influence of the Quraish militated against the propagation of his message. Most of the work was done at Medina. There was hardly any opportunity for the teachers to do field work among the tribes.

The Peace of Hudaybiyyah was a decisive landmark in the history of the missionary work. Henceforth, the new influence spread like a wildfire throughout the Peninsula. The fall of Mecca completed the movement of expansion and growth which had been already initiated by the Peace of Hudaybiyyah and the major portion of the Arab population came within the fold of Islam after this great event.

Historic Efforts

It would be interesting to study the organisation and technique of the method of propagation in the case of at least one particular region in order to make clear the basic principles on which the work was planned. The first pre-requisite for initiating missionary activities in a particular area was political security.

Yemen had attained a higher level of cultural and social life than the rest of the Peninsula. This region had its contact with Iran and Abyssinia while during the pre-Islamic period it had been occupied by the Iranians. The Yemenites were a maritime people and had trade relations with India and other countries. Their economic condition and cultural and social advancement gave them a special priority in the tribal confederacies of the Peninsula. The problem of missionary work was all the more complicated by the racial issue because the Yemenites did not belong to the same stock as the people in the north. The Christian influence which came to Yemen through Abyssinia was fairly strong in this region and the Christians like that of Najran who were governed by prelate had ancient traditions of a national church and clergy.

Hence a number of distinguished teachers were selected to work in the area and they were deputed to different parts of Yemen.

Muslim Missionary : The chief distinction of the Muslim missionary from the earliest times is that he has never been only a missionary. The very spirit of Islam fought against the growth of priesthood as a separate class and every Muslim who travelled in the capacity of a merchant or a soldier, carried with him the inner urge of propagating the message of Islam. It has been introduced into the heart of the Dark Continent, the impenetrable forests of Indonesia, or the distant regions of Central Asia by men who combined their worldly vocations with their missionary work.

The inspiration had its origin in the days of early Islam. The first officers sent by the Prophet were teachers, judges, revenue collectors and administrators at one and the same time but the mission of teaching held a place of premier importance in their programme.

According to al-Istiab, the Prophet appointed Muadh bin Jabal, a Qadi for Jund (army) in Yemen in order to teach them the Quran, the laws of Islam and to perform the function of Qaza (Judiciary). He was also put in charge of the collection of charities from the ummals (officers) in Yemen.

And in his parting counsel to Muadh he instructed him into the programme of teaching as planned in three stages, and ended by calling upon him to fear the curses of the oppressed because there was no partition (Hijab) between the cry of the oppressed and God. He insisted mainly on the teaching of the formula of Tawhid, the five prayers and injunctions on charities.

The Prophet cross-examined him also on his method of deciding cases before he left for Yemen. Muadh told that he would seek guidance from the Quran, the Traditions and failing there he will rely on his Rai or judgement.

Some of the revenue collectors also worked as teachers. For instance, Abu Musa al-Ashaari was sent to Yemen as a revenue officer. Abu Musa, the golden tongued reader of the Quran was a very happy choice because he personally belonged to a Yemenite tribe. He was sent to the areas of Zubayd and Aden.

Work among the Higher Classes : Jarir bin Abdullah Bajalli propagated the new message among the ruling princes of Yemen and was successful in converting Zul Kalab Humayri who wielded a great influence among the people of Yemen. On one occasion when he was acclaimed as the over-lord of the people, one hundred thousand men had bowed down in prostration, before him, a custom which had been borrowed from the Iranians.

His conversion was a red-letter day in the history of Yemen because he liberated four thousand slaves to celebrate the occasion. Some of the ruling princes visited the Prophet and received personal instructions from him. Hajr bin Wail, a prince of Hazr Mut stayed for a number of days at Medina and was held in high respect by the Prophet. He returned with a letter of authority from the Prophet. The letter is given by Qadl Ayaz in Shifa and by other writers. It contains instructions which had a special significance for the social and economic life of the home region of the chief. Hajr was also granted a piece of land by the Prophet.

Ali had been deputed to the tribes of Hamadan with a letter from the Prophet. As a young man he felt rather diffident about himself when the Prophet decided to send him to Yemen but the Prophet reiterated his faith in him and sent him on the Mission. The whole tribe of Hamadan accepted Islam at his hands. Ali worked also in the land of the Jazimah.

In the beginning the deputations of teachers were accompanied by soldiers. There was an obvious need for such precautionary measures because there had been cases of perfidy and in one case, a whole body of Qura or Quran Readers had been butchered to a man through a subterfuge. These missions of teachers which went with parties of soldiers are named *Saraya* by historians. Khalid bin Walid had stayed with the tribe of Hamadan for six months when he was followed by Ali who converted the tribe to Islam.

Tribal Missions : Another method of propagation was through those tribal Missions who visited Medina, stayed in the mosque or elsewhere and acquired instructions from the Prophet on important matters. They would return to their people and instruct their people. Sometimes they carried back with them written instructions from the Prophet. Theirs was the Bayat al-Arabiyyah and not Bay at al- Hijrah.

For example, Malik bin Juwayrith came with a deputation, stayed for twenty days, and returned to his people. On the eve of his departure the Prophet said, 'Return to your people and teach them the laws of the Shariat and pray as you have seen me praying.

A class of teachers whom the Prophet trained under his personal supervision were the People of the Suffa. They were extremely poor and depended on the Prophet for their maintenance.

They did not have more than one cloth on their bodies which they tied round their neck and let it fall so that it served both for the upper and the under garment.

It is interesting to learn that they did not depend on the people for their maintenance. They brought faggots from the forest and the proceeds of the sale was divided into two equal parts, one half went to the poor and the destitute while the other half went into the common fund for the maintenance of the group.

They had hardly any leisure time during the day so they devoted the night time to learning and teaching.

Ubadah bin al-Samat, the great teacher who was sent to Palestine on an educational mission by Umar during his regime was one of the teachers who belonged to the people of Suffa. According to Abu Daud, he taught the People of Suffa Quran and the Art of writing.

Functional Education

According to Plato, "Knowledge is Virtue", and in view of the practical experience of Greek thinkers, knowledge was essentially identical with virtue because it was interpreted in Greek life as synonymous with wisdom, a stage which is not reached by skimming over the placid waters of bookish information but discovered after a process of continuous moral and intellectual struggle; it is the fruit of long and hazardous adventure of exploration and discovery. But when the scholastic philosophy cast its spell on the schools which had already been divorced from life and activity under the influence of the Church, knowledge became a stranger to action and since then the efforts of the greatest educators have been ever more directed towards recovering once more this elusive principle of education, the activity principle.

New Education aims at bridging over the gulf between knowledge and activity and has opened out fresh channels of free and joyous expression for the superabundant energy of the child, but the vistas opened out belong mainly to the field of physical and intellectual activity; it would be unjust to prefer the charge that the New Education has failed to appreciate the moral and the social implications of the educative process, but there is no gainsaying of the fact that they have certainly failed to inspire those concerned with Education with a burning enthusiasm for high moral values. It is not the denying of moral values in new education, it is the recognition of a lack of emphasis.

Inter-dependence of Knowledge and Action : Modern psychology has discovered a close interdependence between action and knowledge; action helps in placing the other on a secure basis of practical reality and assists in the integration process of experience, while knowledge reveals the social, moral and intellectual implications of a particular activity and makes it purposeful and interesting. Knowledge and action are the two supports which maintain the moral and social integrity of an individual and according to Sufiyan Thauri, "When knowledge hails action and the latter replies in the affirmative, well and good, otherwise it bids the person his last farewell."

Reconciling Liberal and Vocational Education : The tremendous influence of the Industrial Revolution in the growth and development of modern civilisation and primarily the social and economic crises into which humanity has been betrayed, have led the educationist to emphasize a system of education based essentially on a closer relation between knowledge and experience. Deway says, it could result in the reconciliation of two apparently exclusive aims, the liberal and the vocational and would help in creating a bond of human kinship and understanding between the working classes and their masters. It is true that handwork is being advocated on a psychological and moral basis as well but the driving force behind the tendency is primarily sociological and political.

The unprecedented world situation which made the educationist adopt such a course in education did not exist in the early days of Islam. In those days when the bitterness between labour and capital was not so pronounced, when the great Prophet held the spade and tended the goats in person; when the hatchet of his Companions echoed in the forest and they collected firewood for their livelihood; when the vocation signified a calling for life and not the despised pre-occupation of the unlettered class, when human relations were more telling a factor in social life than economic and industrial considerations, there was no place for handwork in the schools for purely sociological reasons and the psychological basis for their inclusion in the curriculum remained yet to be discovered. The vocational training lay in the hands of master craftsmen who combined the joy of artistic creation with the process of production. Hence the urge for a closer harmony between knowledge and action was not satisfied through manual activities in schools but was cultivated at the higher reaches of moral life and social service in school and society.

Guiding Gems

The Quran has accented at more than one place the intimate correlation between knowledge and the development in the spiritual and moral sense.

> "Verily it is the Ulama (The People of knowledge) out of the Creation of God who fear God, and according to another verse of the Holy Book knowledge leads the way to emotional and moral Catharsis "and verily those who have been given knowledge shed tears."

Legacy from Ancient Prophets : This much desired inter-dependence of knowledge and action has been recognised as the basic factor of a well integrated personality from the earliest days and the Muslim writers trace its formulation and practice throughout the grand hierarchy of Prophets who had preceded the Founder of Islam.

According to Ibn Abi-al-Darda, a divine message was revealed to some of the prophets that "those who pursue knowledge without the object of realising it in daily practice were persons who moved about among the people in the garb of harmless goats but at heart they were more ferocious than the wolf; their speech was sweeter than honey but their hearts were more bitter than the aloe."

The Bible disapproves the fruitless venture for learning in case the person has not been successful in resolving the conflict between his actions and previously acquired knowledge. "Don't you seek knowledge which you do not know so long as you have not realised into action all you know." According to Jesus Christ, action comes as natural to a person who knows, as vision to one who has eyes to see. Once he spoke thus to his apostles, "Verily one who tells the word of wisdom and the other who listens to him both are co-sharers in the process but the precedence will be his who earns it by first acting upon it." "O Israelites! a blind man gains nothing although he is covered with the glory of the sun because he cannot exercise his sense of wisdom and a scholar never benefits by the abundance of his knowledge if he makes no use of his capacity for action."

Educational Catastrophe : The Prophet was keenly alive to this tragic disassociation between knowledge and action in the case of schools maintained by the Jews and the Christians and he had warned his people of such an educational catastrophe.

When the Prophet talked of the time when knowledge would be wrested away from the people, some body remarked that they should insist on the teaching of the Quran again and again to women and children.

Thereupon the Prophet quoted the instance of the Jews and Christians who taught the Torah and Bible but they could hardly check their moral deterioration.

In fact the Jews of Medina presented a lurid example of a sophisticated people whose sense of morality had been stifled under the crushing weight of their religious and racial pride.

They had perhaps the best organised system of education in the Peninsula and the town of Medina had its Dar al-Madaris where regular instruction was imparted in the Torah. Traditions narrated by Kaab, the great scholar of the Jewish lore have a special significance in this context.

According to Kaab, the scholars who did not act upon their knowledge were often like those who went about in a lamb's skin but their hearts were more bitter than the bitterest medicine.

According to another Tradition "Where knowledge does not lead to good action, it is better to adopt the religion of the men of the desert or the school children." (Who are simple and naive and act according to the dictates of their hearts rather than that of acquired knowledge).

A group often Companions used to hold learned discourses in the Mosque of Kaaba and once when the Prophet came upon them he remarked, "Learn however you may but unless you act upon your words. God will never grant you a reward for it."

Rich Imagery : Traditions on this subject contain a wealth of rich imagery which present the idea in a colourful language and emphasize the truth by means of analogy. In one of his Traditions, which is reminiscent of the lurid imagination of Dante's inferno, he describes the punishment of a scholar who advised others to follow the path of virtue and refrained himself from pursuing it. Such a scholar would be cast into the infernal blazes and his entrails would burst out of his abdomen and he would turn round and round like a donkey moving the millstone."

The poetic justice which hardly loses its efficacy by being poetic is a suitable punishment for those who gained knowledge as a pander to their baser self and they are condemned to suffer under the grievous burden of sterile knowledge which they had been building up to enormous proportions in their worldly career.

Knowledge which does not function as a dynamic factor in moulding the personality of a person and the building up of sentiments is styled as the death-knell for the heart or emotional life. It makes the springs of heart brackish and bitter and they turn into a barren salty desert where the raindrops from above fall and turn into saline crystals. A scholar who fails in turning his knowledge into virile action is a diseased man who is himself deprived of the blessings of health but grows eloquent on the efficacy of a recipe or a starving person who talks of delicacies and gloats over their details although he could never dream of enjoying them.

A close harmony between knowledge and action is the *sin qua non* of moral life and is essential for establishing the integrity of character and unity of disposition in an individual but on the teacher and the savant it imposes a double responsibility.

Work of Reality

He should not only be true to himself but true to his pupils also. In the opinion of the Prophet, he cannot lay claim to the proud title of a scholar if he is not true to himself. "A person hardly deserves the name of a scholar if he does not fashion his life activities according to his scholarship."

The responsibility of an action grows seven-fold for a person who knows its moral implications than in the cause of one who is ignorant. According to Ibn Abi al-Darda, "For one who does not know, there is a single perdition, but for one who knows and does act upon it, there are seven."

The fact that the pupils take the teacher as their ideal in social and moral affairs makes his position all the more significant. The relationship of the teacher to his pupils resembles the relation of the engraved plate to the plaster which receives its impression or that of a piece of wood to its shadow. If the plate has no engraved designs, it would have no effect on the plaster and if there is a warp in the wood, the shadow will suffer from want of symmetry. The kinks and the deformities in the teacher become all the more pronounced in the pupil through suggestion and imitation. Hence, the greater need of a reconciliation between knowledge and action for the teacher.

In fact a teacher who does not create harmony between his doings and profession leaves no lasting impression on the minds of his disciples and his words of counsel slip away from the mind as rain drops slide over a stone. Ibn Masud condemned the teaching of such persons and remarked that Quran was not revealed to be prescribed as a textbook for the schools.

4

Founding Father

Muhammad was born of noble parentage; the family of Hashim was the noblest amongst the Quraish; his grandfather Abd-ul-Muttalib was the custodian of the Kaaba. The same year which saw the destruction of the Abyssinian invaders, and which formed an epoch in the history of the Arabs,' witnessed the birth of Muhammad. He was born on the 12th of Rabi-ul-Awwal (Rabil), (now forming the third month of the Moslem calendar,) in the 40th year of the reign of Chosroes the Great, Kesra Anushirvan, the magnificent and successful rival of Justinian.

He missed all the parental care which forms the blessings of childhood. His father had died before he was born. He was bereft of his mother, when only six years of age. The charge of the orphan child fell to his grandfather, who loved him dearly. On his death-bed Abd-ul-Muttalib confided his young charge to his son Abu Talib, a nuterine brother of Abdullah, the father of Muhammad.

In the house of Abu Talib, Muhammad passed his early life. Endowed with the most amiable qualities, he won the affections of all who came in contact with him, A touching incident of the attachment subsisting between nephew and uncle is preserved by Moslem historians. Abu Talib determined to make a journey to Syria, leaving Muhammad with his own children at Mecca. When Abu Talib was on the point of mounting his camel, Muhammad clasped his knees and cried, "O my uncle, take me with thee. "The heart of Abu Talib melted within him and the little orphan nephew joined the commercial expedition of his uncle. They travelled together into Syria. During one of the halts, at a place called Basra, they met an Arab monk of the name of Bahira who, struck by the signs of future grandeur and intellectual and moral qualities of the highest type on the countenance of the orphan child of Abdullah, recognised in him the liberator and saviour of his country and people. He impressed his convictions on Abu Talib, and enjoined him to guard his charge with the tenderest care from the paths of danger and the machinations of his enemies.

The Deputy

Very soon after, the sacrilegious wars of the Fijar broke out between the Quraish and the Bani-Hawazin which lasted with interruptions for nine years. In two of the contests Muhammad, though only fourteen or fifteen, accompanied his uncles in this tribal war; and proved himself a worthy descendant of the sturdy and patriotic defender of the Kaaba.

From this time till the twenty-fifth year of his age, Muhammad scarcely appears in public life. His kindliness of heart, and his gentleness of manners, combined with his fidelity, his honesty, his truth, and his unsullied character, had acquired for him the goodwill and affection of all his fellow-people, and the surname of al-Amin, "the True." In the twenty-fifth year of his age, Muhammad had occasion to travel once more into Syria, in charge of the merchandise of his kinswoman Khadija, a rich widow lady of the tribe of Quraish. The faithful prudence and exalted probity with which he discharged the trust reposed in him created a deep feeling of gratitude in the bosom of Khadija. A marriage was soon arranged between Muhammad and his noble kinswoman which was solemnised amidst universal approbation. The bride was given away by her own uncle, Amr bin Asad, her father Khuwailid having died before or during the wars of the Fijar.

This marriage acquired for Muhammad great consideration among his compatriots. He loved his wife devotedly and watched her with the most tender care. He managed her affairs and looked after her interests with unrivalled prudence. When Halima, his nurse, came to him and told him her poverty, he solicited for her the benevolence of Khadija, who gave the old and poor Bedouin woman a flock of forty sheep.' As long as Khadija lived, he never availed himself of the Arab custom of taking several wives. During her lifetime his love was unswerving; after her death he never recalled her memory but with the deepest emotion. Raised above the common cares of life by the gratitude and affection of Khadija, he devoted himself entirely to meditation and spiritual communion with God.

A Stranger : As yet Muhammad was a stranger to the outside world. He now added to his reputation among his fellow-men by taking a prominent part in the resuscitation of an old league called the Federation of the Fudhul (Hilf-ul-Fudhul), formed in ancient times for the repression of acts of lawlessness within the walls of Mecca. Such deeds of oppression and reckless audacity had become terribly frequent; and acts were done in broad daylight at which every soul possessed of a spark of humanity revolted and shuddered. This led to a new compact between four or five of the chief families of Mecca for the protection of the weak and the oppressed. Muhammad was one of the most prominent movers in this federation, the revival of which mainly resulted from his efforts.

In his thirty-fifth year, he settled by his decision a grave difficulty which had sprung up during the reconstruction of the Kaaba regarding the placing of the sacred stone, and which almost threatened to plunge the tribes into another of their ever recurring wars.

Act of Patriotism : But history will always remember him during this period for an act of patriotism the deep significance of which has been overlooked by all our historians excepting Ibn-Khaldun. Just before the reconstruction of the Kaaba, Mecca had been saved from a conspiracy to rob her of her independence. Uthman, son of Huwairith, an Arab who had embraced Christianity in the court of Constantinople, had come to Hijaz, backed by Byzantine gold, to throw Mecca into the hands of the Greeks. His design was exposed and the conspiracy proved abortive, through the exertions of Muhammad. The Western world lauds, till the heart grows sick, the successful exposure of Catiline by Cicero; the foul deed of Brutus assassinating his benefactor; or the murders committed by the two Athenian youths, as the greatest achievements in the history of freedom. But the merit of Muhammad, in saving his birthplace from falling under the yoke of the miserable despots of Byzantium, must always deserve the thanks of humanity. Muhammad had thus already served his country faithfully. He had tried also to discharge some of the debt of gratitude and obligation he owed his uncle Abu Talib, by charging himself with the education of Ali, one of his sons. Abu Talib who had a large family, had not the means of bringing them up as they deserved. Muhammad, rich by his alliance with Khadija, and Abbas, the brother of Abu Talib, were the most opulent citizens of Mecca. During a severe famine which afflicted the country, Muhammad persuaded his uncle Abbas to adopt one of the sons of Abu Talib, whilst he adopted another. Thus Abbas took Jafar; Ali; and Akil remained with their father. Muhammad had lost all his sons in early infancy. In the love of Ali, he found consolation for their loss; and the future marriage of the son of Abu Talib with the youngest daughter of Muhammad, Fatima, sealed the bond of love and devotedness.

Act of Humanity : Muhammad had also about this time set an example to his fellow-citizens by an act of humanity hardly surpassed by any recorded in history. A young Arab of the name of Zaid, son of Harith, was made captive by a hostile tribe and sold to a nephew of Khadija, who presented him to her. Muhammad, struck by the gentleness of Zaid, asked him as a gift from Khadija; and the moment he was made over to him, Muhammad enfranchised the young boy. Sometime after, Zaid's father, who was tenderly attached to his son, came to Mecca in order to ransom him. Muhammad said to Zaid, he was free to remain with him or go with his father; and young Zaid preferred to remain with his benefactor.' But whether engaged in these acts of benevolence or in assisting his fellow-citizens to frustrate the plans of conspirators, or to settle public questions, the mind of Muhammad was always busy on the future destiny of his race. His two visits to Syria had opened to him a scene of moral and social misery beyond conception. Before him lay his own country, and he beheld his people sunk in absolute barbarism. His noble heart bled for degraded humanity. With the keen foresight of an inspired Teacher, he saw that every hope of social and political improvement rested on a moral regeneration.

Profound Meditation : Whether in the bosom of his family or in the depth of solitude, he passed his time in profound meditation. Solitude had indeed become a passion with him. Every year, the month of Ramadan he spent with his family on the mount of Hira, devoting his time entirely to prayer and to the succour of the poor and famished wayfarers who came to him.' Here he often remained whole nights plunged in the profoundest thought, deep in communion with the unseen yet all-pervading God of the Universe.

The poetry of the soul can go no further, when it is said, he heard even the stones and rocks and trees, calling on him to fulfil the task an Almighty Power was directing him to undertake. The mental visions and the apparitions of angels at these moments were the bright though gradual dawnings of those Truths with which he was to vivify the world. Often in the dark and benighted pathways of concrete existence, the soul of every great man has been conscious of unrealised yet not unseen influences, which have led to some of the happiest achievements of humanity. From Samuel, that ancient seer, wild and awful as he stands there, deep in the misty horizon of the Past, to Jesus in the wilderness pondering over the darksome fate of his people and the magnitude of his work, listening to the sweet accents of the God of Truth;—from Jesus to Muhammad in the solitude of his mountain-retreat, there is no break in the action of these Influences.

In the still hours of the night, in the sweet calmness of the early dawn, in the depth of solitude when no human sympathy is near, a Voice comes to him from heaven gently as the sough of the gentlest breeze, "Thou art the Man, Thou art the Prophet of God;" or when wrapt in sleep, it comes in mighty waves, "Cry in the name of the Lord " The over-wrought mind at these moments raises a Vision before the eye, a Vision of the celestial ministrants who are believed to form the medium of intercommunication between the God of heaven and the man on earth. 'The Father of Truth chooses His own prophets, and He speaks to them in a voice stronger than the voice of thunder. It is the same inner voice through which God speaks to all of us". That voice may dwindle away, and become hardly audible; it may lose its divine accent and sink into the language of worldly prudence; but it may also from time to time assume its real nature with the chosen of God, and sound in their ears as a Voice from "Heaven."

We can appreciate the severe mental conflicts, the intensity of feeling, which wrung the heart of Muhammad, when we are told that before he had himself realised his Mission, he was almost driven to the verge of suicide, when a voice from within,—a Voice which proceeded from the Author of the Universe who had selected him for the salvation of his people—recalled him to his duty to mankind.

His was not the communion with God of those egoists who bury themselves in deserts or forests, and live a life of quietude for themselves alone. His was the hard struggle of the man who is led on-wards by a nobler destiny towards the liberation of his race from the bondage of idolatry. His destiny was unfolded to him, when wrapped in profound meditation, melancholy and sad, he felt himself called by that Voice from Heaven, which had called those who had gone before him, to arise and preach,—"O thou, enwrapped in thy mantle, arise and warn, and "glorify thy Lord." And he arose and girded himself for the work to which he felt himself called. Thenceforth his life is devoted to humanity. Preaching with unswerving purpose amidst frightful persecutions, insulted and outraged, he held on in his path of reproof and reform.

Pioneering Status

Khadija was the first to believe in him and his mission. When he had confided to her sorrowfully and despondingly, the early struggles which preceded the enlightenment of his mind by divine truths, she consoled him and expressed to him her belief that he would be the chosen one for regenerating his people. Now that his mission was revealed, she was the first to abandon the idolatry other people, and to join with him in purity of heart in offering up prayers to the All-Merciful.

In the beginning Muhammad opened his soul only to those who were attached to him, and tried to wean them from the gross practices of their fore -fathers. After Khadija, Ali was the first to believe in the mission of Muhammad. Often did the Prophet go into the depths of the solitary villages around Mecca, with his wife and young cousin, that they might together offer up their heartfelt thanks to the God of all nations for his manifold blessings Once they were surprised in the attitude of prayer by Abu Talib, the father of Ali: And he said to Muhammad, "O son of my brother, what is this "religion that thou art following?"

"It is the religion of God, of His angels, of His prophets and of our ancestor Abraham," answered the Prophet,"—"God has sent me to His servants to direct them towards the Truth; and thou, O my uncle, art the most worthy of all. It is meet that I should thus call upon thee, and it is meet that thou shouldn't accept the Truth and help in spreading it." "Son of "my brother," replied Abu Talib, in the true spirit of the sturdy old Semite, "I cannot abjure the religion of my fathers; but by the Supreme God, "whilst I am alive none shall dare to injure thee." Then turning towards Ali, his son, the venerable patriarch enquired what religion was his: "O father," answered Ali, "I believe in God and His Prophet and go with him." "Follow him," said Abu Talib, "he will invite thee to nothing but what is good."

Soon after Zaid, the son of Harith, who notwithstanding his freedom had cast in his lot with Muhammad, became a convert to the new faith. He was followed by a leading member of the Quraish community, of the name of Abdullah, son of Abu Kuhafa, who afterwards became famous in history as Abu-Bakr. His influence drew several other converts to the new faith, and the Prophet had the satisfaction of seeing his followers increase in number. It is a noble feature in the history of the Prophet of Arabia, and one which strongly attests the inspired character of his teachings and the intensity of his faith and trust in God, that his nearest relations, his wife, his beloved cousin, and intimate friends were most thoroughly imbued with the truth of his mission and convinced of his inspiration. Those who knew him best, who lived with him and noted all his movements, were his most sincere and devoted followers. If these men and women, noble, intelligent, and certainly not less educated than the fishermen of Galilee, had perceived the slightest sign of earthliness, deception, or want of faith in the Teacher himself, Muhammad's hopes of moral regeneration and social reform would all have been dashed to pieces in a moment. They braved for him persecutions and dangers; they bore up against physical tortures and mental agony caused by social excommunication, even unto death. Would they have done this, had they perceived the slightest backsliding in their master? But even if these people had not believed in Muhammad with such earnest faith and trust, it would furnish no reason for doubting the greatness of his work or the depth of his sincerity. For the influence of Jesus himself was least among his nearest relatives. His brothers never believed in him, and once they even went so far as to endeavour to obtain possession of his person, believing him to be out of his mind. Even his immediate disciples were not firm in their convictions. Perhaps this unsteadiness may have arisen from weakness of character, or it may have resulted, as Milman thinks, from the varying tone of Jesus himself; but that it is a fact is undeniable. This intense faith and conviction on the part of the immediate followers of Muhammad is the noblest testimony to the purity of his motives and the truth of his doctrine.

Quiet Efforts : For three years he laboured thus, quietly to wean his people from the worship of idols. At last, he determined to assemble all his kinsmen in his house, in order to explain his mission to them. They came; but mocked his efforts, and taunted Abu Talib about the enthusiasm of his son on behalf of Muhammad. Having thus failed to make any impression on his kinsmen, he commenced preaching openly to all his people. Little success attended these efforts. But his denunciations of their idols, his reproofs, his vehement exposure of the grossness of their worship lashed the Quraish into fury, as the reproofs of Jesus had roused the anger of the Jews in Sanhedrim before. Several times they sent deputations to Abu Talib, asking him to stop his nephew from preaching against their religion. At first, Abu Talib turned them away with soft and courteous words. But as Muhammad grew firmer in exposing the weakness of their idols, they expelled him from the Kaaba where he was preaching, and then came in a body to his uncle "We respect thy age and thy rank," said they, "but our respect for thee has bounds; and "verily, we can have no further patience with thy "nephew's abuse of our gods, and his ill-words against our ancestors; wherefore, do thou either prevent him from so doing, or thyself take part with him, so that we may settle the matter by fight, until one of the two parties is exterminated." Having thus spoken, they departed. Abu Talib was unwilling to separate himself from his people, neither did he like abandoning his nephew to the tender mercies of the idolaters. Sending for Muhammad, he informed him of the speech of the Quraish, and begged him to renounce the task he had undertaken. Muhammad thought his uncle wished to with draw his protection: but his high resolve did not fail him. "Even at this moment," Firmly he replied: "O my "uncle, if they placed the Sun on my right hand, and "the Moon on my left, to force me to renounce my "work, verily I would not desist therefrom until God "made manifest His cause, or I perished in the attempt." "But the thought of desertion by his kind "protector overcame him." He burst into tears, and turned to depart. Then Abu Talib called aloud: "Son of my brother, come back and he came. And Abu Talib said: "Say whatsoever thou "pleasest; for by the Lord, I shall not abandon thee, "nay never. The Quraish made another attempt to persuade Abu Talib to deliver up his nephew to them. They offered, in exchange, a young man of the family of Makhzum, but it was of no avail The declared intention of Abu Talib to support his nephew excited their fury, and they renewed their menaces of violence. The venerable patriarch appealed to the sense of honour and pride of the Bani-Hashim, the kinsmen of Muhammad, to protect a distinguished member of their family from falling a victim to the hatred of rival clans. Abu Talib's energetic appeal was nobly responded to by the Hashimites, with the exception of Abu Laheb, "the father of flame".

The fury of the Quraish, however, increased every day; and though, in the beginning, the powerful influence of Abu Talib had the effect of warding off an immediate attempt on the life of Muhammad, yet the outrages, to which he and his disciples were exposed, were fearful. The hostile Quraish followed him wherever he went; they threw stones at him and his disciples when engaged in their devotions; they threw dirt on him during his meals. They stopped him from offering his prayers near the Kaaba. They organised a regular system of persecution; each family taking upon itself the task of strangling the new religion among its members. The hill of Ramdha and the place called Batha became thus the scenes of cruel tortures. The men or women whom the Quraish found abandoning the worship of their idol-gods, were exposed by them to the burning heat of the desert, where when reduced to the last extremity by hunger and thirst, they were offered the alternative of adoring the idols or death. Some recanted; but the majority held firmly to their faith. They killed with excruciating torments Yasar and Samiya, his wife; they inflicted fearful tortures on Ammar, their son. Muhammad was often an eyewitness of the sufferings of his disciples, sufferings borne with patience and endurance as became martyrs in the cause of Truth. And these were not the only martyrs in the early history of Islam. Like the Pharisees tempting Jesus, the Quraish even came to Muhammad with temptations of worldly honour and worldly aggrandisement, in order to draw him from the path of his duty. One day, says the chronicler, he was sitting in the mosque of Hijr, at a little distance from an assembly of the opposing chiefs, when one of them, Utba, son of Rabia, came to him and said to the Prophet, "O son of my brother, thou art distinguished by thy qualities and thy descent. Now thou hast sown division among our people and cast dissension in our families; thou denouncest our gods and goddesses; thou dosttax our ancestors with impiety. We have a proposition to make to thee; think well if it will not suit thee to accept it." "Speak, "O father of Walid, said the Prophet, "I listen." "O son of my brother, if thou wishest to acquire riches by this affair, we will collect a fortune larger than is possessed by any of us; if thou desirest honours and dignity, we shall make thee our chief and shall not do a thing without thee; if thou desirest dominion, we shall make thee our King; and if the spirit (demon) which possesses thee cannot be overpowered, we will bring thee doctors and give them riches till they cure "thee." And when he had done, "Hast thou finished, O father of Walid," asked the Prophet. "Yes," replied he. "Then listen to me." "I listen," he said.

> "In the name of the most merciful God. This is a revelation from the most Merciful: a Book the verses whereof are distinctly explained, an Arabic Koran, for the instruction of people who understand; bearing good tidings, and denouncing threats: but the greater part of them turn aside, and hearten not thereto. And they say, "Our hearts are veiled from the doctrine to which thou invitest us; and there is a deafness in our ears, and a curtain between us and thee: wherefore act thou, as thou shall think fit; for we shall act according to our own sentiments" "Say, Verily I am only a man like you. It is revealed unto me that your God is one God: wherefore direct your way straight unto Him; and ask pardon of Him for what is past. And woe be to the idolaters; who give not the appointed alms, and

> believe not in the life to come! But as to those who believe and work righteousness, they shall receive an everlasting reward." When the Prophet finished this recitation, he said to Utba, 'Thou hast heard, now take the course which seemeth best to thee."

Profoundly afflicted by the persecution of his disciples, whose position every day became more and more unbearable, he advised them to go to Abyssinia and remain there, till some change for the better occurred in the feelings of the Quraish. Some immediately availed themselves of the advice, and sailed, to the number of fifteen, to the hospitable shores of Abyssinia. This is called the first Flight in the history of Islam. These emigrants were soon joined by many more of their fellow-sufferers and labourers in the cause of Truth, until their number amounted to eighty-two or eighty three men and eighteen women But the untiring hostility of the Quraish did not allow them rest or peace even here. The Quraish sent deputies to the King of Abyssinia (Najashi, Negus) to demand the delivery of these refugees in order to put them to death. They stated the chief charges against them to be their abjuration of the old religion and their adoption of a new one. The king sent for the exiles and enquired of them, whether what their enemies had stated was true "What is this religion for which you have abandoned your former faith?" asked the king, "and adopted neither mine nor that of any other people." Jafar, son of Abu Talib, and brother of Ali, acting as spokesman for the whole body of emigrants, spoke thus:

> "O King, We were plunged in the depth of ignorance and barbarism—we adored idols; we ate dead bodies; and we spoke abominations; we disregarded every feeling of humanity, and the duties of hospitality and neighbourhood; we knew no law but that of the strong, when God raised among us a man, of whose birth, truthfulness, honesty and purity we were aware; and he called us to the Unity of God, and taught us not to associate anything with Him; he forbade us the worship of idols, and enjoined us to speak the truth; to be faithful to our trusts; to be merciful and to regard the rights of neighbours; he forbade us to speak evil

> of women, or to eat the substance of orphans; he ordered us to fly vices, and to abstain from evil; to offer prayers, to render alms, to observe the fast. We have believed in him, we have accepted his teachings and his injunctions to worship God and not to associate anything with Him. For this reason, our people have risen against us, have persecuted us in order to make us forgo the worship of God and to return to the worship of idols of wood, and other abominations. They have tortured and injured us, until finding no safety among them, we have come to thy country, and hope thou wilt protect us from their oppression."

The demands of the Quraish were scouted by the king, and the deputies returned in confusion to Mecca.

Here, we may pause for a moment in the course of our history, and recognise the deep significance of this touching episode. The words of Jafar contain a comprehensive summary of the entire teachings of Muhammad. No person has ever succeeded in equalling the burning enthusiasm of that man, pleading the cause of his fellow-religionists and persecuted kinsmen.

Whilst the disciples of Muhammad were seeking safety in other lands from the persecution of their enemies, he himself stood bravely at his post, and amidst every opprobrium, insult and outrage pursued his mission. Again they came to him with promises of honour and riches in order to seduce him from his duty; the reply was as before, full of life, full of faith.

> "I am neither desirous of riches, nor ambitious of dignity, nor of dominion; I am sent by God, who has ordained me to announce glad tidings unto you. I give you the words of my Lord; I admonish you. If you will accept what I bring you, there is happiness for you in this world and in the next; if you reject my admonitions, I shall be patient, and leave God to judge between you and me."

> They asked for miracles to prove his mission. Remark his reply. "God has not sent me to you to work wonders He has sent me to preach to you. If you will accept what I bring you, you will have happiness in this world

> and the next. If you reject my admonitions, I shall be patient, and God will judge between you and me."

The sublimity of these words have been hardly recognised even to the present day. Disclaiming every power of wonder working, Muhammad rests the truth of his divine commission entirely upon his teachings. "Listen to what say, and happy will be your lot here and hereafter" is his invariable appeal to his hostile and idolatrous people. "I am but a man like you," he says, "but I bring you hope fill tidings." The answer he receives breathes a fierce animosity paralleled only by the darkest days of Arian or Pelagian prosecution in Christendom. "Know this, O Muhammad," said they, "we shall never cease to stop "thee from preaching, till either thou or we perish."

Supported, however, by a firm conviction in Divine assistance, and upheld by the admonitions of the heavenly voice within, which he believed, in the sincerity of his heart, to be the voice of God, conveyed to him by the administrators of heavenly mercy, he continued his preaching undeterred by the hostility of his enemies, or by the injuries they inflicted upon him. In spite of all opposition, however, slowly, but surely, the new teachings gained ground. The seeds of truth thus scattered could not fail to fructify. The wild Arab of the desert, the trading citizen of distant townships, who came to the national fair, heard the words of the strange man, whom his enemies thought possessed, listened to the admonitions, in which he poured forth his soul; listened with awe and wonder his denunciations of their divinities of wood and stone, and of their superstitions; and carried back to distant homes new light and new life, even unconsciously to themselves. The satires, the ill-names his enemies heaped upon Muhammad tended to make his words more extensively known. A Yathrebite wrote to the Quraish of Mecca, and holding up the examples of bygone ages, exhorted them not to become embroiled with civil dissensions and warfare. He also advised them to give a hearing to the new preacher:

> "An honourable man has adopted a certain religion, why persecute him? for it is only the Lord of the heavens who can read the heart of man! Follow the true religion: our eyes are fixed on you; they follow the right track who keep always in view the highest points."

About this time, also, Muhammad had the satisfaction of seeing his uncle, Hamza, and the well known Umar, both men of great energy, adopted his religion. Hamza, indeed, was the prototype of Ali in bravery, generosity, and chivalrous grandeur of character.

The accession of strength brought to the new faith, by the loss of Abu Talib and Khadija, in the same year, (619-620 A.C.). The venerable chief of the Bani-Hashim had stood faithfully by his nephew. For three consecutive years previous to his death he and his kinsmen—the children of Hashim and his brother, Muttalib,—had been beleagured in their own quarter, and subjected to every privation by the Quraish in order to force them to deliver up Muhammad. This siege was the result of a regular league among the various families opposed to the Prophet. Reduced to the last extremities for want of provisions and water, the Bani-Hashim were only saved by the breaking-up of the league against them in consequence of external dissensions.

Abu Talib did not survive this event many months; and in him Muhammad lost, not only the head of the family, who had kept it united, but a protector who had hitherto shielded him from the fury of his enemies. The death of Khadija was a loss equally severe. In the hard struggles of life; in the many afflictions and trials which he had to undergo. She was his sole comforter; and her death, following immediately upon that of Abu Talib, fell heavily on Muhammad.

Persecution Redoubled : The death of Abu Talib became the signal for the Quraish to redouble their persecutions. The family of Hashim, deprived of its head, could not afford an efficacious protection to Muhammad. The injuries and outrages to which he had been already exposed were renewed with increased fury.

Weighed down by the loss of his venerable protector and of his cherished wife, hopeless of turning the Quraish from idolatry, he determined to proceed to Taiyef, and preach to its inhabitants the unity of God. Accompanied by his faithful servant Zaid, the son of Harith, he arrived among the Thakif. But, instead of making a favourable impression, his words roused their fury: they drove him from the city; and the rabble and the slaves followed, hooting and pelting him with stones until the evening, when they left him to pursue his way alone. Wounded and bleeding, footsore and weary, he betook himself to prayer under the shade of some palm trees, which afforded a welcome shelter to the thirsty and famished wayfarer. Raising his hands towards heaven, and with tears streaming from his eyes, he cried:

> "O Lord! I make my complaint unto Thee out of my feebleness and the vanity of my wishes. I am insignificant in the sight of men. O Thou Most Merciful! Lord of the weak! Thou art my Lord. Do not forsake me. Leave me not a prey to strangers, nor to mine enemies. If thou art not offended, I am safe. I seek refuge in the light of Thy countenance, by which all darkness is dispersed, and peace comes here and hereafter. Let not Thy anger descend on me; solve my difficulties as it pleaseth Thee. There is no power, no help, but in Thee."

Muhammad returned to Mecca, sorely stricken in heart. He lived there for some time, retired from his people, preaching occasionally, but confining his efforts mainly of strangers congregated in Mecca, and its vicinity, during the season of the annual pilgrimage; hoping, as Tabari expresses it, to find among them some who would believe in him, and carry the truth to their people.

One day, whilst thus sadly and sorrowfully, but yet hopefully working among these half-traders, half-pilgrims, he came upon a group of six men, from the distant city of Yathreb, conversing together. He asked them to sit down and listen to him; and they sat down, and listened. Struck by his earnestness, and the truth of his words they became his proselytes, (620A.C.); and, returning to their city, they spread the news, with lightning-rapidity, that a Prophet had risen among the Arabs, who was to call them to God, and put an end to their dissensions which had lasted for centuries.

Next year these Yathrebites returned, and brought six more of their fellow-citizens as deputies from the two principal tribes who occupied that city.

On the self-same spot which had witnessed the conversion of the former six, the newcomers gave in their adhesion to Muhammad. This is called the first Pledge of Akaba, from the name of the hill on which the conference was held.

The Pledge they took was as follows:

> "We will not associate anything with God; we will not steal; nor commit adultery, nor fornication; we will not kill our children; we will abstain from calumny and slander; we will obey the Prophet in everything that is right; and we will be faithful to him in weal and in sorrow"

After the Pledge, they returned home with a disciple of Muhammad to teach them the fundamental doctrines of the new religion, which rapidly spread among the inhabitants of Yathreb.

The interval which elapsed between the first and second Pledge is remarkable, as, one of the most critical periods of Muhammad's mission. The sublime trust of Muhammad in God, and the grandeur of his character never stand forth more prominently than at this period. He was sad at the sight of his people so sternly wedded to idolatry; but his sorrow was assuaged by the hope that the truth would in the end prevail. He might not live to see it; but as surely as darkness flies before the rays of the sun, so surely falsehood would vanish before truth. Regarding this epoch, a few words of unconscious admiration escape even the lips of Muir: "Mahomet, thus holding his people at bay; waiting, in the still expectation of victory, to outward appearance defenceless, and with his little hand as it were in the lion's mouth; yet, trusting in His Almighty power, whose messenger he believed himself to be, resolute and unmoved—presents a spectacle of sublimity, paralleled only in the Sacred Records by such scenes as that of the Prophet of Israel, when he complained to his Master, 'I, even I only, am left."

This period is also remarkable for that notable vision of the ascension, which has furnished worlds of golden dreams for the imaginative genius of poets and traditionists. They have woven beautiful and gorgeous legends round the simple words of the Koran: "Praise be to Him who carried His servant "by night from the sacred temple to the temple that is more remote, whose precincts we have blessed, that we might show him some of our signs! For He is the Hearer, the Seer." And again: "And remember we said to thee, verily, thy Lord is round about mankind; we ordained the vision which we showed thee." "All that Mohammedans must believe respecting the Meraj is, that the Prophet saw himself, in a vision," transported from Mecca to Jerusalem", and that in such vision he really beheld some of the greatest signs of his Lord. It must be evident to the reader that the visions also of a prophet are a mode of divine inspiration."

The following year (622 B.C.) the Yathrebites, who had adopted the new religion, repaired to Mecca, to the number of seventy-five, in company with their idolatrous brethren, to invite the Prophet to their city;- but the idolaters had no knowledge of the intention of their companions.

The Promoters

In the stillness of night, when all hostile elements appeared slumbering, these pioneers of the new faith met under the hill which had witnessed the first Pledge. Muhammad appeared among them, accompanied by his uncle Abbas, who, though not a convert, yet took a warm interest in the progress of Islam. He opened the conference and vividly described to the Yathrebites the risks they incurred by adopting Islam, and inviting its teacher to their city. They replied with one voice they adopted the religion though conscious of the dangers that surrounded them. "Speak, O Prophet of God," said they, "and exact any pledge for thyself and thy "Lord."

The Prophet began, as was his wont, by reciting several passages of the Koran; he then invited all present to the service of God, and dwelt upon the blessings of the new dispensation. The former Pledge was repeated, that they would worship none but God—that they would observe the precepts of Islam—that they would obey Muhammad in all that was right, and defend him and his even as they would their women and children. "And," said they, "if we die in the cause of God, what shall "be our return?" "Happiness hereafter," was the reply. "But," said they, "thou will not leave us in the hour of prosperity, to return to thy people?" The Prophet smiled and said: "Nay, never; your blood is my blood; I am yours, you are mine" "Give us then thy hand;" and cach one, placing his hand on the Prophet's hand, swore allegiance to him and his God. Scarcely had the compact been concluded, when the voice of a Meccan, who had been watching this scene from a distance, came floating on the night air, striking a sudden panic into the self-denying hearts there assembled. The firm words of Muhammad restored their presence of mind.

The Pledge : Muhammad then selected twelve men from among them,—men of position, pointed out to him by the voice of the people, as his delegates (Nakibas). Thus was concluded the second Pledge of Akaba.

The Meccan spy had already spread the news of this conference through the city. Astounded at the temerity of Muhammad and his followers, the Quraish proceeded in a body to the caravan of the Yathrebites, to demand the men who had entered into the Pledge with him. Finding no clue, however, as to the persons who had taken part at the meeting, they allowed the caravan to depart unmolested. But this apparent moderation on the part of the Quraish formed only a prelude to a furious persecution of Muhammad and his disciples. The position of the latter became every day more and more perilous. The Prophet, fearing a general massacre, advised his followers to seek immediate safety at Yathreb; whereupon, about one hundred families silently disappeared by twos and threes from Mecca, and proceeded to Yathreb, where they were received with enthusiasm. Entire quarters of the city thus became deserted; and Utba, the son of Rabia, at the sight of these vacant abodes, once so full of life, "sighed heavily," and recited the old verse: "Every dwelling-place, even if it has been blessed ever so long, will one day become a prey to unhappiness and bitter wind." "And" he sorrowfully added, "all this is the work of the son of our brother, who has scattered our assemblies, ruined our affairs, and created dissension amongst us."

As it was with Jesus, so it was with Muhammad; only with this difference, that in one case the Teacher himself says: "Think not that I came to send peace on earth; I came not to send peace, but a sword: for I am come to set a man at variance against his father, and the daughter against her mother, and the daughter-in-law against her mother-in law." In Muhammad's case it is one of his most persevering opponents who accuse him of creating dissension in families.

But throughout this period, when the storm was at its height and might at any moment burst over his head, Muhammad never quailed. All his disciples had left for Yathreb; alone he remained, bravely at his post, with the devoted Ali and the venerable Abu Bakr.

Meanwhile the clouds were gathering fast. Fearful of the escape of the Prophet, an assembly of the Quraish met in all dispatch in the town-hall (*Dar-un-Nadwa*), and some chiefs of other clans were invited to attend. The matter had become one of life and death. Stormy was the meeting, for fear had entered their hearts. Imprisonment for life, expulsion from the city, each was debated in turn. Assassination was then proposed; but assassination by one man would have exposed him and his family to the vengeance of blood. The difficulty was at last solved by Abu Jahl, who suggested that a number of courageous men, chosen from different families should sheathe their swords simultaneously in Muhammad's bosom, in order that the responsibility of the deed might rest upon all, and the relations of Muhammad might consequently be unable to avenge it. This proposal was accepted, and a number of noble youths were selected for the sanguinary deed. As the night advanced, the assassins posted themselves round the Prophet's house. Thus they watched all night long, waiting to kill him when he should leave his house early in the dawn, peeping now and then through a hole in the door to make sure that he still lay on his bed. But, meanwhile, the instinct of self-preservation, the instinct which had often led the great Prophet of Nazareth to evade his enemies, had warned Muhammad of the danger. In order to keep the attention of the assassins fixed upon the bed, he put his own green garment upon the devoted and faithful Ali, bade him lie on his bed, "and escaped, as David had escaped, through the window." He repaired, to the house of Abu Bakr; and they fled together, unobserved, from the inhospitable city of their birth. They lay hidden for several days in a cavern of Mount Thour, a hill to the south of Mecca.

The fury of the Quraish was now unbounded. The news that the assassins had returned unsuccessful, and Muhammad had escaped, aroused their whole energy. Horsemen scoured the country. A price was set upon Muhammad's head. Once or twice the danger approached so near that the heart of old Abu Bakr quaked with fear. "We are but two," said he. "Nay, "said Muhammad, "we are three; God is with us." And he was with them. After three days the Quraish slackened their efforts. All this time Muhammad and his companion were sustained by food brought to them at night by the daughter of Abu Bakr. On the evening of the third day the fugitives left the cavern, and, procuring with great difficulty two camels, endeavoured to reach Yathreb by unfrequented paths. But even here the way was full of danger. The heavy price set upon Muhammad's head had brought out many horsemen from Mecca, and they were still diligently seeking for the helpless wanderer. One, a wild and fierce warrior, actually caught sight of the fugitives and pursued them. Again the heart of Abu Bakr misgave him, and he cried, "We are lost;" "Be not afraid," said the Prophet, "God will protect us." As the idolater overtook Muhammad, his horse reared and fell. Struck with awe, he entreated the forgiveness of the man whom he was pursuing, and asked for an attestation of his pardon. This was given to him on a piece of bone by Abu Bakr.

The fugitives continued their journey without further molestation, and soon they reached the territories of Yathreb. It was a hot day in June 622, of the Christian era, when Muhammad alighted from his camel upon the soil which was thenceforth to become his home and his refuge. A Jew watching on a tower first espied him, and thus were the words of the Koran fulfilled, "They to whom the Scriptures have been given, recognise him as they do their own children. Muhammad and his companion rested for a few days at a village called Quba, situated only two miles to the south of Yathreb, and remarkable for its beauty and fertility. Here he was joined by Ali, who had been severely maltreated by the Idolaters after their disappointment at Muhammads's escape. Ali fled from Mecca, and journeyed on foot, hiding himself in the daytime, and travelling only at night, lest he should fall into the hands of the Quraish. The Bani-Amr-bin-Auf, to whom the village belonged requested Muhammad to prolong his stay amongst them. But the duty of the Prophet lay before him; and he proceeded towards Yathreb, attended by a numerous body of his disciples. He entered the city on the morning of a Friday, 16th of Rabi I corresponding (according to M. Caussin de Perceval) with the 2nd of July, 622.

Thus was accomplished the Hijrat, called in European annals, "The Flight of Muhammad," from which dates the Mohammedan calendar.

5

Education in Book Form

The Traditional literature provides interesting material for providing a consistent view of the place of poetry in life.

The Prophet has laid down in clear and unambiguous terms the role that poetry should play in the building up of the individual and society but he is far more forceful and emphatic in stating what poets and poetry should not be.

The Poetry

Poetry, according to the Traditions, should not serve merely as a channel of expression for high strung, hypersensitive personality, or an outlet for the ventilation of suppressed feeling; it should not pander to erotic pleasure or rioting in sound and symphony; it is a purposeful activity opening out channels of communication between one individual and another, making them co-sharer of some valuable experience realising thereby the democratic ideal in the cultural, social and moral sense. According to Tolstoy: "That was how men of old—Socrates, Plato and Aristotle looked on art. Thus did the Hebrew Prophets and the ancient Christians regard art. Thus it was and still is understood by the Muhammadans."

The Chapters on Poetry in the collections of Traditions reveal a discriminating attitude towards the poets and their compositions.

Poetry according to the Traditions should enshrine a philosophy of life and should convey a message to the reader. The Prophet disapproved very strongly the fulminations of the contemporary poets, but always maintained that there were honourable exceptions.

"There are descriptions charming like magic, knowledge as dark as ignorance, poetry instructive like philosophy and speech harmful like a calamity."

On another occasion when poetry was mentioned in his presence, he stated "poetry is nothing but expression; if it is good it is praiseworthy and if bad it should be condemned." And the chapters on poetry contain forceful denunciations of bad poetry, bad as interpreted according to the verse of the Holy Book—the poets who are followed by the be guided ones,' the main charge laid down against them being that they attempt to explore all the valleys and are evidently not governed by any unity of purpose or noble ideas. And when poets are denounced by the Quran as persons who roam in every hill and profess what they do not act upon, it does not imply an outright denunciation of poets. It is followed by the usual saving clause which invariably follows as a corollory. "Except those who believe in God, do good deeds and pray abundantly."

The Prophet seemed to have no patience with poets whose preoccupations with their erotic pastime left them no leisure for the more serious and essential business of life.

Once he came across a man in the suburbs of Mecca who suddenly appeared before him and began to recite poetry. The Prophet said, "Catch hold of this Satan. Verily filling one's intestines with puss is better than stuffing it with poetry."

Here also his remark does not imply a sweeping denunciation of all poetry, good or bad. It is specially directed against that erotic form of poetry, which fills a man to brim' and leaves no room for prayer, Quran reading or meditation (Fiqh).

Plato on Homer : Such a discriminating attitude towards poetry is a legacy shared by all great minds. Plato has devoted a special section of his chapter in 'Republic' (on the Arts of Education) to the denunciation of poetry which may have an adverse effect on the young mind. He forwards a fervent plea for such a critical attitude towards the works of some of the greatest names in Greek poetry, "and we must beg Homer and the other poets, not to be angry if we strike out these and similar passages, not because they are unpoetical or unattractive to the popular ear but because the greater the poetical charm of them, the less are they met for the ears of boys and men who are meant to be free and who should fear slavery more than Death".

Place of Good Poetry : In the beginning, poetry did not form a regular feature of the school curriculum among the Muslims because it was in the air and it ran its passionate course in their blood but later on when it was felt that it deserved a regular place in school, some great thinkers sedulously excluded poetry from the text prescribed for children. Umar bin Atba in a letter to the tutor of his son instructs him to teach him only respectable (Afif) poetry.

Although fully conscious of the pernicious influence of bad poetry on the Site of individuals and society, his personality had a grand rhythm of its own.

The Quran has an awe inspiring grandeur of style and the Traditions are couched in an infinitely human, intimate and emotional style. They express in words the grand sympathy of the soul which throbbed in his moral frame.

He would revel in the sheer beauty of oral expression, the rhythmic cadence and harmony which gurgled out so mellifluously from the mouth of the desert Arab. Once when a Beduin came to visit him and opened a speech in the true Beduin style, the Prophet remarked. "Verily, there is description (as effective) as magic and there is poetry (as true) as *Hikmat* (Philosophy)."

The conception of good poetry, according to the traditions, is that of a moral force which serves some high social purpose and looks refreshingly modern when we compare it with the opinions held by that particular school of critics who subscribe to this view. According to Tolstoy, "Formerly people feared lest among works of Art there might chance to be some causing corruption and they prohibited art altogether. Now they only fear lest they should be deprived of any enjoyment art can afford and they patronize any art. And I think the last error is much grosser than the first and its consequences are far more harmful."

The Appreciation : Hence he always approved of the poetry of men who were inspired with ideals. Out of the poets of Jahiliyah, he expressed high appreciation of the poetry of Umayyah bin Abi-Salt, one of those who followed the creed of the Hanif, a group of sincere seekers after truth who believed in Unity of Godhood and high morals. He saw the rise of Islam but did not enter its fold. The Prophet prized high the poetry of Labid bin Rabiah Ansari for its moral vigour and noble appeal and would often quote with high approbation his well known line on the unrivalled eminence of the Lord. He described two lines by him as the truest words ever versified by a poet.' His opinion was supported by Farzdaq in a unique manner. When a couplet of Labid was recited in his presence, he made a prostration and said, 'There is prostration (Sijdah) for the verse as there is prostration for Quran.'

It is said that the contemporary poets prostrated themselves on the ground for him when he recited a well known Qasidah of his.

It is said that Labid had embraced Islam and he sang joyously of the new Faith in these lines:

> "Thanks are due to God that death did not overtake
> me until I had donned the garments of Islam."

Poets of the Prophet : The most important poets attached to the Prophet were Hassan bin Thabit, Kaab bib Malik and Abdullah bin Rawaha. They were all masters of satire and he would put their talent to use when he requisitioned their devastating power of satire for giving a rejoinder to the withering sarcasm of the poets of Quraysh. All the three had a satiristic vein in their style. But there was a difference in outlook and approach. The forte of Hassan and Kaab was the denunciation of the genealogy, or other failings of the Quraysh of Mecca. Abdullah on the other hand, wrote lampoons on their lack of faith, their worship of idols and their other religious malpractices. The Meccans used to say that the poetry of Abdullah bin Rawaha was more grievous to them than the vilifications of his fellow poets.

The need for such an action arose as a defence mechanism against the bitter satires that the Meccans wrote against the Prophet. Some of them employed slave girls to sing scurrilous verses about him in accompaniment of a musical instrument. When the Prophet decided to give a rejoinder he sent someone to Abdullah bin Rawaha and asked him to compose a reply to the verses written by the Meccans. But his attempt was not approved by the Prophet. Next he tried Kaab bin Malik who also did not come upto the mark.

Then Hassan bin Thabit came to him. The Prophet felt gratified at his appearance and welcomed him as 'the lion who thrashes people with his tail' and with these words, the Prophet took out his tongue and moved it. This lion of verse used to wag his tail most vociferously. Hassan, the erstwhile court poet of the House of Ghassan, was confident about the devastating venom of his verse. When he was told to compose verses against the Meccans he declared that he would tear them to shreds just as one tears a piece of leather or skin. In this way Hassan became the chief satirist of the Muslims.

The Prophet would often incite him to recite poetry against his enemies. "Revile them," the Prophet would say, "and may Jibbrail be with you." On another occasion he had said, "Send horsemen (of thy verse) against Banu abd Munaf because by God, your poetry is more grievous upon them than the swords (that come down on the tribe) in the dark of the night."

And Hassan would use his powerful talent for vilification with disastrous effect for the Quraysh of Mecca. In this he was helped by the genealogical knowledge of Abu Bakr who was a good scholar of Ilm al-ansab.

The Prophet had singled him out for the supreme honour of ordering a pulpit for him whence he could declaim the eulogies of the Prophet, "Verily" he would declare, "the Holy Spirit (Ruh-al-Quds) is with Hassan."

Hassan had three distinctions which were denied to others. He was the poet of Ansar in the Jahiliyyah, the poet of the Prophet during his life time and the Poet of Yemen after his death.

But the Prophet would always discriminate between true and false poetry and when Hassan recited beautiful verses celebrating hollow claims without substance he would have nothing but an indulgent smile for him. Once Hassan recited certain verses in which he described how he rose in the morning among his people with a gleaming sword about his girdle.

The Prophet smiled at him because he knew that with all his vauntings, Hassan had never taken part in a serious engagement.

In the Battle of the Ditch he was quartered with women and children in a fortress and when a Jew approached the fortress with hostile intentions, Safflyah bint Abdul Mutallib, an aunt of the Prophet asked Hassan to go and kill the Jew. Hassan said, "May God pardon thee, O' daughter of Ibn Mutallib, I am not the man for it." Then Safiyyah herself got down and killed the man, with a tent peg. When she returned, she asked Hassan to go and plunder him. This he refused to do.

The Dewan of Hassan bin Thabit has been published and it contains his panegyrics of the Prophet. It contains also a funeral song which he wrote on the death of the Prophet.

But even more genuine and spontaneous was the poetry of those tribal poets who would often accompany their people to the Prophet and describe in a language coloured with deep emotions the great inner change that has come over them.

The embracing of Islam was a thrilling experience for these sensitive souls and a number of companions have composed touching lines on such occasions. They sing in beautiful words of their great joy at their new spiritual adventure and their deliverance from the superstitions of the Jahiliyyah.

When Jarud came with the deputation of Abd al Qays in A.H., he sang "How the daughters of his heart had responded with open declaration and zeal." And when Tharwan ibn Fazzarah saw the Prophet he sang in the classical style how his she-camel had sped along for four days at a stretch without food or drink.

They would often rejoice in verse on the victory of the one God over a whole host of gods who held people in the grip of ignorance and superstition.

Rashid bin Hafsa was a devotional attendant of Suwa, the idol of Banu Sulaym and when the Prophet entered Kaaba after the Fall of Mecca, he sang:

> "And my beloved said, "Come along, let us talk (of love) but I said, 'No'. God and Islam has prohibited it. If thou had seen the Prophet and his people on the

> fall of Mecca when he smashed the idols you would have observed the Light of God, glorious and resplendent and the face of idolatory covered with the darkest clouds."

An interesting incident had turned Rashid against the tribal god. He was the priest of the idol and when he saw one day two foxes urinating over it, he could hardly restrain his spite and indignation and he burst into these verses:

> "Have you a right to be called a god when foxes urinate over your head. Verily one who is watered by the fox is despicable."

He attacked the idol which was made of some fragile substance and smashed it into pieces. After that he came to the Prophet and embraced Islam.

These poets would often mention their favourite idols in verse by name and heap dishonour on them. The poet of Saad al Ashirah broke the idol of Farradh into pieces and sang, "Who should take the tidings to Saad that I have brought to them something eternal for that which was evanescent."

Abu Sufiyan, the veteran general of the Meccans and one of the shrewdest and the most inveterate foe of Islam in early days sang in a melancholic vein of those days.

"By thy life, on the day when the standard was raised that the host of Lat (the name of a Mecca idol) may vanquish the army of Muhammad. On that day I was like one who had strayed into the dark and what a darkness it was! But today I have been shown the light and I have received it."

And this great leader of the host of Lat sang in a different vein when he stood nonchalantly holding the reins of the Prophet's mule on the battlefield of Hunayn as the main body of the Muslim army ran helter skelter, when they had to face a surprise attack of the Hawazans in a mountainous defile.

He sang, "Verily I am the brother of battle and I ride on its sharpest edge. I have taken my stand before the Messenger of God and I have no fear."

Tribal Poetry : They would often sing of their heroic resolution to embrace the new faith and when Zamil of Bani Azrah visited the Prophet he said, "O Prophet of God, I have turned the face of my ride in your direction and I have forced it to cross the expanses of the sandy wastes of the desert. I resolve to help the best of man," and he continues "I have attached a cord from thee to my own and I will follow the path as long as my shoes burden my feet."

A personal contact with the Prophet would often bring to their hearts a comforting sense of self–confidence and awakened in them the supreme urge for sacrifice.

A poet of the Banu Sulaym said, "When I came to Muhammad I strengthened my right hand by a union with the best of hands. I have shared my religion with him and I have given him one thousand men with the lightest of hearts." The poet could not fulfil his promise but his tribe honoured his words and sent the contingent.

This ecstatic joy on discovering the light and emancipating oneself from the darkness of sin and sordidness would often touch the cords of the most unpoetic hearts and they jingled out in strains of genuine poetry.

When Abu Hurayrah appeared before the Prophet after a long and dangerous journey on which he was deserted by his slave he sang, "O what a long and terrible night, only it rescued me from the land of Unbelief."

The tribal deputations that waited on the Prophet from different quarters of the Peninsula were often given presents, by the Prophet. Some of them received a caress over their head, or faces.

These pretty moments of their visits were commemorated by the tribal poets in verse. A poet of Bani al Bakka sang how his father was caressed on his head by the Prophet and how he presented him with some white sheep of a high breed, "which regaled the deputation to overbrimming at night and repeated the process in the morning."

The caress given by the Prophet to a member of the deputation of Halal bin Amir was commemorated by the poet in a verse, and he described how the glory of the blessing lent a lustre to his face until he made his resting place in the grave. The compositions of these tribal poets are not high class examples of poetic expression. In fact it was not easy to produce such poetry under the limitations imposed on this form of expression by the Prophet. But they symbolize the widespread enthusiasm which the new faith had awakened among the desert Arabs.

Events of social and political life, friends and foes, tribal and personal loyalties, wars and battles, even journeys and travels and sometimes the most trivial incidents of daily life provided subjects of purposeful poetry for the desert Arab. The struggle of life was so keen and relentless that it hardly left much leisure for the contemplation of his inner self or the world of nature. There was not much scope for sheer contemplative or romantic poetry.

Life in the desert as bare and barren as the sandy wastes of the Sahara and even the minor occupations of life which were dull, uninteresting and irksome had to be made more attractive through rythmic prose or poetry.

Hence there arose an irresistible urge to break the monotony of the physical psychological landscape by striking a correlation between art and life. It was the most effective panacea against the inertia and enervation produced by the life in the desert. The other alternative for driving away this oppressive feeling of monotony was to indulge in tribal warfare.

The prosaic and tiring work of camel driving received an added charm by the march songs of the camels and the Prophet had a number of songsters or Hudat for this purpose. Zad-ul-Maad gives a list of persons who had acted as his hudat.

Once he was travelling along with ladies and Anjushah, one of the camel drivers, was singing a marching song for the camels (hudi). The music had probably a quickening effect on the movement of the camels. Thereupon he asked him to proceed softly and with such care as if his camels were laden with glassware.

Amir bin Akwa was also one of the hudat. On their night march for the siege of Khyber, Amir bin al Akwa, the reciter of the camel songs of the Prophet, was requested by his companions to recite some verses. He got down from his ride and began to recite the following:

> "If it were not for God, we would have never seen the light.
>
> We would not have given in charity and we would not have turned to prayers.
>
> O God, make steadfast out feet when we encounter the foe and pour on us the blessing of peace."

He was singing in this vein when the Prophet heard him and said. "Who is he?" When he was told that it was Amir, he said," May God bring peace unto him."

Amir died in this campaign.

Poetry as a Physical Stimulus : Poetry was recited as a physical stimulus to action when engaged in physical labour. It is said that he had recited verses when engaged in carrying stones for the building of the Prophet's Mosque.

> "O God, there is no good except the good of the world to come. Render help to the Ansar and the Muhajirin. This is the great burden, the burden of Khyber is nothing (to it). This is the more pious, more sacred, O God."

According to Zahri, he had never composed any verse except these lines and he had never expressed any desire to do so. The lines have been described as rajm and have in common with war poems, the quality of stimulating physical activity.

It is interesting to know that a number of verses were composed on this occasion by Ali and others. They helped to alleviate the strain of physical labour and expressed a spirit of joyous enthusiasm for cooperative effort.

When a stone struck his finger on the day of Uhud and it bled, the trickle of blood brought to his mind his great destiny in facing ordeals in the way of Lord. How comforting are these lines to one who feels the ecstatic joy of self–sacrifice. "Thou are but a finger which is bleeding. Thou have met this fate on the path of the Lord."

Poetry as a Leisure Time Activity : Recitation of poetry as a leisure time activity was permitted and enjoyed by the Prophet.

Out of the poets of Jahiliyah he had a high opinion of Umayya bin Abi Salt, a poet whose compositions were inspired with a deep moral fervour. Umayyah lived to see the days of the Prophet but he did not enter the fold of Islam. The Prophet had described once a line by Umayyah as the best verse composed by a poet.

He loved to hear recitation and according to Shurayd bin al-Suwayd, once his father was seated behind the Prophet on the camel's back and the Prophet asked him to recite the verses of Umayyah. He recited a couplet. The Prophet cried encore and in this way he recited one hundred couplets in all.

Recitations of Poetry were often made in the Prophet's assembly. According to Jabir bin Samurah, he had the opportunity of attending the assembly of the Prophet more than hundred times. On these occasions the companions would recite verses and relate things about Jahiliyyah. The Prophet would sit quietly and would often smile.

Very often he entered into the spirit of the recitation and blessed the poet with a good word. When Nabighah al Jadi came to him he recited the following:

> "I visited the Prophet when he came with guidance and he read a book radiant like the stars. We had reached the skies in glory and ancestral pedigree and we aspire a station still higher than that."

The Prophet asked, "Whereto O Aba Laylah," and he replied "towards paradise" and he blessed him with the words, 'by the grace of God, you will' and he prayed that may his mouth never lank in. It is said that he retained excellent teeth upto the end of his life.

The Poetesses : The Prophet had expressed appreciation of the poetry of Khansa, the greatest elegy writer of the age. She was unprecedented in the art and exercised the special privilege of raising a standard over her tent at Ukaz with these words blazoned in purple, "The greatest elegy writer of the age."

She came to the Prophet with a deputation of her people, Banu Sulaym. It was usual for these tribal deputations to bring their best poets and orators with them. When Khansa began to recite, the Prophet was obviously moved. He waved his hand and encouraged her with the words, "On with it, O Khansa."

The Prophet had described her as the best of poets and when Adi bin Hatim of Tay came to see him and claimed that the tribe of Tay had amongst them the greatest of poets, the most generous of men and the bravest of warriors, the Prophet remarked that Khansa was the greatest among the poets.

According to Ibn Abd al-Bakr, she joined the battle of Qadisiyyah with four of her sons all of whom fell heroically in the battle. Each one of them is credited with a war poem which he recited on the occasion. Umar bin Khattab appreciated the great spirit of Khansa who had encouraged them with word and deed alike and he transferred the stipends of all her sons in her name. It amounted to 800 Dirhams. She died in 50 A.H. during the period of Muawiyyah.

Another poetess who had made a deep impression on the Prophet was Qutaylah, the sister or according to another source, the daughter of Nadhr bin Harith.

When she came into his presence and recited her moving verses on the death of her brother, the Prophet was deeply moved by this expression of filial affection.

Nadhr had been made a captive in the battle of Badar and was put to the sword. Her elegy is a deeply moving piece written in a simple and direct style. She says:

> "O thou, the rider, take my message to the Dead because the riders have always wandered about with my messages, and give him the tiding of my tears, those that roll down for him who had conserved their store for himself and the tears that have choked me up."
>
> "And if thou hail Nadhar he would listen to you if the dead speak and listen. Verily it was the swords of his kinsmen that destroyed him. I wonder over the kinship that was thus shattered to pieces."

She adds a singularly beautiful line in praise of the Prophet at the end and appeals to him in the name of kinship that he should have granted a reprieve to the unfortunate youth.

The Prophet remarked on hearing these verses. "I would have pardoned him if I had heard these verses in time.

Poetry in the Prophet's Family : There is abundant evidence to prove that poetic talent or at least a knack of versification was fairly widespread in the Prophet's family. It is said that Abdul Mutallib had called up six daughters of his to his death bed and asked them to sing to him the funeral ditties with which they would bewail his death.

Ibn Hisham gives at length the funeral songs of Safiyyah Barrah and Atikah. Safiyyah speaks of her tears that would roll down her cheeks like glistening pearls. She was followed by Barrah, Atikah Um Hakim, al Baydah and Umaymah.

It is said that Abdul Mutallib approved of their compositions by nodding his head as he was too weak to speak.

Three of the Prophet's aunts outlived him and wrote mourning ditties (Marthiya) on his death. They were Urwa, Atikah and Safiyyah. It is doubtful how far these pieces are genuinely authentic because they have the air of a formal elegy about them. But nevertheless there are snatches of genuine emotion which reveal how deeply the writer had been aroused by the great tragedy.

Atikah sang, "Who would come now to the rescue of the needy who was being pushed out, from all sides and being driven out ignominiously; one who was in bonds and complained of the grievous burden of his chains."

In these lines she is obviously referring to the usual practice of the Prophet who would liquidate the debts of those who could not pay them. Thereby he saved them from indignities at the hand of the creditor who had the right to turn him into a vassal and keep him as a slave in the days of Jahiliyyah. The scene of a creditor dragging the debtor with a cord tied about his neck was not uncommon in the days of Jahiliyyah.

Atikah was a poet of fairly good talent and Abi Tamam has included in his well known selections a piece of hers in his chapter on the Hamasah. It has been written to commemorate the Day of Ukaz, the last event of the war of Fijar, an engagement in which the Prophet had taken part. In the skirmish which gave the finale to a rather long drawn war. The Quraysh finally defeated Qays bin Ghaylan. The piece is a forceful specimen of war poetry and represents the sense of glorious pride that the poetess feels for the victory of her people. She presents a realistic picture of the encounter drawn with a few powerful strokes. It looks marvellous with what economy and effectiveness the poetess has used her colours.

In a neat small piece of six lines, she has drawn a gorgeous picture of the battle array, how the resplendent brightness of the helmets dazzled the eyes of the spectators. And then the final catastrophe. How Malik fell in battle, treacherously betrayed by the rabble rout and the finale; how his corpse lay on the far stretching plain and was being devoured by beasts of prey. The Prophet had himself participated in the battle of Fijar and must have enjoyed these lines.

The most prolific poet of the Prophet's family whose verses have been abundantly quoted by Ibn Hisham is Abu Talib, the uncle of the Prophet.

He quotes several poems by Abu Talib, verses which he wrote in those perilous times when the Quraysh plotted to alienate his sympathies from the Prophet.

His forceful Qasidah Lamia and others seem to be pieces of old world oracles hurled with the flaming eloquence which grows out of prolonged persecution. It is the cry of a ferocious but noble beast of prey turned to bay.

Ibn Hisham does not vouch for the authenticity of the entire piece but even if they are not authentic they describe entire piece in a bold, and forceful style, the heroic determination with which Abu Talib had steeled his mind to support his nephew.

He has two other pieces to his credit, one composed on the eve of that infamous conspiracy which drove the Prophet's family into the Shaab Abu Talib and another on the breaking up of their enemies' alliance after a period of three years.

He enthuses over the great event in a lyrical vein and says, "Have our exiles beyond the sea (emigrants to Abysinnia) known how God has been considerate to them in their exile." He has a word of glorious praise for those who had taken the lead in its abrogation.

He compares them to the eagle, which sails steadily in its 'long armours'. When faced with great crisis they are like a firebrand which is ever blazing in the hand of one who holds it.

One of the finest pieces said to be composed by Abu Talib expresses his great determination to protect the Prophet even at the sacrifice of his life.

In an impressive, rather awful atmosphere he describes the solemn pledge he had taken for this purpose. He says how he presented himself before the Kaaba with his partisans and his brethern and he caught hold of the sacred drapery. He stood against its magnificent gate, where stands the man who takes the solemn oath of his innocence. In this solemn setting with Isaf and Nailah, the two idols on one side where the stream flows by, he took the redoubtable oaths. By the God of men, and by the mountain of Thaur and Thabir and by the Kaaba and the Black Stone!

After giving an impressive array of the great symbols of sanctity, he rises to an acme of moral indignation and hurls denunciations on his opponents. He tells them about the fiery resolution with which they will rise, laden with weapons like she-camels loaded with water skins. And how they will retaliate 'measure for measure',

It is said that in later years the Prophet would often recall these lines written by Abu Talib in those troublous days and indulged in grateful reminiscences of the great sacrifices which his uncle had made for him.

According to Ibn Hisham, once when he went out to pray in a year of drought and it began to thunder and rain he said to Ali, "If Abu Talib had been alive today, it would have cooled his eyes because he had written, "He is such a glorious one that rains are sought by his face." The lines were composed in praise of the Prophet.

And when the Prophet surveyed the great dead of the Quraysh lying on the battlefield of Badar he turned to Abu Bakr and said, "if Abu Talib had been alive he would have seen how our swords had overtaken the nobility of the Quraysh." Then he quoted a verse of the Qasidah Lamia of Abu Talib in which he had denounced the Quraysh who had practically incarcerated him and his family into the Shaab of Abu Talib. He had sung how their swords will be driven into the bodies of the noblest among them.

Companions' Poetry : Ali the son of Abu Talib, had inherited the literary traditions of his family and his verses are informed with a high ethical tone. According to al Mubarrad the author of Al-Kamil, one of the finest pieces ever written on keeping a secret are ascribed to Ali.

But he is more known for his splendid Rajm or war heroics which he had recited on various occasions. The war scene seemed to have awakened in him the spirit of moral and physical indignation that found its expression in extempore verse of a fairly high order. His rajm on the battle of the Ditch and Khyber have been preserved by the chroniclers.

His authorship of Nahj al Balaghat is of doubtful authenticity but his literary bon mots and his sparkling wit embellish many a chapter on Adab (manners) and education. His literary interests were inherited by Hassan and Hussain. The latter has described in an inimitable style his love for his wife Rabab and his daughter Sakinah.

Out of the Prophet's wives, Aishah seemed to have inherited a literary taste from her father. Her expression revealed a fine literary flavour and there were often lightening flashes of poetic beauty in her talk. She would often quote verses in her intimate chats with her husband.

Once when she saw droplets of perspiration sparkling on the brow of the Prophet she quoted the well known lines of Abu Kabir al-Hudzayli which he had composed about his stepson Tabat Sharra, the well known poet. When I look upon the lineaments of his face, they sparkle like the flashes of a lightening cloud.

She had a ready line on her lips for all occasions. According to Ibn Abd al-Bar she had learnt 12,000 lines of Labid, the favourite poet of the Prophet by heart. And according to her favourite pupil Hisham bin Urwah, he had never seen a woman more learned than her in poetry, medicine and law.

Abu Bakr was not a poet but he was a fine connoisseur of poetry and the cords of his heart would vibrate if struck with a sympathetic note. He has written more than one elegies of the Prophet. They do not rise much above the average, but there are flashes of genuine feeling in some of the lines. "When I saw my Prophet going into the dust, the halls with all their vastness looked so oppressively narrow to me".

"Armies of sorrow and grief made their charges and counter charges throughout the night. And they had fractured my physical frame as if they were stones."

Even a puritan like Umar could hardly escape the contagion. It is said that he was keenly interested in poetry. He would quote poetry, discuss ideas expressed by poets and illustrate his own by quoting verses.

He has been credited with a funeral ditty and other pieces which he had composed when aroused.

When he performed his last pilgrimage, the memories of the old days flooded his mind. His family was not counted among the rich in Mecca and he had to tend the flocks of his father al-Khattab in the valley. The severe old man would find fault with him even if he performed his duty and would thrash him in case of default. These melancholic thoughts moved him to recite verses on the vanity of life and its glories. He had also celebrated the fall of Mecca in verse.

Atikah the wife of Umar bin Khattab was a master of elegy. Few verses could vie with the deeply tragic note that Atikah bint Zayd struck on his murder. The lines thrill with the great personal loss suffered by the poetess and the tragedy that had overtaken the poor and the destitute; "Who would help now a soul that has been attacked by the counter-charge of grief and who can console the eye which has emaciated on account of prolonged sleeplessness."

It was the fate of this talented woman to write a number of elegies for illustrious men who took her as wife one after the other and all of whom died through violence. According to Ali "if any one desired a ready martyrdom, he should marry Atikah."

She has mourned the loss of Umar in more than one elegies and the recurring refrain of all these songs is the terrible disaster that has overtaken the poor, the friendless, the debtor, and the destitute.

Different Styles

There is evidence to prove that the Prophet was interested in the technique of poetry and would some time invite a poet to discuss his method of composing verses with him. Once Abdullah bin Rawaha was passing by the Prophet's mosque when he was sent for by the Prophet. When he went to him he said to him, "How do you manage to compose poetry when you have a desire to do so." It appeared as if he was expressing a pleasant surprise on Rawaha's versatility and genius. "I must get a few moments before I could give a reply to this question," said Abdullah, and then he extemporised some lines on the Unbelievers.

Freedom of Expression

There were no restrictions on the writing of purposeful poetry during the period of the Prophet and Abu Bakr. By the time of Umar, tendencies of erotic poetry seem to have been revived and Umar imposed restrictions on them. According to his instructions no poet was permitted to compose, or at least recite in public Nasib or erotic poems.

The order was not relished by the poets and Humayd bin Thaur the well known poet wrote as a protest a fantastic love lyric about the 'trees of Malik' opening with the line, "God desires that the trees of Malik may be tall."

It appears that Umar had laid restrictions on the public recitation of Nasib but he had not banned recitation in private. Once Umar objected when he heard a companion reciting Nasih in his house. Thereupon he replied. "We recite within our houses what others recite." Thereupon Umar kept quiet and made no further comment.

There were no restrictions on the recitation of good poetry. Once Umar disapproved Hassan reciting poetry in the mosque. But Hassan retorted that he had been reciting like that in the presence of one who was better than him (the Prophet).

During the life time of the Prophet, recitations of poetry were often made in the mosque and he would himself enjoy them. Umar provided a separate site called Batiha for this purpose. As the name indicates, it must have been a piece of spacious level ground.

6

The Perceptions

Islam, the greatest experiment in social and cultural democracy on an essentially human and spiritual basis was a reaction against the parochial outlook of tribal life, the narrow individualism of other religions and the domination of a privileged class in Mecca who jealously preserved their vested interests in the face of an evergrowing class of paupers. The Islamic belief and observances, players and social usages, the tithe (zakat) and the fasting penance, all fostered a consciousness of corporate life among the old and created a social environment of the highest educative value for the young. It awakened among the desert Arab, the dormant desire for human association and gradually widened the sphere of their loyalties from the narrow circle of tribal life to the universal brotherhood of man.

Philosophical Basis

According to the greatest thinkers of Islam, human society is not based on the nasty and brutish individualism of Hobbes where the deeply laid instinctive suspicion of one another forced men to associate together in order to safeguard against the danger of fratricidal strife and anarchy. According to them, the origin of human association is mutual love and attraction and the Shariah has seized upon this innate tendency and has tried to foster it through religious observances. Ibn Maskwayh writes as follows while discussing the origin of human association, its recognition by the

Shariah and the means by which it has attempted to place it on a sound foundation.

Basic Principle of Life : "The temporal love develops out of associating with one another.... and its origin is the innate tendency of association and company which is inherent in man's nature. Man is not unimpressionable by origin nor does he abhor company and the term Insan is derived from Uns in the Arabic language.

We should try our best that this feeling for comradeship may not be atrophied; rather we should try to foster and cultivate it as far as possible. Hence the Shariah and goodly usage have approved of the feasts and gatherings for cultivating this spirit. The Shariah has ordained all men to attend the mosque five times daily. It has enjoined prayer in company in preference to prayer in private, in order to nurture this innate feeling for association which is potential until it issues forth in action. The Shariah has strengthened it by inculcating it through religious belief and inhabitants of every street or alley can easily attend such gatherings every day.

Concept of a Cooperative Society : It is incumbent on the citizens to meet together once a week on Friday in a mosque, spacious enough to contain all of them; the inhabitants of the town and the neighbouring villages must come together twice a year in the plain outside the town in order to revive this sense of social solidarity among them and may knit themselves in bonds of unity under the influence of this integrating love.

Again it has been made obligatory that all should meet once in their life at Mecca and no specific year of one's life has been appointed for its performance in order to provide facility for the people of different lands to meet together, just as the citizens of a single town gather together and develop a sense of camraderie and sympathy of virtue and grace like those who congregate annually, weekly or daily.

They flock together under the urge of the natural feeling in order to do good in common and to revive in them love of the Shariah.

Reaction on Education : Such a conception of human society was bound to have a strong reaction on the system of education and the social outlook of such a system has been inspired by that religious faith in corporate life and human camraderie which is the life breath of Islamic thought and practice. A great achievement of the system was the development of a closer relation between community and education; the absence of a privileged class of the clergy precluded any possibility of knowledge degenerating into a preserve of the Elect; under the influence of this new movement of democracy. Education was primarily meant for the masses and not for the classes. The contents of education were selected from the social viewpoint and the criteria for such a selection were not determined by a ruling class or an intellectual hegemony; they were primarily chosen for their social values, social in the sense that they help the individual in the moral and intellectual regeneration of his people and along with that provide scope for his individuality and personal contribution without which all human progress is impossible.

Teachings of Prophet

A close study of the Traditions on the subject provide plenty of evidence in support of such a conception of Islamic education. The Traditions accept frankly the inherent similarity of the function of a Prophet and a Teacher, the nature of Apostlehood and the educative process. According to them, the difference lies in degree rather than in quality. The teacher is described as the rightful heir of the apostles of God; he is the caliph of the Prophet among his people; a patriarchal figure like the Prophets of the Old Testament on whose shoulders lay the responsibility of social and intellectual leadership of his people.

Role of a Teacher

The function of the Prophet and the scholar appears to be essentially similar in nature according to certain Traditions. They throw interesting light on the social role that a teacher is expected to play in the Islamic society. In the first place, he shares with the Divinity, the quality of Knowledge. According to the Prophet, "The Lord revealed to Abraham 'Oh, Abraham, I am 'Alim (One who knows) and I love all who have knowledge". According to another, the teacher is the Trustee of the Lord on Earth. Another set of traditions emphasise the likeness of the function of a teacher with that of an apostle. According to a tradition, the groups nearest to the rank of Apostlehood are the teachers and the martyrs. One who offered prayers behind a teacher, gained the merit of offering prayers behind an Apostle and one who prayed behind an Apostle received absolution for all his sins. Elsewhere the Prophet declared that there are two groups among his people. In case they were sound, the rest of the people were also sound; but when they were in the wrong, the rest also were in the wrong; one of these groups, according to him was that of the teachers. Commenting on these traditions, Ghazzali remarks how closely the Prophet has associated knowledge with Prophethood.

Great savants have also expressed the same idea in a similar vein. According to one, none was gifted with anything more valuable in this world than Prophethood and next to it is Knowledge. Another has said that one who desires to attend the Assembly of the Prophets should visit the Assembly of Teachers".

Teacher and Recluse : The traditions on the comparative merits of the teacher and the recluse indicate abundantly the pronounced social bias in Islamic education and the uncontested superiority of the teacher, the symbol of social good over the recluse who represents individual idealism in the religious sense. Social good and the welfare of the group as a whole outweighs all considerations of personal weal even in the field of self-edification. According to another set of Traditions, the teacher stands higher than a martyr in the estimate of the Prophet. One is a positive and constructive force who is building up the Palace of Truth tier after tier and generation after generation until its pinnacles kiss the glorious heaven; the other is essentially a negative force under whose thundering blows the citadel of Evil is tottering to pieces.

Scholarly Position

The rank of the teacher in the Old Testament is held by the patriarch and according to the Prophet, the teacher deserves the same honoured status of social leadership and guidance in the Islamic society. "The superiority of the scholar over the recluse is that of the full moon over the rest of the stars and the learned scholars are the inheritors of the Messengers of God. Verily the legacy of the Prophets is neither gold nor silver; their legacy is knowledge and one who receives that (princely heritage) should be deemed fortunate. The simile of the full moon which bathes the whole earth in its light and makes dull and dark objects shine with her reflected glory is an illuminating symbol of the teacher while the stars, illuminous bodies in themselves, resemble a recluse who cannot shed a circle of light which may flood a world besides their own. The scholars have been aptly styled as light-houses on land.

According to another Tradition, "The learned savants among my people have the status of the Prophets among the Israelites." On another occasion, he explained in a more pointed and lucid manner the exact place of the Savant on the social ladder. "The priority of the savant over the recluse is akin to my superiority over my people." According to 'Umar, "the demise of a thousand recluses is easy to be borne than the death of a single discriminating person who knows lawful from the unlawful." The mathematical finality with which the verdict is given in favour of the teacher is a clear and indisputable indication of the social outlook of Islam and the conditions which it implies for the growth of an efficient system of education.

In fact, Islam deeply imbued as it is with the social spirit could hardly recognise much good in the individualism of a recluse who sought salvation of the self in vacuo, and not through that fuller realisation of the self which is achieved by self- surrender and sacrifice for the larger interests of the group.

Teaching and Praying : Optional prayers as distinct from the obligatory which are offered in group and gain thereby a social value peculiarly their own, aim mostly at individual salvation and are considered less meritorious than teaching as the latter involves a social process resulting in the moral and the intellectual development of the entire community. It is very important to make a pointed reference to this comparison which occurs with such a significant frequency in the Traditions and which throws light on such an aspect of the educational thought in Islam which is in the truest consonance with the social spirit of the religion.

"Teaching is praying", says Ibn Masud and when another savant was asked whether he preferred night long prayers over the writing of a single Tradition, he replied that he would certainly prefer the inscribing of a single Tradition; another would place the study of a chapter of knowledge above one thousand prostrations. According to Shafii, the illustrious founder of a school of Islamic law named after him, search after knowledge is more laudable than optional prayers (Nawafil). The superiority of the search after knowledge over optional prayers is implied in the Tradition that "search after knowledge is obligatory on every Muslim"; the author of Tadhkiratus Sami advances other arguments on the subject. The benefit of knowledge, according to him is universal while that of the optional prayers is confined to an individual; Prayers stand in need of knowledge and are dependent on it while knowledge is independent of them; the scholars are the inheritors of the Prophets while it is not so in the case of the devotees; submission to the scholars is obligatory on all; the blessing of knowledge continues after the death of the scholar while that of the optional prayers stops with the death of the individual and in the preservation of knowledge lies the regeneration of Shariah and the protection of the symbols of the people.

Learning and Praying : The above remarks are potent with an important significance as far as the educational problems of Muslims are concerned. The Muslim backwardness in education has become a byword and there can be no more effective remedy for the propagation of knowledge among them than the wider publicity of this aspect of the teachings of the Prophet and the savants, teachings which are certainly more in harmony with the Islamic spirit than the attitude of legions of Muslims who prefer to occupy their leisure moments in religious meditation and optional prayers. Their time would be much better occupied if they devote it to the nobler task of educating the illiterate members of the community.

There is the instance of a great savant rating the pursuit after knowledge higher than obligatory prayers. It is related by Ibn Wahb that he was once studying with Malik b. Anas when the time for the noonday or the afternoon prayers approached near. He was reading and studying in his presence. Then he gathered his books and prepared to depart for prayers. Malik asked what for he was leaving. He said, "For prayers". Upon this Malik exclaimed that it was strange for his present occupation, if prosecuted in the right spirit was superior to that one for which he was departing.

Roots of Wisdom

The teacher is a dynamic force for good and a quiet and silent crusader against evil. According to a Tradition, a savant is a thousand times more calamitous for the Evil One than the devotee; certainly so because he does not hide his light under a bushel like a recluse and the forces of evil recede before his radiating refulgence as the pitch black night disappears before the approaching dawn. According to a savant, the teacher can be described as a lighthouse on land which sheds its lustre far and wide. He would be seated on a pedestal of light on the Day of Judgement, a poetic reward for one who had been a radiating centre of light and learning in this world. "Three groups will enjoy the right of interceding for others on the judgement day, firstly the Prophets who would be followed by the scholars and the savants. There is an instructive legend describing the visit of the Evil One to a recluse who was easily misled by the intriguing problem whether the Lord could originate the entire universe from an egg while the savant showed the traditional ingenuity of a dialectician in evading the issue and hurling upon him a crushing rejoinder.

The teacher is a holy warrior who wages the battle for truth while the Martyr wages war against evil; the enemies of the Faith one represents the positive and the other the negative aspect of the process of moral and social progress; one acts as the surgeon and the other as the dietician of the body politic. Hence, according to Tradition, "one who enters my mosque to learn Good or impart it to others has the rank of a warrior on the path of Lord." According to another Tradition, "One who is overtaken by death during the process of learning dies a martyr."

Scholar: One Rank Higher : The nature of the service rendered by the teacher to the community is positive, comprehensive, extensive and more lasting in ordinary circumstances than the service of a martyr; also a scholar can expect to earn the merit of a martyr during his life time at any moment but the reverse cannot hold true. Hencc a number of Traditions place the scholar above the martyr in merit. The scholar stands one rank higher than martyr and on the Day of Judgment although both the groups shall have the privilege of interceding for others, the scholar will come first in priority. One who honours a teacher has earned the merit of honouring seventy prophets and one who honours a pupil earns the merit of honouring seventy martyrs. There are Traditions of rather doubtful authenticity which state that the ink of a scholar shall be weighed against the martyr's blood on the day of judgement and according to Hassan Basri the ink will outweigh the blood. When Ibn Abbas was asked about the Holy War, he replied whether they would like to know something more valuable than the Holy War and he added, "It is erecting a mosque and teaching therein the law of inheritance. Traditions and Fiqh."

Social Orientation

If education is defined as the self-perpetuation of culture by the younger generation, then no method of informal education can be more effective in realising the objective of education than the method adopted by the Prophet. The fundamental principle of informal education is the direct association of the young and the old through communication on a basis of equality, equality in the sense that we treat the younger members of the society as responsible beings in their own limited way who are expected to react as vigorously to external influences in their characteristic manner as any adult and are not the lifeless automations of the school whose physical and intellectual movements are controlled by the dimensions of the writing desk. The sense of responsibility is awakened by treating them as responsible persons and no persons could have a higher regard for the delicate feelings of the younger generation than the Prophet.

Faith in Childhood : He had implicit faith in the younger generation and they justified the confidence reposed in them by rising always equal to the occasion and performing in war and peace what was expected of them. His glorious confidence in man ignited in the heart of the young a spark of moral fervour and they discovered for themselves a heartening faith in personal merit and an independent outlook on life. The chief drawback of our present day social life in general and the educational system in particular is that the younger generation has lost all faith in the ideology and the experience of the older people.

Complete Loss of Faith : And there seems to be some ground for such a complete loss of faith. Somehow or other the older generation does not appear to know the younger and a proof of such a devastating generalisation lies in the fact that teachers, parents and others concerned with the training of the younger people ignore very conveniently that fundamental principle of child education which emphasizes treating the child as a responsible being and not meeting him half way condescendingly with a physical and intellectual lisp. Experiments in child psychology have proved abundantly that children when treated as responsible beings become actually responsible persons with a high sense of duty and moral vigour and those who have studied children closely and sympathetically know what a glorious spirit of idealism can be released in a young person when he learns that he is the repository of such a confidence.

Respect for the Child's Personality : "Honour your progeny and educate them well," says the Prophet and like a true educator that he has, the respect for the child's personality has a precedence with him over his training. He never lost a single opportunity for bringing home to the younger people the profound regard which he entertained for them. When he saw a party of children and women returning from a marriage feast, he rose on his feet and greeted them thrice in the following words, "You are dearest to me of all humanity."

When he came across young people on his way he would greet them by invoking peace on them while in the older company he had a scrupulous regard for their feelings. Once a young boy was seated on the right hand of the Prophet while some elderly persons were occupying seats on the left. He desired to treat them with a drink and preferred to start with the elder members of the company. But in deference to the usual custom of always beginning from the right, he sought the consent of the young boy to start from the left which he frankly refused. He was not prepared to waive of his privilege of partaking from the drink of the Prophet before others and the Prophet allowed him precedence over other in consideration of his feelings.

Keeping Promise with the Child : It is common for the parents to hold out petty little promises to their children, sweet nothing, never meant to be fulfilled for cajoling the child; the practice militates against a harmonious development of the child's personality, introduces a note of insincerity and is a direct insult to the self-regarding sentiment of the child. The Prophet discouraged it in undisguised terms. Once he was visiting a family when the lady of the house called her children aside and promised them something sweet. The Prophet asked what she was giving to them upon which she replied that it was a date. He approved of her action and added that if she had not given anything, the sin of telling a lie would have been entered against her in the Account.

Legally young children were given a free option of choosing the parent with which they decided to stay in case one of them had embraced Islam while the other still remained a non-believer. He would address the child who stood most probably between the two parents in benignant terms, "My dear boy, here is your mother and there stands your father; now make a choice for yourself."

Advice for New Generation

The confidence reposed in the younger generation by the Prophet found a faithful reflection in the thought and practice of the Companions; 'Umar would send for the younger people when faced with a crisis, took their counsel on important matters of state and availed himself of their innate intelligence in the affairs of administration. They constantly reminded the younger generation of the heavy responsibility which they were expected to shoulder in future and for which they should make preparation in right earnest from the very beginning. "Learn", said Hassan Ibn Ali to his son and nephew "because although you are the younger members of the community today, you will be their great ones tomorrow. "Ibn-al-Zubayr advised his son in the following words, "Learn from me because it would not take long when you would be the leader of the people".

Nothing Wrong

The spirit of mutual trust and understanding was all the more strengthened by the absence of any feeling of false prestige among the older people and their frank recognition of the merits of the younger persons when they had supplied sufficient proof of it. Hamidi, a disciple of Shafii, relates how he accompanied the great master on his journey from Mecca to Egypt and on the way he learnt from him the laws of religion (Masail) while Shafii took lessons from him on Traditions. A person describes that he saw Abu Hanifah sitting in the company of Malik as a child sits in the presence of his father and he observed all this decorum in spite of the fact that he was older than Malik.

These instances remind one of the well known episode of the intelligent boy who played the judge in the story of the two merchants and the jar of olives, in the days of the good Harun al-Rashid. The story of the Arabian Nights tells tale of a tradition of high intelligence and innate shrewdness of the Arab youth which was frequently availed of by the adults.

The children of Medina in the days of the Prophet were second to none in intelligence and shrewd repartee; they were ready witted and were gifted with a readier tongue. There exists the account of a group of children frolicking about in the street when 'Umar appeared suddenly on the scene. All the children sneaked away with the exception of Abdullah bin Zubayr who showed early signs of that undaunted spirit which brought him one day to a glorious end. When Umar asked why he did not follow the example of his companions he replied, "I have not done anything wrong that I may be afraid of thee and the path is not so very narrow as required my removal for broadening it for thee. Such boldness was the fruit of an atmosphere surcharged with educative influences of the highest order.

7

Education for Knowledge

As a system of faith and action which holds rationalism to be the very essence of religion, Islam emphasized the importance of Reason and a number of Traditions deal specially with the specific role of reason in human affairs. The study of these Traditions will make an interesting reading in the light of the present day tendency in some circles to belittle intellectual development in comparison with the emotional and the intuitional. The confusion of thought has grown on account of a dual conception of personality, a divided self driven by two mutually exclusive, rather antagonistic urges, *Ishq* (emotions) and *Aql* (intellect).

The Prophet was credited with a great sense of justice and acumen even before he had proclaimed the message of Islam. He was called Amin or the Trusted one and his timely decision (Tahkim) on the occasion when the tribes of Mecca were disputing over the privilege of erecting the Hajr-e-Aswad during the repairs of the Kaaba indicates in the opinion of Ibn Saad, that he used to exercise the authority of Hakm in the period of Jahiliyyah.

According to a Tradition, 'Wisdom of all creation right from the beginning is like unto a particle of sand quantitatively as compared with the wisdom of the Prophet which may be likened to the sand dunes of the whole world.

The Essence

Ultimate greatness lies in Divine Essence and approximation to it provides a measurable criterion for the relative greatness of others.

The Throne of the Almighty is high and exalted on account of its proximity to the Divine Presence but a Tradition emphasizes that 'Reason is more exalted than the Throne.' It belongs to the Divine Essence.

In the next world the greatest reward promised to the virtuous is the contemplation of Divine Appearance, and as wisdom constitutes the Essence of the Divine the grades of the virtuous will be determined according to their wisdom; their proximity to the Divine Being will be determined by this criterion. Wisdom has been recognised as the touchstone of Divine Grace because it helps man in distinguishing Good from Evil.

The Philosophy

In the opinion of Ghazzali, the word (Noor) Light in the Quranic verse 'and verily God is the Light of the heavens and earth' signifies wisdom. In fact, it is Light 'which illumines for him his (right) path among men,' and one of the greatest blessings for him is that God rescued him from the Dark and brought him into Light.

Knowledge which is acquired through Wisdom has been described as 'The Soul' 'revelation', and 'life'. For according to the Quran, 'Verily we sent (Awhayna) unto thy Soul by our Command.' In another verse 'We have given life to one who was dead and made for him light with the help of which he moves among the people.' Hence it is Wisdom which is the cause of our spiritual, intellectual and physical being.

The Tradition lays special accent on moral or ethical intelligence and reason as defined in the literature of Traditions is synonymous with this kind of intelligence. According to the Prophet, "He is only wise who obeys the Lord and unwise is he who disobeys Him, and the degree of intelligence attained by a person is to be assessed by this criterion. The varying degrees of intelligence acquired by different individuals are also determined by this criterion. 'Verily he is the wisest among you who fears the Lord most and one who has the deepest insight in matters which are ordained and forbidden.' And reason will also provide the ultimate measure for the assessment of human actions on the Day of Judgment.

A number of Traditions reveal the importance which the Prophet attached to Reason. According to him it is the most perfect of all creation.

When Lord had created Reason, He asked it to stand face to face. Then He commanded it to turn over. After contemplating it closely, the Lord felt triumphant on His achievement and said, 'I swear by my Honour and Greatness that I never created anything more worthy than you. I will reward by thee and condemn by thee.

Thus intelligence constitutes the standard by which men and their actions will be judged by the Almighty. Traditions like these have formed the chief argument for those who support the Doctrine of Free will (Ikhtiyar) against that of pre-destination (Qadr).

The comprehensive term 'Aql' which is more akin to the Greek conception of wisdom appears to be an all pervasive, all- embracing force which directs and guides the individual in various spheres of life.

One of the Traditions is extremely illuminating in this context and emphasizes pointedly the comprehensive nature of its directive influence on human affairs.

People of Faith

Every thing has its Kit and the reason is the Kit of the Faithful. Every thing has a ride and the ride of man is reason. Every thing in the world has a support and the support of religion is reason. Every nation has an end and the end of humanity is reason. Every tribe has a watchman and the watchman of the pious is reason. Every trader has his wares and the wares of those who strive on the Path of the Lord is reason. Every house has a manager and the homestead of the True ones is managed by reason. Every wilderness has a population and the population of the next world is reason. Every person leaves a belonging behind on account of which he is remembered and associated. The inheritance with which the True ones are commemorated and associated is reason. Every journey needs a tent and the tent of the Believers is reason.

The Ideology

The above discussion relates to the inborn innate wisdom, of both kinds, theoretic and moral. But the Traditions of the Prophet lay a great emphasis on the Empirical kind also which is acquired through experience and human associations. He has said that the old man is unto his tribe as the Prophet is among his people. And in one of his Traditions he has told that leadership lies in Wisdom; when he asked the Archangel Gabriel wherein lies leadership, he replied 'in wisdom.'

The Wisdom

According to Ghazzali, whose conclusions are generally based on a very intimate study of the Quran and the Traditions, there are four kinds of intelligence. The first is the general kind of intelligence which is innate or inborn. This is the apperception of theoretical knowledge. He describes it as the basic, inborn intelligence. It has the same relation with learning as the eye has with the power of sight while the Quran and the Shariah are akin to sunlight.

Other kinds of intelligence which he enumerates is the capacity of understanding axiomatic truth like two and two make four. The third kind of intelligence is empirical which is acquired through experience and experimentation. The fourth is the moral and ethical intelligence.

In a rather lengthy tradition from Abdullah bin Salam, the Prophet says The angels asked the Lord whether He had created anything greater than the Arsh (throne) and the reply was 'Yes. Reason is greater than the Throne!' Then they asked for a measure of wisdom in the quantitative sense and the reply came that their knowledge could not comprehend it. 'Can you count the particles of sand!' The angels said, "no." Then the Lord said, "I have created Reason in varying quantities like the particles of sand. Some persons were given one Mithqal, others two, three or even four. A few were gifted with one Farq (about seers) and some were given a camel load of it."

According to Ghazzali, this particular Tradition refers to three kinds of Reason, the theoretic, the empirical and the ethical. The fourth which helps the individual in comprehending axiomatic truth is found in all and has not been measured out in varying quantities to different individuals.

The above Tradition throws light on a subject which has been investigated by modern psychologists and seems to affirm their findings that there are varying grades of intelligence. The climax of this development is reached in the Prophets. According to a Tradition the intelligence of the entire humanity is like a particle of sand as compared with the Intelligence of the Prophet which is like the sand-heaps of the entire earth.

These individual differences in grades of intelligence demand from the educator a careful study of individual pupils and an adaptation of his teaching methods to the standards and needs of the individual pupil.

Ghazzali has made a pointed reference to a Tradition which indicates that individuals differ in their level of theoretic intelligence and this fundamental difference has a specific significance for the educator because of the close correlationship between the level of intelligence and the receptivity of educative influences on the part of the pupil. There are persons who would comprehend and improve through their inborn intelligence. Others won't register any change without training and education. The third won't improve in spite of all training and education."

Education's Significance

The Prophet was keenly conscious of the importance of wisdom not only for the spiritual but for worldly affairs. In fact there was hardly any quality between the two and wisdom helped in the secular and in the spiritual sphere of life.

On his return journey from the Battle of Uhud, some one started discussing the fortune of battle and praised the chivalry of one and the experience of another. Thereupon the Prophet said, "Verily men fought in accordance with their intelligence and their success was in a measure with it and each one of them attained to different stages of (Divine Grace)."

And when Aishah asked wherein lies precedence for men in worldly affairs the Prophet replied, "in intellect here as well in the next world."

Thereupon Aishah asked whether reward in the next world was to be determined by actions. He replied that men did good and evil in accordance with their intellect and their reward would be commensurate with their actions.

Reason not only directs a person on to the right path; it helps him in reaching the goal and assists in the completion and the final summing up of the whole process. According to the Prophet, "Good morals are not perfected until reason receives perfection, because it is then that a person's faith acquires perfection and he surrenders himself to the Lord and repudiates his enemy, the Satan."

Reason and Morality : One of the most illuminating and irresistible inference from a study of the Prophet's Traditions is the undeniable fact that he has emphasized on the perfection of reason and intellectual development of the individual as a means for spiritual edification and not as an end in itself.

According to a Tradition. Wisdom is synonymous with self-surrender to God.

Out of all the Believers, he is the most loved one of the Lord whose wisdom is perfect, who counsels his lower self and acts according to reason throughout his life. And the most perfect in reason is he who has the greatest fear of God and has the greatest insight of positive and negative commandments although he may be less rigorous in prayers.

For the Believer who is a wayfarer on the highway of life, wisdom is the traveller's kit; it is his ride or means of conveyance and the tent which protects him from the inclemencies of weather.

It does not form the essence of Faith but it is the prop and the pillar on which it rests. The pillar determines the strength and the support of a building and according to a Tradition, "All things in the world are supported by another and the support of the Faithful is reason. His piety will be in accordance with his reason. For verily the unbelievers will say when they are cast in the fire of hell, "If we had listened and understood, we would not have been the inmates of hell."

But when it is said that intellectual development is only a means to an end and not an end in itself, it implies the first three kinds of intelligence. And these in their own turn function as means to an end which lies in the fourth, the ethical or the moral intelligence. When the Prophet said that every group has an end and the aim of humanity is reason, he meant the last kind.

In fact the educative process is an ever-developing, ever-growing unfolding of personality and its enrichment in the knowledge and control of physical, mental and the social aspect of life. The first three kinds of intelligence help in the comprehension and control of these three worlds and they pave the way for a conscious control of the fourth kind of intelligence which serves the spiritual or the moral world.

The entire process of educational development as conceived in these terms is not static. It is an evergrowing process both as regards means and ends.

Basis of Knowledge

According to a Tradition, "Reason is a guide. The abundance of reason leads a man towards Hidaya and saves him from perdition."

This negative aspect of reason which ensures man from going astray from the Right Path finds expression in a Tradition where reason is described as the Watchman of the Pious. When a person was being praised in the presence of the Prophet, he enquired about his wisdom. They protested and told that they were discussing his piety and charitable disposition and there was hardly any reason for enquiring about his intelligence. Thereupon the Prophet told that a well intentioned fool may commit more sins than a wicked person through his ignorance.

8

Various Disciplines

Different Branches of Knowledge

The earlier literature of the Arabs does not contain treatises providing a systematic and well-documented account of the events of the past. The historical material mostly comprised the knowledge of days, a graphic and passionate account in prose or poetry, of some historic day of a battle or a tribal catastrophe. They failed to appreciate that there was a Divine purpose running through the gamut of human affairs and that the history of mankind was not a discontinuous account of unrelated episodes; it is an integrated scheme of things unrolling into milleneums where days and months are the tiny snippets of the grand Film Roll of Time.

The Continuity : The Prophet seized upon this continuity in the history of mankind, ever emphasizing, ever reiterating the great lessons of morality in a higher sense which the catastrophe of one nation after another brought into prominence.

Divine Purpose : For him, history is not a gorgeous film roll of the past nor an intellectual amusement which may pander to imagination and love of romance. For him the entire history of Man is governed by divine purpose and is directed by the undeniable, irresistible principle that any people who did not respond to the call of Truth were doomed for ever. He allowed his Companions to study the History of the Israelites, not for the Code of Laws which it laid down for the Jews but for the sublimity of its moral teachings and great lessons in socialised living and cooperative effort.

He has permitted relating facts of Jewish history and according to another authority, once conversation about the history of Jews continued in his company upto the prayer time. According to authorities on Islamic Traditions, their history is not so reliable as that of the Prophet and his period on account of the lack of a proper chain of evidence and the passage of time.

History in the Prophet's Mosque : He had a benevolent spirit of tolerance for those who indulged in the tales of the Days of Jahiliyyah in his presence. We have it on the authority of a person who had visited his Presence hundred and odd times that his Companions would often recite poetry and talk of the Days of Jahiliyyah. The Prophet listened to them quietly and very often a smile played on his lips in the course of these narrations. (Perhaps at some pleasant anecdote, the period being so full of witticisms and bon mots).

Tales and Accounts

Story telling became popular in the days of the early caliphate and 'Umar was the first Caliph to allow Tamimad-Dari to relate stories. He did so in a standing posture. The story teller must have confined himself mostly to the account of the Prophets and people in the past as narrated in the Quran. In the opinion of 'Umar, the story of Joseph in the Quran was to supply the criterion for this kind of literature.

Most of the Qasis or historical stories told in the Quran deal with the people of the Old Testament and other nations who proved recalcitrant and were visited by Divine wrath in a way which was exemplary for others.

The Traditions supplement to some extent the historical information given by the Quran but they deal primarily with those episodes or aspects that have a significant moral value. For instance, the story of Joseph and his brethern occurs in the Quran but it does not find a prominent place in the Traditions. While the episode of Moses, Solomon, David, Abraham and Ismail occur frequently in moral contexts. The life story of Moses had received a detailed treatment in the Quran but his great Quest for learning as evidenced in the account of his travels presents the patriarch of the Old Testament in an extremely interesting light. The episode has been supplemented to some extent by the Traditions. According to the Traditions when Moses rose one day to address his people, he was asked, "Who is the greatest knower of all" and Moses said, 'I', and God sent him on his travels as a punishment because he had not used the saving clause of grace that the Lord was the best knower.

Three Queries by Moses : The entire story of the three queries put by Moses and answered by his Companion is narrated on similar lines in the Quran and in the Traditions, with a single addition in the Tradition. As the Moses and his Companion got into the boat, a sparrow came and sat swinging on the rim of the boat and dipped its beak in the sea. The Guide pointed to the sparrow and said, "May knowledge as compared with the Lord's is something like the small drop of water which the sparrow has taken out of the sea." The Guide is named Khizar in the Tradition.

Educative Value : Writers on education have drawn several instructive conclusions from the episode of Moses and his companion, the first being the excellence of travel for the sake of learning.

One must learn the virtue of being patient and bearing the trials and travails of the quest after knowledge in a patient manner.

It teaches the great lesson of humility to the scholar and makes him realise like Newton how limitless is the ocean of knowledge and how trivial is the amount that we acquire through our efforts.

On the one hand, it teaches the pupil to be patient. On the other, it provides the lesson of forbearance for the teacher. Khizar in this story patiently answers three questions which in his opinion were unwarranted and uncalled for.

Arithmetic : The Prophet laid great emphasis on a sound knowledge of the law of Inheritance (Ilm al-Faraiz) and according to Ibn Hurayrah he had advised his people to learn the science and impart its knowledge to others because it formed one-half of the Shariah. He continued that the law of inheritance was the first branch of learning which would be taken away from his people when they fall on evil days. On another occasion, he foretold the evil times when his people would befriend riches and forget accounts (arithmetic).

The Science of Inheritance : The Science of Inheritance is defined by one of the authorities as a branch of learning which deals with the fundamentals of Fiqh and Arithmetic which determined the shares of all the claimants in the case of a particular inheritance. When the Prophet enjoined on the Faithful the learning of the law of inheritance, he was virtually pronouncing a religious decree in favour of learning Arithmetic. Elsewhere he declared that the knowledge of Religion comprised three things and the last but not the least of them is the knowledge of an equitable law of inheritance.

The Prophet entered business quite early in life and one of the caustic jibes flung at him by the unbelievers of Mecca was the claim of a person to apostlehood who ate like others and frequented the bazaar like a commoner. Most probably, he was well versed in the easier processes of arithmatic. The Books on inheritance enumerate a number of cases decided on the spot by the Prophet and they evidence a good knowledge of Arithmetic and the Rules of Ratio and Proportion.

A Feat of Mathematical Calculations : From the earliest, the Muslims have shown an uncanny alertness in problems of mathematics and some of their feats were so remarkable that they have left a mark in the annals of the period.

Khawaharzada mentions in his Sharah that Ali was wonderfully ready with numbers. Once a Christian asked him what reason he could give for the discrepancy in the period of somnolence in the case of the Seven Sleepers as stated in the Quran and the Old Testament, the period being 309 years according to the Quran and 300 years in the Bible. Without a moment's hesitation, Ali explained the discrepancy on the basis of the two different systems of measuring time in the two cases, in one case the lunar system of computation and in the other the solar.

It appears that a knowledge of the Science of Inheritance was highly prized in those days and raised an individual with such an accomplishment very high in the estimate of the people. Umar was once informed that a certain tribe had appointed an enfranchised slave as their religious chief (Caliph). He was surprised at such a preferment, but they justified the selection by explaining that he was a Reader of the Quran, a Master of the law of inheritence and a judicious person for deciding cases.

Arithmetic Enforced by Umar : Mathematical calculations were not only involved in determining the shares of the inheritors, they embraced the entire span of social and economic life; everyday business transactions, sale and purchase, security or lease, all required a knowledge of arithmetic and 'Umar was so zealous in carrying out the laws of Shariah that he threatened his people with the lash if they did not learn the religious injunctions on sale and purchase. Hence the well known saying by Ibn Dawwam, "Teach your son Hisab (Arithmetic), before putting him on to the Kitab (Book)."

Role of Languages : There seems to be present a widespread misunderstanding that the contents of education in the days of the Prophet were only the Quran and the Traditions. There is reliable evidence to prove that the curriculum was not so narrowly circumscribed by religious considerations. The talks and discussions even in the courtyard of the Prophet's Mosque wandered frequently into the secular domain. The evergrowing contacts and conflicts of the Muslims with the neighbouring countries forced upon them the study of foreign languages and conquests abroad necessitated a more intimate knowledge of the culture and the language, the administrative and the social system of the conquered people.

The term Diwan for Audit and Accounts was borrowed early from the official terminology of the Persians and a wholesale borrowing of their system of account keeping implied a considerable amount of knowledge which was of a purely secular nature. Often the very nature of religious learning implied knowledge of secular nature. The custom of learning foreign languages had been established in the Prophet's life time and we have a tradition on the authority of Zayd bin Thabit how the Prophet received letters written in the Syriac language and he did not like to send for a Jewish scholar to read the contents of the letters. So he asked Zayd to learn the language; Zayd learnt it within the short period of sixteen days and henceforth he used to interpret the correspondence received from the Jews and wrote out replies to them.

When Prophet Spoke Words of Foreign Languages : We know on the authority of Ibn Anas that the Prophet could speak a few words of Persian and once when Salman Farsi (the Persian) visited him, he said "Darust... etc". According to Muhammad bin

Amail, the words implied most probably a hearty welcome for the visitor. He is said to have used an Abysinian word also in his talk with a child. The Prophet kept a scribe named Sijl and there are traditions of rather doubtful veracity on the drying of writing with earth and using the back of the ear as a pen- holder. But there is evidence to show that there existed a class of scribes in those days who knew more than one language.

Astrology : The Muslims have made splendid contributions to the development of astronomy in the past. Their calendars and astronomical charts, their observatories and appliances, technical names derived from Arabic that occur so abundantly in the terminology of modern astronomy, all prove that this science was a respectable branch of learning from the earliest days. But when the spirit of scientific method was overshadowed by a superstitious belief in the influence of stars in directing human destiny, Islam stood boldly and nonchalantly and pronounced an outright condemnation of such an attitude.

Accordingly it is astrology and not astronomy which has aroused the disapprobation of the Prophet. Astronomy is recognised in the Quran as a branch of mathematics which deals with the movements of the heavenly bodies. "And there is a measure for the sun and the moon." Again, "We have assigned to the moon its stages until she reverts like an old sprig."

According to al-Ghazzali, the science of astronomy deals with the relation of cause and effect and predicts the movements of the planets as a physician presages the imminent attack of a virulent form of disease from its symptoms.

The Prophet has forewarned his people against the times when the Science would degenerate into astrology and the stars become the means of divination and superstitious belief. "I fear three calamities for my people in the days to come and one of them is their belief in astrology."

Umar was more explicit when in his crisp and commanding tones he made a sharp reference to its practical utility and tolerated no nonsense about it. "Learn the Science of Stars only as a guidance for direction finding on sea or land and don't proceed further with it."

9

Role of Teachers

There are good many Traditions which illustrate in figurative language the social and the spiritual significance of the teacher's role in society.

Roots of Knowledge

The teacher is generally compared to a luminous body radiating light and illuminating the darkness of others' souls. They are the "light-houses of the towns and cities" they may be likened to stars and guiding lights in the darkness that covers land and ocean and when they disappear, the guides would certainly lose their way. "The teacher is a light-house for the land and a spring of fresh water for the town."

There is no end to the graceful similes which throw up realistically and forcefully the creative aspect of the teacher's function in society; he is likened to those great forces of nature whose creative efforts refreshen the world and animate it with new life and ideals. The Prophet quoted once the parting counsel of Luqman to his son that he should seek the company of Savants and listen to the words of wisdom because God resurrects the heart of the dead with the Light of Knowledge just as the barren soil begins to throb with vegetable life under the genial influence of rainfall. Another tradition likens the Assemblies of Teachers to the flower-beds of heaven and the companions are enjoined to browse on so delectable a stuff whenever an opportunity arises.

There are teachers and teachers and the fine distinction between the grades among them is illustrated in another metaphor by Ali, according to whom knowledge may be likened to a melifluous current, while the teacher merely stroll on the banks, the thinker struggles midstream while the Arif (knower) enjoys a ride in the barge of salvation.

Mystic Qualities : The spiritual reward for teaching others is great; it is light as the rainbow coloured clouds and genial like the rainfall. In one of his accounts, Abu Hanifa describes the account of an individual whose Good and Evil actions would be weighed in the Balance on Doomsday and the Pan for evil would indicate a downwards tendency but then suddenly from some unknown quarter would appear a cloud which would turn the balance in his favour. This cloud is the grace of knowledge which he (so profusely) bestowed on the people.

We have mentioned elsewhere how the entire universe appears to be involved in the educative process, the aim of which is the social and moral regeneration of this ace of creation man; and for the teacher who is the Divine instrument for working such a transformation in man, "the angels above, the ants in their anthills and the fish in the sea send their blessings."

Such a dynamic element in human life is essential for its existence and continuity and all men are active participants in the sharing of experience either in the capacity of a teacher or a learner because life ceases to be worthy of its respectable name when man degenerates to the level of inert, static existence. According to Ali, "Men may be classified broadly into three groups, firstly, the goodly teacher, then the pupil traversing the path of salvation, while the rest of humanity are all stupid fools who take their cue from any claimant." (Naiqorerier)

Another tradition urges every man to be a dynamic factor in the educative process which works in the cyclic order of morning and evening and that every man should discover in himself the young Galahad ready to launch on a voyage of moral and intellectual adventure.

There are savants who refuse to recognise such a person as human being who has never been a teacher in his life. Al-Ghazzali quotes Ibn Mubarak according to whom "the only creation which deserves the exalted rank of Man is the teacher because only knowledge distinguishes man from animal."

Trained by Holy Prophet : The first persons who were entrusted with the duty of teaching under the Prophet were Masaab bin Umair and Ibn Um Maktum. They had been deputed by the Prophet from Mecca on the request of the Ansar of Medina who desired some teachers of religion and Holy Quran. Masaab used to make house to house visitation and frequented suburban areas also it was through his pioneer efforts that the message of Islam was propagated in this area.

Masaab bin Umayr, a great dandy of Mecca was converted in the days when the family of the Prophet was living in exile in the defile of Abi Talib outside Mecca. Hc had a phcnomenal success and was known as Muqarri or the teacher and he stayed in the enclosure of Asad bin Lurarai, one of the earliest Medinites to be converted to Islam.

His teaching activities aroused the suspicion of tribal chiefs like Saad bin Maad and Usayd bin Hudhayr.

Usayd actually went to Asad, the host of Masaab and complained how he was maintaining a person who was misleading the people of Medina and ensnaring the weak minded. But when he heard Masaab and his companions reciting the rythmic verses of the Quran, his naive and sensitive heart was deeply moved. He made an open confession of his faith on the spot.

Saad bin Maad followed suit. He began by abusing the host who was his cousin for lodging suspicious characters but Saad was also struck with the awful grandeur and beauty of the Quranic verses and a spark of enthusiasm for the new faith was kindled within Saad who brought his family of Abdul Shah within the fold of Islam after a direct appeal to their sense of loyalty for their chief.

Teachers were sent to the tribal areas by the Prophet from time to time. They were generally sent on the request of those deputations from the tribal areas which came to visit Medina.

Some of the companions had specialised as teachers and they continued their work of propagation of knowledge long after the Prophet. One of them Maadh bin Jabal worked in this capacity in various parts of the Peninsula. These teachers seem to have dedicated their whole life to educational work among the tribes and other distant parts of Arabia.

Service to God : In the beginning, Maadh bin Jabal worked in this capacity as a judge in Yemen and would receive injunctions from the Prophet in reply to his queries. He worked as a teacher of Quran and Fiqh in Mecca when the Prophet had left for the Battle of Hunayn. Under Abu Bakr he had offered himself to go on Jihad to Syria and later on Umar I deputed him to Hims as a teacher of Quran and religious knowledge from whence he proceeded to Palestine where he met his end in the plague epidemic during the period of Umar I.

He exercised the authority of issuing legal decrees (Ifta) during the lifetime of the Prophet and Abu Bakr in Medina. Another great teacher, Ibn Masud described him as 'Amat' "Qanit" (a leader faithful to God), the attributes which are used for Ibrahim in the Quran.

According to Ibn Masud, Amat is a person who teaches people about 'Good', and 'Qanit' is one who is subservient to God.

Great Teachers : The most well known scholars of Quranic readings in the days of the Prophet were Uby bin Kaab, Zayd bin Thabit, and Abdullah ibn Masud. Abu Musa-al-Ashaari was more known for his melodious voice than for the Qirat.

Uby bin Kaab was acknowledged as the greatest scholar of the Quran by Umar I and others and he was associated with its study from the earliest days.

It is related that the Prophet had told Uby that he had been ordained from above to recite to him the Quran and when Uby asked whether the Lord had named him in particular, the Prophet replied in the affirmative. Upon this, tears of joy ran down the checks of Uby whereupon the Prophet recited, "And it is due to the beneficence and grace of God. They should be happy because it (Quran) is better than what they collect".

The Prophet had trained a class of Quran Readers or Qaris at Medina. It appears that these persons who belonged in most cases to the people of the Suffa had dedicated themselves entirely to the Great Cause and had placed themselves at the disposal of the Prophet.

They used to recite the Quran and were engaged in teaching and learning the Holy Book at night.

In the day-time they were occupied with bringing water for the mosque. They would go into the jungle, bring faggots and with their sale they would provide meals for the people of the Suffa and the needy. Haram, a maternal uncle of Anas bin Malik also belonged to this group.

These Quran Readers who lived apparently in the mosque were often sent on teaching missions. Once seventy Ansars, all of whom were Qura were sent to a tribe who slaughtered them to a man.

One of the greatest authorities on the readings of the Quran was Abdullah Ibn Masud who had been described as a chest full of knowledge.

He was elder to Zayd bin Thabit, another authority on the Quranic text and according to him he had learnt seventy surats from the Prophet at a time when Zayd bin Thabit was merely a beardless youth. He kept his side tresses and used to frolick about with children. He was one of those few persons of early Islam who have been described as Allama.

The comprehensive scope of his knowledge has been described by Masruq in an impressive simile, "I would compare him to a reservoir. There are reservoirs that would satiate one or two persons. There may be others which may quench the thirst of a hundred people but Abdullah Ibn Masud was like unto a reservoir that could suffice for the whole world."

The Prophet was deeply moved by the recitation of two companions in particular; they were Ibn Masud and Abu Musa-al-Ashaari.

Once he asked Ibn Masud to recite to him the Quran and Ibn Masud replied, "How can I recite to you, O Prophet of Allah, when the Holy Book has been revealed unto you." But the Prophet insisted and Ibn Masud recited to him the Surat-al-Nissa (Women) and when he read the verse, 'And Verily we will bring witnesses out of all these people and appoint you a witness over all of them', he saw that the eyes of the Prophet were overbrimming with tears.

Then he said, "If anyone desires to recite the Quran as it was revealed, he should read in the style of Ibn Um Abd (Ibn Masud)".

According to Ibn Abbas, the greatest scholar of Exegesis in early Islam, he preferred the Qirat of Abdullah Ibn Masud over the rest because the Quran was recited twice during the Ramadan in the last year of the Prophet's life. In those day Ibn Masud says the Prophet and he came to know of the verses which had been deleted or changed.

Education's Development

Umar Ibn Khattab had organised a well laid out plan for the propagation of learning in areas that had been recently conquered and for that purpose, he selected important centres like Kufa and Basrah in Iraq, Damascus and Hims in Syria and Jerusalem in Palestine. He selected the most outstanding scholars and teachers for this purpose. It appears that some of them received annual emoluments from the state.

Ibn Masud was sent to Kufa by Umar Ibn Khattab and he wrote to the people that he had preferred Ibn Masud to himself and they should acquire knowledge from him. It is said that Ibn Masud used to receive an allowance of 6,000 dirhams.

The Caliphs used to keep a keen vigilance over the activities of these teachers. Once Umar Ibn Khattab had criticised Ibn Masud for relating too many Traditions to the people of Kufa.

At a later period a group of Kufites who had been students of Ibn Masud came to visit Ali who cross-questioned them so closely about their teacher that they had a suspicion that the Caliph was going to give them a test. Finally Ali expressed a high appreciation of the character and learning of Ibn Masud.

Ibn Abbas and Abu Hurayrah had started their teaching work at Basrah. According to Ibn Saad, Ibn Abbas was the first teacher who acquired a great reputation in that town.

Abu Hurayrah had an extremely busy time as a teacher attending to the large concourse of students who attended his narrations. Once he was reminded of a Tradition of the Prophet when he was surrounded by a throng of pupils that a day would arrive when people would come to him in search of knowledge from distant parts and that he should greet them with a welcome on such occasions.

Abu Musa-al-Ashaari, the golden tongued reciter of the Quran was also at Basrah during the period of Umar Ibn Khattab.

Grand Selection : Umar Ibn Khattab had selected a group of three teachers for the propagation of knowledge in Syria and Palestine. They belonged to Ansars who had specialised in the compilation and presentation of Quranic knowledge. The original plan was that three teachers should start their teaching work at Hims, and should train a number of persons who had the talent and capacity to receive such a training. Later on they should proceed to Damascus and Jerusalem.

These three teachers, Maadh bin Jabal, Ubadah bin Al-Samet and Abu-al-Darda by name stayed for some time at Hims and then Abu-al-Darda shifted to Damascus where he continued his teaching work in the Great Friday Mosque of the town till the end. Ubadah stayed at Hims while Maadh went to Palestine. Their main work was the teaching of Quran and the propagation of religious knowledge.

When selecting members of missions the early Caliphs made it a point to include very often some Ansars who were considered to be very faithful keepers of the traditions of the Prophet.

Umar Ibn Khattab sent a mission of the Ansars which included Qarzah bin Kaab Ansari to Kufa for the propagation of the Traditions of the Prophet.

Umar did them the signal honour of accompanying the mission upto the mosque of Dharar on the road from Medina to Kufa. In his parting instructions he asked them to emphasize more on Traditions or Sunan and Fraiz rather than on accounts of battles.

The Most Learned : Ali was one of the greatest scholars of Quran in his days and he had great confidence concerning his knowledge about the particular context in which a verse of the Quran had been revealed. According to Ali, "Ask me about the Book of Allah because there is no Ayat (verse) about which I don't know whether it had been revealed at night or in the day, on even ground or on a hill top." He knew the reason, the place and the person about whom it was revealed.

Such an exact knowledge about the chronological sequence of the Quranic verses led him to plan the collection of the Quran on his own initiative and it appears that he was deeply engaged in this work during the period when Abu Bakr was elected to the Caliphate.

He had been late in taking the Bayt with Abu Bakr and when the latter asked him about it he told that he had taken a vow not to put on his sheet for any other purpose except offering prayers until he had compiled the Quran. It is said that he had compiled it according to its chronological order but he did not appear to have made it public.

According to Umar Ibn Khattab, Ali has been recognised as the greatest authority on Qaza (Legal judgement) in Medina. Umar Ibn Khattab would pray to God to save him from a difficult situation where Abu al Hassan (Ali) was not close at hand to give his counsel. He would seek his legal advice in personal matters and preferred it to that of others.

As a young man, the Prophet had appointed Ali once the Qadi for Yemen. It was a great distinction for a young man to be appointed a judge for this part of Arabia.

Yemen had reached a more advanced stage of social and political development because of its intimate relations with Iran and Abysinnia and Hadrat Ali was not very much in the wrong when he felt slightly diffident about the success of his office.

According to Ibn Saad he had said, "O Prophet, you are sending me to a people who are ancient and great. They are old and experienced and I fear that I may not be able to perform my duties efficiently." Thereupon the Prophet prayed for him and said, "May God give strength to your tongue and guide your heart."

According to Amir, among the early Muslims, the office of the Qadi (judge) was held with special distinction by Umar, Ali, Zayd bin Thabit and Abu Mussa-al-Ashaari.

Zaid bin Thabit, the Katib (copyist) of the Prophet was the greatest scholar of Ilm-al-Faraiz (Law of inheritance) and when he died, he was described as the 'scholar for men' i.e., the savant who dealt with the law of human rights.

He had been described as the greatest scholar of Al-Faraiz by the Prophet and Umar Ibn Khattab. He was retained in Medina and continued to hold the *Riyasat* (Headship) in Qaza, Ifta, Faraiz and Qirat till his death in 45 A.H. He was appointed an officer of judiciary by Umar Ibn Khattab and was granted an allowance. One of his distinguished followers in Qaza was Said bin-al-Musayyib, the well known savant and doctor of law who continued the legal traditions of Zaid bin Thabit in Medina.

Abdullah ibn Abbas was undisputedly the greatest scholar of Tafsir and he has been styled as Sultan-al-Mufassirin (the king of Exegesis) or Habr-al-Ummat (the savant of Ummat), and the Prophet had prayed that God may bless him with Hikmat (wisdom) and the Exegesis of Quran.

Ibn Abbas represents the cultured person of the period who had received a broad liberal education and who used his great learning for the clarification of the text of the Quran.

With Quran as the basis he would develop his lectures according to a scheme of coordinated studies, wherein Arithmetic, History, Literature and geography all would combine into a united whole, the great integrating principle for this unifying process being the Quranic text.

He would illustrate the use of a particular word or phrase occurring in the Quran by quoting the verse of a poet. He was equally sought after for the study of genealogy, accounts of battles and poetry.

He had his week days divided according to a set time-table. He would lecture one day on Fiqh, the next day on Exegesis, the third day on History of battles. Special days were appointed for the teaching of poetry and the history of Arabia.

He has been described as an Ocean of 'Ata' on account of his versatility of genius. And according to another, he overshadowed other savants as a tall date-palm overshadows the smaller ones.

He was styled as an Allama by Uby bin Kaab, and it was a signal honour to be designated with this title by one of the greatest authority on Quranic text in the days of the Prophet.

Great Genius : The educational influence of Aishah worked in favour of the most faithful rendering of Traditions and in several cases her exact knowledge of the context in which a particular comment had been made by the Prophet helped in the clarification of issues. For instance, Abu Hurayrah had related that ill lies in a women, a horse and a house but Aishah explained that he had missed to add the qualifying clause that in this case the Prophet was quoting an article of faith with the Jews.

Her intimate knowledge of the context of a particular Tradition often resolved many a controversial issue.

Once Fatima bint Qays claimed in the days of Dinar Ibn Khattab that the Prophet had abrogated the right of a divorced woman to stay at her husband's house for the period of Iddat. Umar Ibn Khattab refused to credit her statement but the ambiguity was removed only when Aishah described the circumstances under which this exception had been made by the Prophet. The husband's house in this particular case was situated in an out of the way place and the Prophet asked the divorcee to leave the house on account of its isolated situation.

Through her close association with the Prophet and her critical attitude she has been recognised as a master of the science of Istidrak, or the higher criticism of Traditions. Her critique has been compiled by more than one scholar out of whom the most well known study is by Sayuti under the title of '*Ayn-al-Asabah fi ma istadrak hu Aishah ala Ashabah*'.

She would lose no opportunity for imparting instruction to others and while on the pilgrimage, she had her tent on the slope of mount of Thabir, and she was accosted by a large number of persons seeking after knowledge. Sometime she would hold classes within the Haram and seat herself under the roof of Zam Zam.

Another medium through which her knowledge of law was being broadcast was through Ifta (legal decrees) as she continued to exercise the authority of issuing legal decrees till the end of her life. Reference on legal points were made to her by Muawiyyah who would send emissaries for this purpose from Damascus.

Her remarkable eloquence was a great asset to Aishah as a teacher. According to a very reliable and honest witness Ihnaf bin Qays, he had the opportunity of listening to the addresses of Hadrat

Abu Bakr, Umar, Uthman and Ali but he never heard a more eloquentadness from any one in the world than that of Aishah.

Hadrat Aishah held a school for the teaching of Traditions at her residence. The place had an additional advantage as it adjoined the Prophet's mosque. Women and younger fold sat within while men took their scats in the out. She had more than 200 pupils which included 88 women. She was extremely particular about the language and expression of her pupils. Once she had criticised the language of two young persons who had come to her as pupils.

She was a great teacher of the subject, and her house was the cradle bed of a regular school of Traditions. She would take young children, maintain them out of her own pocket and give them training in this subject. Urwah, Qasim, Abu Salma, Masruq, Amrah and Saffiyah had been apprenticed to her when quite young.

Out of these Amrah acquired great distinction as an authority on Traditions and when Umar bin Abdul Aziz launched on his great task of preserving Traditional literature, he asked Ibn Hazm, the Qadi of Medina to take special carc in acquiring Traditions from Amrah. He had written to Amr ibn Hazm, "Copy Traditions from Amrah because I fear the loss of knowledge and the passing away of men of knowledge."

In case of women teachers, an important group among their students always belonged to their own family. In case of Aishah, the family of Abu Bakr benefited of a great deal from her teaching.

Hadrat Abu Hurayrah, the most copious narrator of Traditions was one of the most popular teacher of the subject in his later years. He had continued his pursuit of learning with great devotion and self-sacrifice. His only rival in the field was Aishah, the wife of the Prophet and when she told him once that he narrated such traditions on the authority of the Prophet which she had never heard of, Abu Hurayrah replied, "O Mother of the Faithful, I acquired this information at that time when you were busy with your collyrium and your mirror! Aishah had criticised also the rapid speed at which he used to narrate Traditions.

Abu Hurayrah had pursued his great interest in the preservation of Traditions at great personal sacrifice. While the Ansars were busy with their daily occupations like agriculture and the Muhajirs carried on their trade in the market place, he would stick to the Prophet and acquire knowledge of Traditions. For some time, he lived with the people of the Suffa and had experienced terrible spells of starvation in those days. In his own words, "When I could scarcely move between the mosque and the residences of the Prophet's wives which were very close to the mosque without losing consciousness on the way." But nevertheless he continued his pursuit of learning in an unabated manner.

The people of Suffa used to share their meals with the Prophet or meet their needs through those charitable donations of the community which were brought to the mosque.

Abu Hurayrah had an extremely vigilant mind and he used to keep a careful note of the daily activities of the Prophet. He was often accused of being too prolific in his narrations. But it appears that he had acquired such a capacity of concentrated attention and memory that there was hardly anything which escaped his notice or passed out of his wonderful memory. Once he asked a person what Surah the Prophet had recited in the night prayers day before. The man had attended the prayers but he had no idea of the Surah. Abu Hurayrah remembered the whole of the Surah recited by the Prophet on that occasion.

A psychological treatment which helped Abu Hurayrah considerably in improving his memory was made by the Prophet when he complained of bad memory. The Prophet asked him to spread out his covering sheet. Then he sprinkled a few drops of water on it and asked him to put it on again. According to Abu Hurayrah he never forgot a single Tradition after that.

According to another version, the Prophet made a gesture of putting two or three handfuls on the sheet, as if bestowing something on him.

Allowances Permitted : One of the main traditions which provide a sanction for monetary compensation in case of religious instruction has been related by Kharajah bin Salt, a Kufite whose uncle had visited the Prophet for instruction in the teachings of

Islam. On his way back he came across a Beduin who was suffering from an attack of insanity and was bound in chains. His tribal people asked him to treat the sick person. He recited Surah Fatiha, the opening chapter of the Quran and the sick person recovered from the attack. He was offered one hundred goats as a compensation which he refused to accept. He visited the Prophet once again, and asked his opinion on the matter.

He said, "It is your right. Others accept compensation for unlawful treatment of the invalid through (sorcery or enchantment) but you have earned it through a lawful treatment."

According to a tradition, the Prophet had sanctioned payment of compensation in case of those who were engaged in religious warfare; He had compared them to Moses' mother who received payment for suckling her own child. The fighters were paid for defending the Faith.

The Hanafite school has interpreted payment in case of religious instruction as a parallel case in which the tradition is equally applicable.

Umar and Uthman had granted allowances for Muezzin, Imams and teachers and Umar bin Khattab had sent special instructions to some of his amils that those who learnt the Quran should be granted an allowance.

Umar bin Abdul Aziz had sent Yazid bin Abi Malik and Harith bin Yamjid Ashaari to the countryside for teaching purposes and granted allowances for them. Yazid accepted the grant but Harith refused it.

Great teachers who had specialised in a particular science were despatched to important centres in the dominions not only for the propagation of religious knowledge among the masses but also for the training of a class of scholars who would blaze a new trail in their special field of interest. These great teachers functioned as a great educative force for the common people also but their primary objectives was the training of teachers or scholars. For the education of the common man, Umar Ibn Khattab sent a number of Qasas (story tellers), not story tellers in the literal sense of the term but men who would present great religious truths in the form of stories as illustrated in the lives of the Prophets of old. They appealed to the imagination of the common people by their simple, direct and forceful style of teaching. The first persons to be selected for this work were Tamim-al- Dari and Ubayd bin Umayr. They taught traditions and religion.

This class grew in popularity and their services were often requisitioned by later rulers for purposes of political propaganda. They sometimes accompanied the army and incited them to fighting on the battle-field.

Expert's View : Great teachers were inspired by the Divine Command to the Prophet "Say, O Prophet, I don't ask for you any reward for all this."

Ghazzali affirms that the teacher should follow the noble example set by the Prophet and should not expect any compensation in the form of monetary reward, any other form of return or even the gratification of receiving thanks. On the other hand, he believes that it is the taught who lays the teacher under obligation rather than vice versa. According to him, "the pupil is like a landlord who has surrendered to the teacher the barren wastes of his soul for tilling and cultivating. As a sheer economic proposition, the cultivator of the soil stands to gain more than the proprietor. Hence the teacher has hardly any justification for making a parade of his beneficence because the teacher could not have earned the grace of God through his teaching if the pupil had not provided him with the opportunity of earning this spiritual merit.

This approach of Ghazzali which might come as a surprise to some of the teachers in our days introduces a fundamental revolution in the pupil-teacher relations, and raises the level of the professional attitude towards work from the economic to the spiritual. This outlook is indispensable in the teaching profession because the very nature of the efficiency demanded by the educative process demands an approach essentially different from that in other professions. But this does not imply that the economic aspect should be ignored altogether.

10

Teacher's Responsibility

The teacher held an important place in the system of higher education among the Muslims, a pivotal position which determined the plan and the execution of the entire scheme of education.

Teachers for the highest kind of learning existed in the Islamic world long before the colleges came into existence. They continued to work even when that magnificent system had fallen into decay. The study circles of the early period owed their heightened scale of intellectual effort to individual teachers and even the era of colleges failed in the regimentation of their individual traits to the dull uniformity of a college cadre; more often a college was known by the reputation of a great teacher than vice versa. Great thinkers like Ibn Khaldun, Abu Ali Sina and a host of other illustrious names owe their education to the fostering care of individual teachers rather than to an educational institution.

The teachers scaled the heights of social and moral prestige in the community, but their achievement in educational administration was something unprecedented in the history of education and all the more significant in a system which had a religious bias, but was otherwise thoroughly secular in its organisation. The system was essentially different from the education of the monasteries in Medieval Ages in the sense that there was no priestcraft or clergy among the Muslims who held an undisputed monopoly of education. Although secular in this sense the educational system was entirely in the hands of the teachers. The teaching staff exercised the right of autonomy in framing cf curriculum, planning or general organisation. The endowment system had made them more or less free of any servile dependence on the state or other patrons and the management of the endowments was also in most cases in the hands of the teachers themselves and the record of its educational history reveals that the teachers ran the system with credit to themselves and to the people. There are certain dangers in a teacher-ridden system, but they pale into insignificance when compared to the dangers inherent in a system, which is controlled by a political or a religious group or is metamorphosed into a Government bureau by a totalitarian state. In fact the study of the system of higher education in the Islamic world and the role played by the teacher in building up the system acquires a specific importance in a world where education has become a plaything of party politics and where its organisation is, being directed by socialistic or capitalistic planning. It is very conveniently forgotten in a world resounding with political slogans that there is one more way of planning education and it is the teachers way.

If we desire to save education from soulless uniformity and regimentation, we must concede autonomy to the teacher in organising and administering education and it is hoped that the progressive tendencies in educational administration in the democratic and the socialistic blocks will be heading in this direction.

The teacher held a key position in the system of higher education under Islam and an intimate study of the problem will have not only a historical value, it could provide us with certain organisational and administrative patterns which may help us in solving the educational tangle at present.

Teacher's Position

The teacher of higher education enjoyed a specially unique status in the Islamic World. He presented a pattern of moral and social leadership, which remains unexampled in the social structure of the modern world. The social gauge by which the prestige of an individual could be measured were not so precise and prosaic as they are today. Economically the teacher did not reach the high water mark, but it was not an important measure in a world which was more open to fluctuations of fortune for the individual and wherein the value of an individual was assessed by surer and more lasting standards.

Among the people, the prestige of a teacher was known by the size of the assembly which gathered to listen to his lectures, the crowds which would go to welcome him on his arrival or accost him on his departure. The final test of his reputation was the concourse which accompanied his bier on his last journey.

In the educational world, the teacher's worth was determined in the qualitative sense and he was known by the number of distinguished scholars who had graduated under his direction. The quality of his work was also judged by the number of great teachers who attended his lectures, a custom not uncommon in those days.

The common people and the educated class determined the nature and the quality of the reputation of a teacher. It received further recognition through the ruling princes and the nobility. The poets also provided a measure of universal respect in which a teacher was held in those days.

The teachers were held in the highest esteem everywhere, but in their assemblies they could vie with the greatest of the land in authority and prestige. It was not confined to the physical limits of the assemblies, it transcended political or racial boundaries and reached wherever their word was carried.

A witness, by no means favourably disposed towards a teacher describes how he treated the royal summons to appear before the king. The episode has been described at length by Al-Maqarri and his lively narration could bear repetition for our readers.

When the royal slave came with a message to Abu Ibrahim, a teacher in the days of Hakam II of Spain (died. 976 A. D.) that the Caliph desired to see him he replied Go back to thy master and mine (may God pour his favours on him!) and tell him how thou hast found me in one of the houses of God, surrounded by a number of students, to whom I am recounting traditions respecting the Prophet.

Tell him that these students are attentively listening to my words and profiting by my lesson and that it behoves me not to interrupt the subject upon which I am lecturing to them until the sitting be at an end and the hour come for my dismissing them.

The royal slave returned to the palace and came back with the following characteristic reply. "The Caliph has directed me to say that he hopes God will reward thee for the good thou art doing to religion and to the Muslims who are profiting by thy lessons and that when thou has put an end to thy lecture, thou art to go to him straight."

Now Abu Ibrahim was fairly advanced in age and was too weak to ride. He requested the Caliph to order that the gate of the palace nearest to the mosque where he lectured might be opened for the occasion and the Caliph did him the signal honour and issued a royal order that the gate which was continually shut up might be opened for his reception.

The narrator tells that when he passed by the closed gate after the lecture, he saw royal slaves and attendants bustling about in order to accord a suitable reception to the savant.

Role of Kings

There were teachers who had matrimonial relations with royalty and others who refused to maintain them. Osman, the patriarch of the Osmanides took the daughter of Maula Adah Bali, a pious savant of the age as his queen. She was the mother of Ur Khan who ascended the throne after the death of his father.

It is related that Osman Ghazi used to visit the savant at his monastery and would often stay there for a night. Once during his stay there he dreamt that a moon rose high from the residence of the savant and entered the royal citadel. Out of this moon spread out branches which covered the whole of the earth and underneath was a magnificent range of mountains out of which gushed forth springs and humanity availed of these springs, watered their beasts of burden and irrigated their gardens.

When Osman related the dream to the savant in the morning, he read into it the happy augury that the faithful would be benifited by him and his progeny and forthwith he offered him his daughter in marriage.

The daughter of Sheikh Adah Bali became the Queen of

Osman Ghazi while her aunt was wedded to a minister of the state. The mother of Akbar the Great was the daughter of a mystic teacher.

There were teachers who refused the offer of a royal espouse for their daughter and preferred to marry her to a promising young member of their class who could not afford some times even a few dirhams for marriage money.

Position in Courts

The highest offices of the state were open to the class of savants and the names of scholars who became ministers of state occur quite frequently in the annals of the Osmanides and other dynasties. There were others who acted as ambassadors and leaders of diplomatic missions and they conducted this delicate business with honour to themselves and to their country.

In spite of Ibn Khaldun's remarks on the failure of teachers in practical politics on account of their preoccupation with intellectual pursuits the ruling princes availed of the tremendous prestige which the more distinguished of the savants enjoyed in the Islamic world for diplomatic purposes. Great scholars were more widely known than the princes and the kingdom of knowledge extended beyond the frontiers of empires and principalities. Moreover the days when political relationships were determined by personal contacts with the rulers, the social, cultural and intellectual qualities of the envoy were more important than mere diplomatic sagacity and acumen.

In the case of a prince with cultivated tastes a distinguished savant with the gift of eloquence and scholarship was sure to prove a greater success than the diplomat. When the Byzantine emperor saw the ambassador of the Omayyid Caliph Abdul Malik, he was very much impressed by his personality. He wrote back to the Caliph that he very much wondered why the Muslims elected him to the Caliphate in preference to Shaabi, the ambassador. It was a left handed compliment which cut both ways. When the Caliph read out the epistle to Shaabi on his return to the court, the great savant replied with all the unction of a diplomat whose role he was playing that the Emperor would not have made this remark if he had seen the Caliph.

But when a great scholar was dispatched as an ambassador to a Muslim ruler, his reputation was sure to precede him and he was often given a public reception befitting the royalty. Sheikh Abu Ishaq, the first Principal of Nizamiyya College of Baghdad was sent in 475 A. H. by the Abbaside Caliph to Sultan Malik Shah at Naishapur as an ambassador. He was given grand ovations at every town which he passed on his way to the capital of the Seljuq monarch. The towns people preserved the dust under his mule's hoof as something sacred and as he entered the town and passed through the streets, the shopkeepers thrown up their wares to the crowd in sheer ecstasy at his arrival. At Sawah, the bakers, the fruiterers and the sweetmeat sellers all distributed their wares and when last of all he passed through the cobblers street, the people had reached such an acme of emotional fervour that they flung the shoes into the air which were caught by the crowd. And when the savant stopped to rest, he was offered hospitality by such a large number of citizens that he made a polite refusal and stayed in a residence by himself.

There were occasions when they played the role of a peace-maker successfully. Allama Qushji was sent as the messenger of peace by Ulugh Beg, the ruler of Samarkand to the Osmanide Sultan, the conqueror of Constantinople. It is Sultan Ulugh Beg who was not only the patron but also the teacher of Qushji with whom he had studied mathematics and astronomy.

Ibn Khaldun had been sent to Tamerlane when he was investing Damascus in the same capacity. Sometimes a forceful address by a teacher has saved a whole town. Once the ruler of Allepo invested Marrat-ul Numan, the native place of Abul Ala-al-Maarri and fixed his war engines close to the city walls. The siege was prolonged and the town people grew panicky. They approached Abul Ala for help and guidance. He did not speak a word in reply, took a guide, blind as he was, and passed through the gateway which was opened for him on the occasion and went straight to the king. He opened the conversation with a dignified address. The king was so much impressed by his address that he at once announced the amnesty in words eminently suitable for the occasion. He said to the blind poet, 'I present you the town and its people.

The savants were often required to deliver an address on the occasions of grand reception given to foreign missions. Al-Maqarri mentions the eloquent speech which was delivered at the court of Abdul Rahman-an-Nasir who ascended the throne in 300 A.H., when the embassy of Constantine was given a great reception at the royal court. The great scholar Al-Qali had been specially entrusted with the duty of addressing the mission, but he failed to rise to the occasion and it was performed in a most spectacular manner by Manzar b. Said. As a recognition of his wonderful talents, Manzar was appointed Imam of the Friday Mosque of Al-Zahra and later on was promoted to be the judge of Cardova.

Sometimes diplomatic missions headed by scholars were instrumental in developing fresh contacts, cultural and intellectual between two countries and the philosopher diplomats which Akbar the Great of India sent to Shiraz caused a renaiscence of philosophical and scientific studies in India. Some of the royal courts observed a fine grade of ranks and it was scrupulously followed in the seating arrangements in case of ceremonial occasions and functions of state. The gradation of services was generally determined by the salaries received by the incumbent, but the savants and teachers were always given precedence over others without any consideration of the poor pittance which they drew from the state coffers.

A savant who taught in the days of the Osmanides relates how once Maula Lutfi went to see the minister who was closeted at the time with a high dignitary of the state. The savant went up to the minister in his simple dress and took his seat above the distinguished official and none prevented him from occupying the place. On enquiry, he was told that the savants' status was not assessed by their salary but by their learning. This set him thinking furiously and he decided to adopt the profession because although he could hardly hope to attain the status of a noble he could make an effort to win the position of a scholar

On the Indo-Pak sub-continent, the teachers were given the highest precedence at the royal court during the pre-Mughal period. Later on when Humayun drew up his weekly programme for meeting different classes of people, he assigned the first day to ahl-i Saadat, the scholarly class.

Teachers Higher than Kings : The teachers did not play an active part in politics yet they had the potentiality of becoming the leader of a religio-political movement any moment on account of their social status and their influence with the people. It has been said that all revolutions in Egypt had their origin in Jamia-al-Azhar and it can be affirmed with a fair degree of accuracy that most of the revolutions in the Islamic world have been inspired by religious personalities who were closely associated with education.

They educated the people for the great change before it came and educated them into it when it came. Only the scholar and the savant could provide those intellectual and religious foundations which could maintain the interest of its supporters after the first wave of enthusiasm had passed over.

Hasn bin Sabbah, Ibn Tumart, Ibn Muquffah and a host of other personalities form a distinguished group who blazed a new trail in the history of religion and politics. The ruling princes kept a watchful eye over the savant whose influence was in the ascendant and sometimes they could scarcely conceal their nervousness at the spectacle of an entire people paying tribute to a savant.

As Malik Zahir Bayburs watched the funeral procession of Allama Abdul Aziz passing by, he heaved a sigh of relief and declared that for the first time in his life he felt secure because the Allama wielded such a tremendous influence with the people that he could incite them into open rebellion against him. Abu Hamid Isfraini once told the ruling prince that he owned a kingdom of knowledge from which he could not be exiled, but he could expel the prince if he wrote a slip of paper against him to the people of Khurasan.

Imam-al-Harmain, another teacher of Khurasan beard the Seljuk lion in his den and proclaimed his injunctions against the royal will in Naishapur . And when people began to throng in the assembly of Bahauddin, the father of Maulana Jalaluddin Rumi the ruling prince Muhammad Khwarizm Shah felt so nervous that he despatched the keys of the citadel and the royal treasury to the Maulana with the message that this was all that had been left to him of royal prestige and power.

The history of Islamic education abounds with instances of extremely pleasant and intimate relations between the savants and the ruling class. This great spirit of love and regard was actuated mostly by genuine motives, but sometimes political considerations also moved a prince to make a display of reverence for a teacher held in universal respect.

Ruling princes have offered themselves as a sacrifice for a savants in his sick bed. Others have composed elegies celebrating the praise of their scholarship. Some felt themselves honoured by a matrimonial alliance with the teacher while others had to suppress their sense of frustration when a teacher refused the match.

Not only princes and nobility but world conquerors did not forget the homage due to learning and scholarship in their hour of glory and amidst scenes of universal carnage and plunder.

When Amir Taimur plundered Shiraz, one of his ministers requested for an amnesty for Saiyid Sharif Jurjani and the king granted his request. An arrow from the royal quiver was stuck fast on the door of the scholar's residence and all the womenfolk of Shriaz flocked to his house and shared with him the privilege of royal amnesty.

High principled teachers would refuse to act as royal tutors for more than one reason, the primary consideration being the high educative value inherent in group teaching as compared with individual instruction. Any transgression of the classroom etiquette was checked with severity in case of the princes and the nobility. And very often a teacher refused to wind up his lecture in the face of an urgent call from the royal court.

There were others who refused to accept post of the royal tutor because they could not exercise freely their right of chastisement in case of princes. The princes and the nobility regarded good social behaviour as indispensable in case of students and insisted on a strict observation of classroom regulations. The rulers also enjoined on their progeny the maintenance of an attitude of profound reverence towards their teachers. One day Harun-al Rashid saw Asmai, his son's tutor making his ablutions while the prince was pouring water on his feet.

Harun was annoyed with the teacher and told him that he had

not taught the prince good manners. The prince should have poured the water with one hand and washed the teacher's feet with another.

Teachers and the Poets : One of the criteria for assessing the social importance of a personality in the Islamic world is the variety and abundance of panegyrics composed in his praise during his life time and what is even of greater import, the elegies written in his honour after his demise. This form of poetry has served as a vehicle for expressing such sentiments from the days of the Prophet.

This criterion of judging the social rank of a person is a fairly sensitive means for this purpose because the eulogies written in the praise of savants were not inspired by basers motives of monetary gain or reward and when a poet eulogises a scholar or a savant, we can be fairly certain that he is giving genuine expression to his sentiments and representing also those of the people in general.

Panegyrics written in honour of scholars form a class of literature by itself and they have been preserved for posterity by historians and biographers.

They are not mere high flown, hyperbolic encomiums after the style of this kind of poetry, they have a more sincere ring about them and sometimes they throw interesting sidelight on the personality and activities of the teacher.

The inaugural function of a college provided a suitable opportunity for such panegyrics wherein after praising the founder, the poet cap the recitation by a reference to the great teacher who was expected to deliver the inaugural address and occupy the chair at the Institution. The occasion when a teacher cornpleted the study of a particular work with his pupils was celebrated with great eclat and proved a stimulating challenge to the poetical talent of some members of the assembly.

The departure of Abdullah bin Mubarak from his native town of Marw was celebrated by a poet in memorable words. "When Ibn Mubarak departed from Marw at night, with him departed the town's beauty and light, whenever they would talk of great man in any town thou would be the new moon and the rest the stars."

The poet rose to sublime heights sometimes in singing the praises of a scholar, but in most cases this type of poetry has a waddling, pedagogic air about it. Nevertheless it is an expression of genuine sentiments.

There were occasions when the atmosphere of the classroom, vibrated with the rhythm of true poetry and genuine emotion. Fakhruddin Razi was once lecturing in a mosque College when a pigeon chased by a hawk sought refuge under the cloak of the savant. A poet in the audience was deeply moved by the spectacle and he struck off a beautiful panegyric in praise of the teacher on the occasion."

According to a proverb in Arabic, the Death of Alim (Scholar) is the Death of Alam (world) and the elegies written on the death of a scholar gave a passionate expression to the widespread feeling of sorrow on the sad occasion. Sometimes the panegyrics were not actuated by a purely altruistic motive. Poets would approach sometimes a teacher for a recommendation for preferment to a prince and the request was presented in verse, its introductory lines comprising a panegyric for the scholarly patron. Even those teachers who avoided any visit to kings and courts were won over through the sweet music of poetry to intercede for others to a ruling prince.

Status among People

The teachers were expected to maintain a reserved and dignified demeanour and to adhere to it with the most scrupulous care in public. In this case as in others they had to make due allowance for the prevalent notions and norms concerning social behaviour in order to make their moral and intellectual influence felt as intensively as possible. More than once a great teacher had explained that his preoccupation with external appearance and behaviour was primarily actuated by his desire to maintain the dignity of knowledge and those who profess it. While on foot, they were expected to move at a deliberate pace, more so because sometimes their educational activities continued even when on the move. For instance a pupil might be accompanying them with a book in hand or a passerby might consult them on a point of religious law or niceties of grammar, the general standard of cultural and social life being so high that such encounters were not at all infrequent in those days.

The savants would maintain this dignified behaviour irrespective of the demands of kings or their courtiers. A scholar of Spain was once invited by the king to his court and he proceeded with the dignity and decorum due to his high office. The royal messenger asked the judge to mend his pace but he took no notice of his remarks. When he arrived at the court, the king complained of his being late. The judge who had a shrewd sense of humour, took hold of his staff and began to tuck up his cloak. Upon being asked what he was about to do he told that he was trying to prepare himself for a race because it appeared that he was no longer a judge but a police official.

Role in Family

The teachers did not belong to the order of celibates nor they were expected to lead a single life by the religion or society. Family life was a normal feature of the teaching profession and old bachelors were an exception rather than the rule. The biographers always make a pointed reference to such cases. Here as in other aspects of their life, the savants followed the precepts and the example of the Prophet.

The teachers passed a peaceful family life as a rule, but as most of his time was occupied in the pursuit of knowledge or teaching work, an irate wife would often prove as violent in temper as the wile of Socrates. Az-Zuhri's wife did not like her husband's preoccupation with books and once exclaimed in anger that his collection of manuscripts was a worse calamity for her than three rivals, implying that if he had married three other women as permissible by the Shariat, she would not have taken the step so much to heart. Others would wreak their vengeance after the death of the scholar. The wife of a scholar was so much upset by the death of her husband that she threw the major portion of his collection in a tank because the books had not allowed him any leisure for the pleasures of domestic life.

But when an inordinate love of learning was combined with an inadequacy of the means of support, the rightful indignation of the wife would surpass all bounds. Tannukhi relates on the authority of his father that Imam Abu Yusuf the great Qadi of the court of Harun-al-Rashid was in dire circumstances in the beginning of his career and how his wife resorted to all sorts of expedients to keep the two ends together. At last her patience was exhausted and one day when he had gone to attend lectures he spent the whole day there and returned at night to ask for his meals, she produced a dish under cover. When he removed the cover he found his lecture notes within. When the astonished scholar asked her the reason for this change in the menu, she retorted that he was occupied with them the whole day, so he had better take them for his dinner.'

He returned in a dudgeon to his teacher Abu Hanifa who consoled him with the Prophetic remark that one day he would feast on almond paste mixed with shelled pistachios. Teachers were conscious of the evil effects of the lack of harmony and understanding in domestic life and its pernicious influence on the peaceful pursuit of intellectual interests and they would make an effort to provide suitable life companions for their pupils. There is an ancient tradition of students marrying their teachers daughters and it harks back to the days of the Ummayids. Some of these women were highly accomplished scholars and proved ideal companions for their espouses.

Very often the son of a teacher began his education with his father and ended by stepping into his shoes and occupying the chair vacated by the father. As a rule the teachers treated their sons and pupils alike and in most cases they did , the fullest measure of justice to the intellect and ability of students and prized a talented pupil more than the son.

Abu Jafar of Spain was one of such teachers. Once when one of the pupils recited some verses in his presence, he turned to his son who was sitting close by and said, "Here is genuine poetry so unlike the verses with which you pester me every day. If you propose to write poetry, you should better do it in this style otherwise refrain from it." Next day his son wrote two lines in the same style and he attempt was hardly better than a sorry caricature of the composition of the pupil. The teacher quoted next day the verses composed by his son to the pupil, deprecating them in the strongest terms and indicating how his son had emphasized the form at the expense of the spirit. The pupil commented courteously that he did not agree with him and considered the lines superior to his own. This aroused the anger of the teacher who condemned his remarks as sheer sycophancy and an attempt to adorn a falsehood. But the pupils had the highest regard for the teacher's family and Ibn Jamaah lays down specific instructions for the students how they should respect and support the family of the teacher.

Decline of Teachers : In the beginning, the better class of teachers did not wait on princes and the nobility, on the other hand the latter waited upon them. The early Caliphs had a close affinity with the common man which was all the more close and intimate with the man of religion or teacher, synonymous terms in those days. The prestige of the teacher who was a genuine leader in the social and intellectual sense was very high. Political revolutions in Islamic history have often grown out of religious movements and the instances when a prince felt nervous on account of the phenomenal rise of the influence of a savant are not infrequent in Islamic history.

The second period opened with the first foundation of the colleges by the princes and the nobility, an era which corresponds with the beginning of the system of Nizamiyya Colleges in the East and the royal foundations by Nuruddin Zangi and Salahuddin in the West.

"The foundation of the new institutions implied certain restrictions on the appointment of teachers on grounds of personal merit. During this period the influence of the ruling class began to encroach on the intellectual life and high principled teachers would often refuse to accept the offer of an appointment in these colleges. They preferred to work in private institutions or assembly groups maintained by the teachers themselves."

The third period begins with the establishment of a system of state colleges maintained and supported by the state under the Osmanides with daily emoluments and pensions paid from the state exchequer. This era registered a marked decrease in the prestige of the teachers who could hardly be distinguished from other servants of the state; in some cases they belonged to the personal retinue of the ruling prince. The deterioration was equally marked in the social, moral, and intellectual sphere.

With the establishment of an ecclesiastical Department under a Sheikh-ul Islam as its head, the status of the teacher deteriorated still further. A teacher (d. 969 A. H.) who was overbearing in his arrogance used to criticise the Sheikh-al-Islam of the day. The sultan invited a fatwa (legal injunction) on his behaviour and the mufti decreed that he should be dismissed from service and should be banished from the town after receiving corporal punishment. He was brought to the Divan (secretariat) like a criminal and was given the required number of lashes laid down by the Mufti in the presence of a number of witnesses and expelled from the town.

After all these indignities the teacher had the patience to desire a reprieve, was pardoned by the Sultan and was reappointed to one of the eight colleges at Constantinople. Some of the teachers under the Osmanids had amassed enormous wealth and one of them helped once a minister with thirty thousand dinars. This teacher had built a bath over the hot springs near Bursa which yielded good income every year. He had presented this building also to the same minister. Notwithstanding all these rich gifts, the minister did not have a very high opinion of the man.

A teacher of Dar-ul Hadith at Constantinople was charged once with the offence of selling the posts of Muid (Reviser) and other attendants to the highest bidder and he received bribe for the allotment of residential quarters in Hostel. The teacher was finally dismissed by the ruling Sultan. He took it so much to heart that he pined away in sorrow and died.

Appointment of Teachers : During the early period when education had not been institutionalised, the appointment of the teacher was not governed by any strict regulations. But the wideawake interest of the people in education and specially that of the study group taught by the teacher led naturally to the selection of the most suitable candidate. In some cases the nomination was made by the retiring teacher, in others the class group and the general public selected the best of his pupils. The suitability for the post was determined by the esteem in which the retiring savant held the pupil and the candidate's public reputation.

The main factors which determined the selection was the opinion of the class group as represented by its important and influencial members supported by public opinion. The educational system had a vital relationship with community life in those days and the keen enthusiasm of the people for education made sometimes the teachers national figures of great importance. Hence the nomination of the successor was not an election affair of an educational body, but a matter of genuine concern for the entire community.

During the early period, the ruling princes did not interfere in the appointments but they were approached sometimes to persuade a scholar in accepting a post offered to him. The demand for reappointment of Imam Ghazzali to the principalship of the Nizamiyyah College Baghdad came from the students and the staff who made their representation to the Mutawwali (Manager). When the Imam refused to occupy the post the Mutawwali approached the Abbaside Caliph to exercise his personal influence over the savant.

But the best method of appointment was through that training for apprenticeship which the teacher provided to the more promising of his pupils by appointing him as an assistant professor, or giving him a chance to officiate in his place during his absence. Another pupil of his, Ashshashi by name, who later on became a professor worked as an under tutor before his preferment.

The arrangement ensured continuity of pedagogical traditions after the retirement of the teacher and prevented any dislocation of work on account of unforeseen changes in the teaching staff. By the time that the system of colleges had become established, this method of teachers training had a fairly good trial. Khallikan remarks how Imam Shafii would refer persons visiting him for light on debateable issues to Buwayti, his favourite pupil and when he was approached by officers of the 'shurtah' for an inquiry, he would send them to Buwayti whom he styled as his 'Tongue'.

Abu Ishaq Shirazi the first Principal of the Nizamiyyah College of Baghdad served this apprenticeship with his teacher for more than ten years during which period he officiated for the master and also worked as Reviser assistant.

Circles for Studies : In the case of study circles the appointment of the successor was made very often by the savant during his life time. He would give the favoured pupil an opportunity to officiate in his place when he was indisposed or had to leave the town on business.

When Hammad the teacher of Abu Hanifa, the founder of the Hanafite School proceeded to Basra he appointed him to officiate in his place. In his absence the members of the study circle posited a number of queries on topics which had not been discussed by the teacher and Abu Hanifa gave answers on the basis of personal judgement, but he was careful to keep a faithful record of all the queries and his answers. When Hammad returned from Basra after on absence of two months he referred his answers to him. The teacher approved forty out of a total of sixty answers and rejected the rest.

Imam Shafii had selected Buwayti to occupy his lecturing seat in the Friday Mosque after his death and he had trained him for the job during his life time. Whenever a person came to him for his opinion on a legal point or the chief of the police sought information on a legal issue, he would refer them to Buwayti adding that he was his tongue, implying his exactness in interpreting his viewpoint.

Teachers took special care in selecting the most suitable candidate for filling the post. Imam Abu Hanifa gave his parting counsel to his favourite pupil Imam Abu Yusuf and told him that if he were to certify a pupil for the teaching of Fiqh (law), he should attend his lectures in person and judge his efficiency for the post.

If the pupil committed any mistake in the course of his discourse, the teacher should point it out in the presence of the audience.

In later times, the better type of pupil served a period of apprenticeship in the capacity of a Muid or an assistant. Abu Ishaq, the first principal of the Nizamiyya College, Baghdad worked as the Muid or Reviser-assistant of his teacher for ten long years. There were often more than one Muid attached to a teacher and the experience provided good opportunity for training in educational methods in case of young teachers.

There was a keen contest among the favourite pupils for the vacant post and during the last illness of Imam Shafii two of his favourite pupils exchanged hot words on the issue. When another pupil Al-Humaidi declared that Shafii had already nominated Al-Buwayti to the job, the rival candidate called him a liar and the other retorted in a stronger language. Such language was never used in those days of genial urbanity and the episode indicates the intensity of feelings aroused on such occasions.

Thus frustrated Ibn Abdul Hakam, the vanquished candidate occupied an alcove once removed from the seat where Shafii used to lecture while Al-Buwaiti occupied the place of his master. Lecture work under the Islamic educational system was public in the truest sense of the term and when a teacher claimed to profess a subject he could be questioned by any member of the public interested in the subject, during the course of his lecture. Under these circumstances the scholars ventured to lecture only when they had acquired a good command of the subject matter and method of exposition, otherwise they met with disastrous results.

Ibn Jinni a grammarian used to teach syntax in a mosque at Mawsil when Abu Ali-al-Farsi whose well known text has received sanction of countless generations of teachers and pupils, chanced to attend his lecture. On questioning the teacher, he found out that he had no mastery of the subject. Abu Ali left the class with a parting fling at the novice. He said "You have turned into a raisin before you became a fully ripened grape". Ibn Jinni came to know the identity of the learned stranger when he had left the town of Mawsil but so irresistible was the intellectual urge aroused by the remark that he gave chase, overtook him at the first stage of his journey and remained attached to him as a pupil. His educational career came to a close only with the death of his teacher. He ultimately rose to great eminence as a grammarian and a teacher of language.

11

Teaching Programme

The teachers were regular in their work and demanded rigorously the same regularity from their pupils. Maula Muslihuddin Mustafa called the Red Mule for his complexion was a strict disciplinarian and if a student failed to attend his lecture, he visits him in his room in the hostel and minister to him if he was ill. If otherwise, he chastises him most severely.

Once a pupil of his, invited his uncle who was on a visit to see him, to a feast arranged in one of the gardens during college hours and when he requested the savant to grant him leave for the purpose, he flew into a passion and said 'Your entertainment programme made you stop your lesson, could not your lesson make you stop your entertainment. He further told him that the only consideration which deterred him from expelling him instantaneously was the esteem in which he held his uncle.

The same pupil related that he studied with him for a period of two years and his teacher never missed a single lecture, so assiduous was he in these matters. But the teachers could afford to take a more lenient view when they were convinced of the urgency of their need. Abul Ala-al-Maarri once permitted a pupil to leave his lesson in order to see a visitor from his home town.

Abu Zakariya Tabrizi had been studying with his teacher Abul Ala-al-Maarri for two years and during this period he had never once come across a single person from his native province of

Azarbaijan. They were studying in a mosque when suddenly an old friend and fellow countryman came to offer prayers in the mosque. He was overjoyed to see him and Abul Ala although blind perceived his emotional excitement and asked him what had happened to him. When Tabrizi told him about his old companion he asked him to go and have a chat with him. Tabrizi demurred and told that he would prefer to complete his lesson first. But Abul Ala insisted and promised that he would wait for him till he had finished.

The assemblies of world renowned savants attracted pupils from four quarters of the Islamic world and the audience included sometimes distinguished scholars who came to hear a master discant on his favourite subject. According to Allama Zahbi, ten thousand inkpots were kept in the assembly of Abul Mutaqqai (died 251 A.H.) and the august gathering included two hundred Imams.

A lecture by a traditionist Sulaiman bin Harb which was attended by the Abbaside Caliph Mamun in person drew forty thousand listeners while the record number of one hundred and twenty thousand persons came to listen Athim bin Ali discourse on traditions in the days of Harun-al-Rashid. It is said that his assembly usually comprised more than 10,000 persons.

Although lectures on religious subjects specially traditions drew the largest number, those on secular subjects like grammar were also fairly popular. A lecture delivered by Farah Nahwi was attended by eighty judges, besides students of grammar.

The management of such assemblies required a number of assistants called Mustamilis (the dictators) and some assemblies had quite a large number of such assistants.

The assembly of Abu Muslim, the well known author of the collection of traditions known by his name had seven assistants, who dictated from one to another. The assembly had 40,000 and odd persons who wrote besides others. Another had as many as 316 such assistants in his assembly."

These assistants formed a normal feature of class management in the colleges where it was not unusual to come across a class of hundreds if not thousands. The teachers were expected to group the pupils into smaller units for teaching purposes and for revision work after the lecture.

The monitorial system or the institution of a Muid or a Revisor assistant and a khalifah helped considerably in class management. The system was introduced by Dr. Bell in England in the last century and although it proved of a doubtful value in raising the standard of educational efficiency, it helped to propagate education during a period when trained teachers had not become abundantly available Seats in the class group were arranged in the form of a circle (Halqa) and the practice is traceable to the days of the Prophet. According to Zarnuji the pupil should seat himself at a bow's length from his teacher.

The pupils were expected to be properly dressed when attending lectures. The savants themselves took extreme care in matter of dress and enjoined on their pupils to follow their example. 'Make your turbans more imposing, your sleeves more widening' says Abu Hanifa. They would often expel a pupil who was improperly dressed from the class. Sheikh Abu Umar turned out of his class pupils who came without a proper headgear or whose shirt fronts were not properly buttoned up.

The seating arrangement in the class was regulated by a set of rules by which those senior in age and scholarship were given precedence over others, the front seats and those to the right hand of the teacher being given to privileged pupils. In case a pupil showed evidence of superiority over others, he was given a seat in the front rank. When Abu Hanifa attended the lecture of Hammad, he took his seat on the left of the teacher along with other freshers but a few days afterwards he was assigned a seat in the front row.

The pupils were expected to sit at their ease and listen while seated in a comfortable posture. The teachers did not approve a standing position. Imam Malik would not relate a tradition while standing, travelling or when pressed for time and used to say, "I like to feel the meaning of the Prophet's word when I repeat them to others." Books on Education provide instructions on the manner of taking one's seat in the assembly and maintaining an attitude of attention. Class room behaviour was regulated by a formidable list of rules dealing with such minutiae as toying with a button, pulling at the beard or drawing lines on earth with the finger.

There are strictures on different postures for seating and on laughter, coughing, spitting, sneezing and yawning. The pupils would sit in the classes as if they were at prayers or as if birds had roosted on their heads and they would not change a muscle for fear of driving them away.

According to Shafii, the pupils would refrain from turning the page of a book in order to preserve the pin drop silence so incessantly enjoined on the students. But all these stringent regulations do not imply that the system was unnecessarily harsh. Its outer form was determined by the social and cultural life of the people in general, but it was essentially human in spirit. Very often the disparity between form and spirit gave rise to interesting situations. Once a student's nose tickled and he struggled hard to check a fit of sneezing. The situation tickled a fellow student who whispered in his ear that he should not be so much at pains to control it because after all he was not in the presence of God almighty. Physical alertness is a pre-requisite of intellectual alertness and the pupils were expected to sit upright in the class. Once a son of Mahdi, the Abbaside Caliph came to attend the lectures of Sharik (died 177 A. H.) on Traditions and reclined against the wall, for support. The teacher refused to teach him and told him brusquely that he did not mean to insult him, but he could not brook an insult to Prophet's Traditions. The posture was discouraged because it signified an attitude of listlessness and lassitude on the part of the pupil.

Recitation by a pupil was a highly cherished privilege exercised by the pupils in the order of precedence in which they arrived for the day's work, and the lesson was opened by the first visitor. Pupils would often sleep overnight on the spot for availing this privilege in the morning. The right could be waived off in no case, unless the pupil himself ceded it in favour of another.

The pupils were enjoined never to demand a repetition of any portion of the lecture. According to a traditionist the repetition of a Tradition was more grievous than carrying a heavy stone. The students had to be all the more careful in this respect because in certain cases the teachers positively refused to repeat.

The pupil was expected to listen with attention a discourse even on a subject with which he was already familiar and he must feign a look of pleasant surprise on his face.

According to Ata bin Abi Ribah (died 115 A. H.) he had the patience to hear from a youngman a tradition which he had studied even before he was born, all the time showing off discreetly as if he had never listened to it before.

Relations with Students

Authorities on education lay great emphasis on the relations between the teacher and the pupil. They insist on an attitude of deep reverence on the part of the pupil and love and affection on the part of the teacher.

Qadi Ibn Jamaah's Views: The teacher should accost his pupils with a welcome when they visit him and when they are seated, he should make individual enquiries about their personal affairs and those of their dependants after the usual salutations. He should address them with a smiling face, and a spirit of companionship, love and sympathy so that the pupils may lay open their heart to him, be of good cheer and may be encouraged to put questions more freely. The treatment and behaviour of the great masters and their instructions on the subject would often leave a lasting impression on the pupils. In the most depressing hours when Buwayti (d. 231) the pupil of Shafii was weighed down with an iron chain forty pounds in weight in the prison-house of Baghdad, he would experience moments when he hardly knew whether he was in chains unless he felt them with his hand. In these hours of darkest despair he had the book of his master with him in which he had taken down with loving care the parting advice of Shafii, "Be kind and sympathetic to the members of the study circle and do a good turn to the strangers"

It was common among the Arabs and other nations who came under their cultural and social influence to have more than one name for the individual, the proper name and the Kuniat : the teacher was expected to call his pupil and specially those who were distinguished from others by their scholarship by his Kunia or any other name with which he loved to be styled. In this case the savants acted as in other cases, according to the traditions of the Prophet.

Ibn Abbas used to say "Most dear to me is the person who makes his way to me by crossing over others head in order to be close to me (for listening my speech). I would hardly bear a fly sitting on him and bringing discomfort to him."

Lectures were attended as a rule by two classes of pupils, regular and irregular; those who were attached to the teacher as his pupils and casual visitors. The teacher was expected to make enquiries concerning absentees, regular or irregular and obtain information concerning the cause of absence. If he could get no information he must send some one to his house or should visit him at his residence in person, the latter procedure being the best.

According to Ibn Jamaah, "the teacher should visit the pupil if he is sick and should give expression to his sympathy and consideration for him if he is suffering from some loss or bereavement." In case the pupil has departed on a journey, he should look after his family and dependents. He should make enquiries about their needs, supply their wants and provide for them all what he can. He should help them with every thing which they seek from him. If he has no means to help them financially or otherwise, he should express his concern for their good and pray for their well being.

The teacher should in no case make invidious distinction between his pupils as regards attention and regard if they are otherwise equal in age, scholarship, love of study and singleness of purpose. But if any one of them is distinguished by his love of learning, industry or god behaviour, he may select him for special regard and give him precedence over others, but he should make it explicit that his consideration for the pupil arises out of the above mentioned reasons.

How the Teachers helped their Pupils : The economic relations between the teacher and the pupil were determined by a variety of factors, the class of the teacher as regards his special subject, the financial condition of the savant, and the traditions of the country.

As a rule the teachers of religious studies did not accept any remuneration from the pupil although exception was made in case of teachers who lived in extremely poor conditions. The teachers of Spain would enter into an agreement with their pupils for teaching certain subjects.

Imam Ghazzali does not approve that the teacher should receive any remuneration from his pupil. He was against the custom of using pupils for domestic service which was more usually practised in case of school children. In his opinion even the expression of gratitude on the part of the pupils is out of place.

According to Ghazzali instead of expecting from the pupils an expression of a sense of gratitude, "He should feel under an obligation to them because the pupils have entrusted to him the nurturing of their hearts and he has been able to gain merit in the eyes of the Lord through this service". The pupils are like the owner of a plot of land, who has surrendered it to the tenant for cultivation and harvesting purposes. In his opinion the tiller of the soil and not the landlord gets the best out of the bargain. The teacher has no right whatsoever to place his pupils under a debt of gratitude because if the pupil had not offered himself for training, the teacher could have no opportunity to earn a reward in the eyes of the Lord.

The authorities on education impose the help and encouragement of the pupil as an essential duty of the teacher and he is enjoined to use his influence and monctary resources for providing him facilities as far as possible.

According to Ibn Jamaah 'God favours the person who helps his brother in trouble and one who tries to make life easy for another in this world would enjoy an easy reckoning from the Lord in the next, the reward being richer in case the assistance was rendered to a seeker after knowledge.

The teachers of the Islamic world were essentially *loco parentis* for the pupils and helped them with all the means at their disposal in pursuit of learning.

The history of Islamic education abounds with examples of teachers helping the pupils, the tradition has been laid by the founders of the first four schools of Islamic law. Imam Shafii was helped most generously by Imam Muhammad bin-al-Hasn and even by Imam Malik while the help rendered by Imam Abu Hanifa to his pupil Imam Abu Yusuf prevented him in giving up his studies.

Asad bin Furat relates how his teacher Muhammad bin Hasn came to know about his financial difficulties and he sent his compliments to his pupil through a servant at night. He pleaded ignorance of his condition and sent him eighty pieces of gold through the messenger. He had the courteous delicacy of feeling to send the money in the dark.

Parents in impecunious circumstances could not afford higher education for their sons and preferred that they should join an occupation which might bring a timely aid to the poor parents. In such cases a teacher with means would often come to the rescue of a deserving pupil and help him financially so that he could pursue his studies in peace.

Qadi Abu Yusuf, the pupil of Abu Hanifa was forced away from the class by his father who admonished his son not to take after his teacher, a savant who carried a rich trade in cloth, look to his interests and take to a vacation. When the savant had an opportunity to see his pupil again he came to know of his condition ; he gave him one hundred dirhams in secret and told him to inform him again when he needed money and by and by he presented him with another sum of one hundred dirhams.

Qadi Ibn Furat received a purse of eighty dinars from his teacher when he came to know that he could not pave his way with the monetary assistance which his family had provided for him.

The teachers took extreme care that the offers of financial assistance might not injure the self-respect of the pupil, a virtue which they cherished themselves so eagerly. Abu Zakariya Tabrizi, the well known grammarian relates how he used to live in a call under the minaret of the Friday Mosque at Damascus when one day his teacher Khatib Baghdadi came to see him. He started offering, profuse excuses for not visiting him more frequently. Gradually the conversation drifted to those traditions of the Prophet which extol the presentation of gifts to friends. Upon this the teacher turned to him and told that he was going to present him with a gift only to honour the behests of the Prophet on the subject so that he could provide his stationery requirements with the sum. Then he placed the money wrapped in a paper in front of him and took his leave. The paper contained five hundred dirhams. Abu Zakaria relates that he helped him in this way more than once.

Matrimonial relations were other means by which the monetary and other help rendered by the teacher was elevated from a charitable donation to something in the nature of a privilege. The pupils prosecuted their studies to quite an advanced stage of life in the early period and most of them were married. Matrimonial relations with the teachers' family became a regular feature of the educational life in the Islamic world.

There is the anecdote of Abu Wadaah who married the daughter of Said-bin-Mussayib, a gifted woman whose hand was sought by the heir-apparent of the Ommayid Caliph Abdul Malik bin Marwan without success.

The story runs that Abu Wadaah absented from the lectures of his teacher for a number of days after the death of his wife. When he made his next appearance in the class the teacher came to know of the tragedy and advised him to marry again. The pupil pleaded lack of means and asked who would marry his daughter to a person who could not pay more than two or three dirhams for marriage money. Said told that he would do it and performed the marriage ceremony of his daughter with the pupil in the same sitting. Abu Wadaah returned to his house and in the evening he found his teacher who had come to escort his daughter at the door. According to Abu Wadaah, Said had never been observed to frequent any other path except that leading from the mosque to his house for the last forty years and he could not credit his ears when he heard Said asking permission to enter the house from without.

There were savants who did not forget to make some provision for their pupils in their will. Khatib of Baghdad sought the Caliph's permission to spend his property according to his will during his life time. His money which amounted to two hundred Dinars was distributed among the pupils.

When he was lying on his death bed an illustrious pupil of his, Nasir bin Muhammad-al-Turke, by name, who studied history with him complained against the executor of his will and told him that he had received nothing out of the money which he had earmarked for the Traditionists. Thereupon the great savant raised his head from the pillow, and told the pupil to take away his cloak which contained forty dinars. The money helped him in defraying his expenses during his educational career.

The sting was taken out of that extremely embarrassing feeling which grew out of a sense of financial dependence by the refined manner in which the assistance was preferred. The teachers often tried to spring a pleasant surprise on their pupil, the joy of the moment helping to mitigate the inconvenient feeling.

Qadi-al-Laith ibn Saad, a wealthy savant of old Cairo used to have almond cakes made for his disciples and he hide gold pieces in them so that he who ate the largest number of cakes might get most of the money.

A rich savant at Herat (d. 378—988) had gold coins struck which were one and half a times worth the current coin. In his words "The poor rejoices when I make over a small packet to him for he thinks that it contains a silverpiece. On opening it he is pleased to see the yellow of the gold and more pleased still when he finds it heavier in weight than the ordinary current coin".

This sense of delicacy and sheer joy in rendering monetary help was not confined to the Near East. Even today the Delhi dialect retains the proverb "*Khankhana jis ki roti mein Badana*" or Khankhana whose cakes had a stone within. Khankhana, the resplendent lord at Akbar's court and the founder of an academy, secreted gold mohurs in the cakes and distributed them anonymously. The usage reminds one of old Dr. Johnson passing through London streets late at night and placing bright new coins in the palms of street arabs sleeping on the pathway.

When a rich merchant who was a scholar sent to another man of learning a book as a present, he placed a gold leave between each two folios.

The teachers preferring help did not stop at giving the pupils the barest minimum which could keep their body and soul together. Sometimes they would arrange banquets which often stretched into regular feasting for an entire month. A teacher of the Qalandariyya College at Constantinople wrote a good hand and he used to copy out manuscripts at a great speed. Every year he would transcribe a copy of Tafsir-al-Baidhawi and sell it for three thousand dirhams. With the proceeds of the sale he used to entertain his pupils every night in the fasting month of Ramadan until the whole amount was spent up.

The teachers were more considerate and enthusiast in entertaining pupils who were themselves masters in their subject and were attending the classes of another savant in order to specialise in a different branch. Imam Shafii, the founder of one of the four schools of law proceeded to Medina in order to attend the lectures of Imam Malik, the founder of a rival school on Traditions. Malik would serve him at dinner time, and bring water for ablutions in the morning. When he expressed his desire to leave, Imam Malik went in person to hire a ride for the journey and presented him with a purse when he bade him farewell.

And all this becomes doubly significant in the light of the punctilious care which Imam Malik observed in maintaining the dignity of the profession. He had wielded the unique authority of rebuking the Caliph and the princes alike. His classes presented a rare example of decorum and orderliness.

In some cases the college was opened and maintained by a teacher and the students were also supported by the founder himself. If he could afford, he would be more generous than even the rich philanthropist Ibn Batuta describes the sumptuous meals which were served at a college in Bargi where he enjoyed the hospitality of the founder teacher. It is evident from his account that the four courses with an additional sweet dish was the regular menu of the hostel. He describes another college at Wasit which was run by the members of a learned family who belonged to the town. The pupils were supplied with free board and lodging and a suit of clothes at this institution.

Busy Schedule

The daily programme of most of the teachers even today gives evidence of a strange singleness of purpose and devotion to learning on the part of the savants which appears to belong to a different world than ours. Trimingham in his 'Islam in Sudan' gives a day in the life of a teacher in a Khalwa or School which is full of a round of educational activities from morning to morning. A resume of the daily programme is given below:

After morning prayers read the last day's lesson on Khalil, a book on Fiqh.

Corrected the tablets of the learners of Quran. Morning lesson on Khalil.

Lesson on ash-Shatibi's book on reading of the Quran.

Another class in Fiqh.

Noon day prayers.

Mid-day lesson on Khalil

Afternoon prayers.

Class on Tajwid and Fiqh.

Evening prayers.

Recited the text of Khalil from memory with Commentary.

Recitation by the students of Quran-reading while the teacher took rest in a reclining posture.

Night prayers.

The teacher took rest while the students took their supper.

The Quran students recite the *subh* of the day, retired to his Khalwa where a student read to him in the light of the fire lit in his room told the rosary.

Awakened the students for the new lesson. They washed their tablets and wrote the lesson.

Correction of their writing.

Morning prayers.

Tested the last lesson on Khalil.

On holidays he wrote legal judgements.

This programme of work was followed by a teacher who belonged to the frontier regions of the intellectual world of Islam. It might be described as devoid of joy and discovery, but it gives an indication of the selfless devotion with which the teachers pursued their professional work. It is by no means uncommon to find a teacher of indigenous education so occupied in the Madrasas of Islamic world today. In fact the determination and persistent efforts of such teachers have maintained the system under adverse conditions. The singleness of purpose with which the teachers carry on their work is the surest guarantee for the preservation and continuity of its traditions.

Relations with Non-Muslims : Great teachers were no mere pedagogues. They were spiritual and intellectual leaders of the people and they exercised considerable influence on the high and the low. This influence was mostly utilised for the general good and when the call of justice came, it was exercised irrespective of colour or creed. Again in periods of frequent changes in ruling dynasties and princes when kingdoms were made or marred over-night, the only civic organisation which continued to exist in a more or less preserved form was the township. Like the ancient Greeks, the Muslims had a conception of citizenship which was closely associated with that of a town. The feelings of local patriotism as regards one's home town was as strong as nationalism today and Jews or Christians gloried with equal enthusiasm in the achievements of a great fellow citizen and vied with one another in doing him honour.

When Imam Abul Ala used to go from Hamadan to his native town for offering Friday prayers, the towns-people would issuc forth out of the gates to receive him, the Muslims and the Jews forming two separate groups, all of them welcoming the savant home.

The funeral ceremony of a savant was largely attended and Christians and Jews of the town would come out to pay their last respects to the great dead.

Non-Muslim Students : As a rule the non-Muslim students were not enrolled as regulars in the Islamic institutions, but the restriction did not prevent them from attending classes held by teachers in private. The educational system being teacher centered, opportunities for joining these classes were abundantly available, more so when every teacher working in a college was expected to continue his work at his residence also.

A distinction was made in the case of non-Muslim pupils between religious and non-religious studies and non-Muslims were not enrolled as a rule in the classes held for teaching religious subjects. In fact there was hardly any necessity for providing such facilities because the main interest of the Non-Muslim pupil lay in secular and professional education.

A genuine difficulty arose when a text book belonging to a profane subject included Quranic verses or other religious literature. In such cases the more orthodox teachers refused to teach the book to a non-Muslim.

It is said that a non-Muslim desired to take lessons on the well known book on Grammar by Sibwaih from Al-Mazini. He offered him one hundred dinars for his teaching, but he refused point-blank. Thereupon Al-Mubarrad asked him whether he would refuse the offer when he was actually on the verge of starvation. Mazini told that the book contained three hundred odd verses of the Quran and he did not like teaching them to a non-Muslim.

The tradition of non-Muslim pupils enrolling with a Muslim teacher go back to the earliest times and there are instances when a Christian pupil was rejected by a co-religionist and was given facilities by a Muslim savant.

Hunain Ibn Ishaq, the well-known Christian scholar attached to Bait-ul-Hikmat founded by Al-Mamun was expelled by Yuhanna bin Maswaih, the well known Christian physician of the age because he believed in preserving the science as a guarded secret for his own, people. Ibn Ishaq left the teacher in a dudgeon when the teacher had an undignified fling at his expense. He enlisted later on as a pupil of philology and prosody, Khalil bin Ahmad of Basrah gained a wonderful command of the Arabic language. Hunain introduced Kitabul Ayn, the chief work of his teacher, in Baghdad.

In fact talent and singleness of purpose on the part of the students functioned as the open Sesame for many a pupil and helped in removing barriers other than academic. There are cases of teachers who made up their mind not to teach any Zimmi, but had to revise their opinion when they were approached by a talented pupil who showed marked eagerness for knowledge and the pressure which they brought to bear upon for enlisting themselves as his pupil.

Some, of the non-Muslim pupils showed wonderful resourcefulness in winning over an intractable teacher.

Abul Barkat of Baghdad, a Jew intended to eternal himself as a pupil of a Muslim teacher who did not take Jews as his pupils. Abul Barkat arranged with his door keeper for a hiding place in the passage leading to the lecture room where he could secret himself. After an year or so, a debatable point was raised in the class and not a single pupil could give an effective reply. At this juncture, Abul Barkat made appearance from his hide and sought the teacher's permission to join the discussion. On receiving his assent, he began with a relevant quotation from Galens and supplied reference of the date, the tire and the month, when the teacher had made' a discourse on the subject. The aptness of his reply was a pleasant surprise for the teacher who made eager inquiries and found out his clever ruse for overhearing his lectures. He was so deeply touched by his thirst for knowledge that he declared that it would be injustice to deprive such a pupil from learning the subject. Later Abul Barkat proved to be one of his most distinguished pupils'.

Interest in non-Muslim Literature : The traditions of Muslims' interest in Jewish and Christian literature goes back to the Prophet's time. The Quran speaks highly of the Habbarin (Rabbis) among the people of the Book (Jews and Christians) while the parables and the sayings of Christ redolent as they are with a quiet wisdom and deep humanity can be traced in the Traditions of the Prophet and Islamic literature belonging to the earliest period. The Prophet had instructed one of his secretaries to learn the Hebrew language for correspondence work and the History of the Jews formed often a topic of engrossing interest in the assembly of the Prophet. History of the Jews formed an essential part of the general curriculum while there were teachers who developed further interest in the subject and made a special study of these branches.

There were teachers like Abul Fath Kamaluddin Shafii who lectured on Torah and the Bible for the benefit of his Jewish and Christian pupils. He had composed commentaries on both the books for the students'.

Place of the non-Muslim Teacher : Some of the non-Muslim teachers had extremely cordial relations with their pupils and with the student body in general.

Ibn-al-Talmiz, the chief of physicians in Baghdad treated the pupils of the Nizamiyyah college free of charge.

He kept them as indoor patients at his residence which had

often served as a nursing home for ruling princes and presented them with two dinars for enjoying their recovery when they left the place to rejoin their studies.

Ibn Jazlah, the Christian physician of Baghdad who was converted to Islam later on was a great philanthropist and treated all his friends and neighbours free of charge.

During his last illness, he gave all his books as a free gift to the mausoleum of Imam Abu Hanifa.

Their verses often reveals the deep attachment which they entertained for their pupils.

Ibn Butlan the Christian physician of Baghdad who died a bachelor had composed a beautiful elegy on his supposed death expressing how there was nobody to mourn his loss but his pupils.

"And none will let fall a tear over my grave except my assembly and my books bursting in tears."

The more distinguished non-Muslim teachers who wielded considerable influence and prestige in the society of the day attracted a large number of their co-religionists.

Every student visiting the town pay a social call to these great masters. Some of them enrolled themselves as their pupils while others sought recommendations for registering with others. Christian students continued to visit the house of Ibn-al-Talmiz even after his death and Ibn Usaibiah describes the encounter of two Christian pupils with an imbecile son of his, who had been the despair of his father during his life time.

The non-Muslim teachers used all the means of livelihood commonly open to the scholarly class and they would not allow any religious considerations to influence their usual practice. One of their leisure time pursuits was the copying of manuscripts. Manuscripts on religious subjects were specially in demand in those days and the non-Muslim teachers had no compunction in copying out manuscripts of Islamic literature.

Ibn Hamid bin Zakariya, the Logician who had attained to the status of a Rais (chief) in his subject had made it binding on himself the incredible task of copying out one hundred pages or less in twenty four hours.

He had transcribed two copies of that compendious work, the exegesis of the Quran by Tabri for presenting it to some of the neighbouring princes.

The non-Muslim teachers had monopolised certain branches of learning as teachers during the early period. In the beginning the non-Muslims were the chief authority on Greek sciences, philosophy, logic and medicine and their great schools at Alexandria, Antioch and Junde-Sabur functioned as radiating centres of philosophic and medical learning. Furthermore the traditions of medical education took rather a long time in establishing itself among the Muslims and in most cases the profession was monopolised by non-Muslims. In fact the neglect of such an important branch of professional education by the Muslims has been marked by more than one writers on education. For these sciences, the Muslim student often resort to the non-Muslim teachers. Some of these teachers were attached to hospitals and they examine patients and discuss important cases with the pupils on the campus.

Aminuddaulah, the Christian physician of Baghdad who was chief of the physicians and in charge of the Adhdhadi Hospital in Baghdad upto his death used to examine patients with his pupils. He had a class of fifty pupils. Ibn Usaibiah gives the account of his successful treatment of a difficult case and its discussion in the class.

Abul Farj Baghdadi, a distinguished Christian practitioner on medicine taught in the Adhdhadi hospital of his native town and Ibn Usaibiah came across a copy of Aghlotan's commentary of Galens which was read out in his presence in the hospital and was dated 496 A.H.

Teachers in medicine often hold regular assemblies at their residence which was attended by their pupils and distinguished members of the profession.

Yuhanna bin Maswaih who died in the reign of Mutawakkil used to hold an assembly for discussing all varieties of subjects specially cultivated by the ancient Greeks and its meetings attracted persons of learning and knowledge. He also used to lecture to a large number of pupils.

An exact knowledge of the Arabic language was essential for a proper comprehension of the text and the non-Muslim teachers on medicine sometimes provide special facilities for pupils who were backward in the subject.

Ibn-al-Talmiz employed two grammarians for helping those pupils who committed frequent mistakes in their recitation of medical texts, mispronounced words or stuttered in expression. He attached the pupil to one of the grammarians and the pupil was expected to pay the grammarian some tuition fee. These two persons were most probably students of the great physician. They were held in great regard by the teacher and received sometimes presents from him.

A contact with these non-Muslim teachers must have a broadening influence on the outlook of the pupil and brought home to him liberal education in a wider and truer sense.

Some teachers made special efforts in order to educate their pupils into such an outlook. Once two students came to study with Abul Farj of Baghdad and when they visited his house, they were informed that the physician had gone to the church. When they reached there, they came across a rather unexpected scene. They saw the great teacher clad in coarse woolen cloth ; he was bare headed and was going round the altar with a censor in his hand. When he had done with his prayers, he issued forth, mounted a mule and rode back to his house amidst a procession of slaves.

The students presented themselves before him but there were signs of a great surprise and incredulity on their faces. He allowed them to attend his lecture. When the lecture was over he asked them whether they had ever performed the holy pilgrimage to Mecca. They replied in the negative and the teacher told them that their registration as a pupil was conditional to their performing the pilgrimage. The poor pupils had no alternative and proceeded forthwith on the journey. When they returned from the pilgrimage they were tired and out of spirits. Then he enquired them about the ceremonies of the pilgrimage and specially the flinging of the pebbles and the reason for performing the ceremony. They told him that it was a religious obligation and one could not give any reason for these injunctions.

This was exactly the conclusion which the shrewd teacher desired to impress on them and for which he had made them undertake this long and tiresome journey .

The Measurement

The association of the non-Muslims with the educational system within the Islamic bloc of countries paved the way to a closer understanding with the Zimmies and helped in the rehabilitation of these communities in the socio-political structure, but similar contacts in the countries bordering the Islamic world resulted in extremely fruitful cross-fertilisation of ideas and gave rise to scientific and literary movements which had far reaching influences. In the distant west, these contacts in Spain, Southern France, Sicily and other Mediterranian islands blossomed into a renascence in the scientific and according to some writers literary field of knowledge. The Spanish Jews were the first to avail of the new educational opportunities.

The first contact with the non-Muslims were established through the Jewish pupils who in their turn were instrumental in propagating the new learning further afield over the continent. The courts of those Christian princes who were interested in the cultivation of learning also functioned as a meeting ground for these cultural and intellectual contacts. Their patronage extended some times to the Muslim scholars who had stayed within their dominions. Some of the princes and nobles had established academies for the work of translation and adaptation and these centres provided special opportunities of contacts among the intellectual elite.

Sometimes these contacts with the alien non-Muslims were established nearer home. The crusades gave an opportunity for a free exchange of ideas between the East and the West. Campbell mentions how Richard the Lion hearted tried unsuccessfully to secure the services of Maimonides who was attached to the court of Sultan Salahuddin (Saladin).

Maimonides, the Jewish exile from Spain became directly a radiating influence of scientific knowledge in the Middle East. The persecution of Jews in the West had driven them eastwards and Maimonides who was gifted with a rare combination of philosophic learning and knowledge of the Jewish religion became the Head of the Jewish community in Cairo and won for himself also a place of great eminence in the scientific circles of the day.

He taught Greek sciences and philosophy at his residence in Cairo, a town where he acquired a very high status. He was superb in editing books on astronomy and mathematics and two works edited by him were highly praised by discriminating scholars.

Maimonides' personality attracted a number of Jewish refugees from Spain and the North Africa and one of them was Ibn Ishaq-al-Maghribi. He had brought with him from Sabtah a copy of the astronomy of Ibn aflah of Spain and requested Maimonides to prepare an edition of the book. The work was carried out by their mutual collaboration.

The common people were more influenced by the literary traditions of Islamic learning and its universal appeal for the Christian youth is revealed in the lament of a bishop over their neglect of Latin and religious studies.

In the East, the literary curriculum had even a more profound influence in the development of local languages, literature and general education of the non-Muslims. In India it resulted in the growth of communities among the Hindus which adopted the system of Islamic education and their socio-cultural values. Some of the text books written by Hindu scholars were universally popular with students. Special schemes of curriculum were framed with a view to meet the requirements of the Hindu pupils, pursuing these courses and their literary studies included Persian translation of Sanskrit epics and other works of scientific and mathematical nature.

The lure of state service as a secretary or a tax collector also made non-Muslims pursue literary and linguistic studies under great stylists and masters of the language. In certain parts of the Islamic world, tax collection was monopolised by the non-Muslims. The demands of professional training brought all those people within the ambiṭ of Islamic education.

12

Selection of Teachers

As a rule teacher of established reputation did not apply for a post but they were approached with all the deference due to their high position with the offer of the vacant chair. Sometimes the Mutawalli (Manager) or a patron of the college had to marshall all his persuasive powers in order to win over a teacher. When Imam Ghazzali was invited a second time to resume his work at the Nizamiyya College of Baghdad he was supplicated by Ahmad bin Nizam-al-Mulk, the son of the illustrious founder of the college and a minister of state in those days. When he failed to create any impression on Al-Ghazzali who was at that time staying at his native town, the people of Baghdad approached the Abbaside Caliph Mustazhar Billah to persuade the savant to rejoin his post at Baghdad.

An invitation was drafted under the signatures of all the dignitaries of state, and sent to the savant. But Ghazzali would not come. He thanked them cordially for the offer but replied that he could not leave those one hundred and fifty pupils whom he was teaching in a private college of his own in his native town. Again he had taken a vow not to participate in a debate and he was certain that he could not keep that vow in the metropolis. Another formidable obstacle was the economic one. In Tus he had his family property which yielded him sufficient income for making both ends meet while he could not do without monetary remuneration at Baghdad and this he had foresworn to accept for the rest of his life.

The founders of institutions, their managers and sometimes even the ruling princes were always on the lookout for savants who chanced to visit the country and availed of the first opportunity to offer them a post in a college. Teachers who had distinguished themselves in a particular branch of learning were specially in demand for occupying the chairs in the colleges.

When Shatibi, the famous authority on Qirat (recitation) of the Quran came to Egypt from Spain, he was given a-cordial welcome by Qadi-al-Fazil and appointed a professor at the Faziliyyah College founded by him at Cairo where he composed his well known poems, the Lamia and the Raiyah on Qirat. Qadi-al-Fazil was not only a great patron of learning who saved a considerable number of books from the palace library of the Fatimides when it was despoiled during the period of orthodox reaction under Salahuddin, he was also generous in extending his patronage to great scholars and teachers without any consideration of caste and creed.

He had a soft corner of his heart for the scholars from foreign countries. He befriended Maimonides who had been hunted out of Spain and not only saved him from further persecution at the hands of religious fanatics but helped in safeguarding his interests in other ways.

King's Role

In case of royal foundations the appointment of the teacher was commonly made by the ruling prince. It appears that no person could teach in the Friday mosque raised by Mansur at Baghdad without royal permission. Khatib-al-Baghdadi whose life long ambition was to relate traditions from its historic pulpit had to approach the Caliph Al-Qaim-bi-Amrillah with the request and it is interesting to learn that the very nature of his favourite subject provided him an opportunity to win the royal consent. It appears that Khatib came across a book on traditions which comprised a particular tradition that had been related by the Caliph himself. Khatib sought the royal audience in order to verify the authority and when he approached the Caliph with the request the latter made a shrewd guess that the renowned traditionist had some secret motive for the audience. On discovering that his desire was to dictate traditions in the mosque of Mansur, the Caliph instructed the chief of the Naqibs, the official in charge of organising the assemblies in the mosque to arrange for him an assembly in the mosque.

Later Period : So long as the profession exercised a high prestige in national life, the savants were sought after for occupying the jobs, but in the later period the tables turned, it was the scholar who gave a hot pursuit to the posts which often proved a wild goose chase. The appointments in the later period were not made after the implicit desire of the people whose tacit selection was endorsed by the ruling prince indirectly. Under the Osmanides, the authority was exercised by the judge of the armies (Qadi-ul-Asakir) who had to obtain the final sanction of the prince in case of all recommendations made by him and would often incur the displeasure of his master if he acted on personal initiative.

It appears that although the judge of the armies was the chief authority for the appointment of the teachers, powerful ministers exercised influence in certain cases and a weak judge could hardly refuse the recommendation of a minister.

These judges could very well exercise their authority against the expressed desire of a minister because ministers and judges were recruited from the same class and they frequently interchanged places. But the regalia of the ministerial power had tamed the spirit of the savant and he had learnt in some cases to compromise with the demands of the powers that be. A minister asked a Qadi to appoint the tutor of a personal slave of his to a college and the poor Qadi had no alternative but to pray for divine help in order to seek protection from a misuse of his authority.

The Conditions : The appointments were generally open to all persons qualified to occupy the post without any consideration of the race and nationality of the teacher. This usage was a legacy of the democratic spirit of religion and that cosmopolitan spirit which conceived the intellectual world of Islam as a whole. Certain restrictions were laid on the appointment of the teacher of law, who should belong to that particular School of law, for which the endowment had been specifically made. There were state colleges which had four *iwans* for the four Schools of laws and the professorship in each department was held by a savant belonging to that particular School. In some cases the post was held by a Qadi who decided the cases of those litigants who belonged to his sect and he held his court in the department. This practice afford practical training of considerable value to the students of *fiqh.*

But in colleges with a single chair for law, the post was occupied by the teacher belonging to the school, professed by the founder of the institution. This had an indirect influence in the selection of the teachers. Under these circumstances as the foundation had been made in favour of a particular school the majority of appointments in other departments besides Law went as a rule to those savants who followed that particular School.

Abdullah-bin-Hussain of Baghdad was once approached by a group of Shafites who promised to him the chair of Grammar in the Nizamiyya College of Baghdad if he changed his creed. The savant spurned the suggestion and told that if they were to shower on him so much of gold that he was covered from head to foot he would not play the role of a renegade.

But there were teachers and the instance of Wajihuddin Ibn-al-Dahan indicates how the prospects of a college appointment could transform a teacher into a weather cock.

Ibn-al-Dahan who was a Hanbalite changed over to the Hanafite sect and when he started his career as a teacher at the Nizamiyya College of Baghdad he changed his creed once again. A poet satirized him in the following verses.

You became a Hanafite after being a Hanbalite.

And it was because you needed rich food,

You would have never accepted the faith of Shafii

If you had not been sure of gaining all that you desired.

A day will come when you would certainly change over

To the Malikites, so beware of my prophecy.

It appears that reputed masters of their subjects had no difficulty in obtaining recognition of their worth or an appointment even in a foreign country, their reputation often preceding them into distant lands. When Ibn Khaldun went to Egypt he relates how students flocked to him in search of knowledge notwithstanding his insignificant acquirements and would accept no excuse on his part. During his stay in Cairo he received the privilege of lecturing at the Al-Azhar.

In his days the colleges in Egypt were mostly state institutions and the Sultan granted to Ibn Khaldun an allowance usually sanctioned in the case of savants because he held no appointment in a college and when a professorship was rendered vacant at the Qamahiyya College on account of the death of a teacher, Khaldun was appointed to the post by the Sultan.

Inaugural Address : The first day of a newly appointed principal at the college was a red lettered day and his first lecture was more or less an ordeal which he had to stand in the presence of a representative gathering of scholars and savants who were specially invited for the occasion. The function introduced the teacher to a larger audience than the class group specially his professional brotherhood and provided an opportunity for a test of his mettle and scholarship by others.

The inaugural address of the teacher was an outcome of considerable thought and preparation and he marshalled up all his erudition and his literary talent in order to make it imposing and effective. The lectures were often cherished by teachers as valuable mementos of their old glory in later years. Ibn Khaldun for instance records his inaugural addresses ad verbatim in his autobiographical sketch.

In his first address he spoke of the merits of Ulama in supporting a Muslim state, of the rise of states and the patronage of learning by the dynasties of Egyptian Sultans. He invoked blessing on the ruling monarch and praised his justice and sagacity. The address was garnished with pieces of poetry composed by the savant in which he described his voyage from the West to the East, the greatness of Islam and the nascent intellectual movement of those days.

When appointed a professor at the Sarghatmash College for lectures on the Muwattah of Imam Malik he opened his address by an account of the life of Malik, his origin and the diffusion of his doctrines.

The inaugural address introduced the teacher to a selected gathering of savants. Some times the inaugural address was criticised by a member of the audience and the lecturer had to marshall all his intellectual talent in order to satisfy the critic.

A representative gathering of savants attended the function when Muhammad Shah, the son of Maula Fannari was installed as the chief professor of the Sultania College at Brusa during the life time of his father and on the first day he was successful in rebutting the objections of one and all except those of a person who was notorious for his irreligious tendencies.

When his father visited him after the lecture, Maula Fannari told him that he was never so nonplussed as on that day. His father told him that his critic was really a good scholar. Thereupon he remonstrated that an irreligious person could not achieve true scholarship. But his father told him that if the man had not lacked faith, his excellence would have been even greater than he had experienced on that day.

Mode of Payment

There were various sources for the payment of teachers salaries. The main source was the income of the endowment, the amount and nature of the teachers salaries and allowance being indicated in the original deed of the foundation.

Another important source was the public exchequer and this system of grants in aid by the state could be traced to the earliest times.

Umar bin Abdul Aziz was the first Caliph who sanctioned allowances for the teacher in the Empire. Once he despatched two persons to the desert for teaching the Bedouins the traditions of the Prophet. One of them Yazid by name accepted the monetary award made for the service while the other refused it.

But it seems that the monetary assistance given to the learned profession in the earliest days was not liberal.

Khaldun had an opportunity to study the salary registers of this class under Al-Mamun and was successful in discrediting the general notion that the learned class received princely help from the state.

The monetary aid from the state took various forms according to the custom or usage of different parts of the Muslim world. The Osmanides had a regular system of salaries paid on a daily basis followed by superannuation allowances in some cases. The payments were made either directly from the public treasury or made payable from the proceeds of a particular tax levied on a particular town.

In countries like India, there was an Ecclesiastical Department under the chief Divine called Sadr as Sadur who sanctioned monetary assistance to the learned profession. It took the form of grants of landed property free from taxation.

There was a country wide system of free land (Muafi) granted not only to the distinguished members of the profession who were associated with higher learning, but also to the teachers of the Maktabs (Elementary school). Dr. Leitner came across a number of such grants in Punjab as late as the second half of the nineteenth century.

Shahjahan had styled the Eastern part of the United Province (India) as the Shiraz of India, because this tract of land was dotted all over with seats of higher learning and its towns and villages were peopled with scholars and savants who received stipends or '*Madad-e-Maash*' and held free lands granted by the state.

The princes often examined the applicants for monetary assistance in person. During his reign, whenever a scholar applied for a maintenance allowance Madad-e-Maash, Sher Shah examined them personally on Hashiyah-i-Hindi for even then he had much liking for books of history and dynasties of ancient kings.

Besides grants and salaries, the teachers received sometimes munificent rewards from the rulers in lump sum. Mulla Abdul Hakim of Sialkot the well-known scholar and teacher was weighed in gold and received the amount as a present. According to another version he was weighed in silver and received six thousand rupees as a present.

The teacher was expected to maintain the dignity of his profession by not frequenting the presence of the rich without a proper excuse. He was permitted to visit them in case of financial necessity or for some religious purpose. Writers on education defend such visits on the authority of Imam Shafii; Al-Zahri and others. Shafii had intimate relations with the House of Banu Abdul Haq in Egypt and they had presented him once with one thousand dinars and acquired another contribution of two thousand from a merchant and their other friends for him. These exceptions are made on the basis of urgent financial need of the savant. Public subscriptions were an important source specially in the case of the Elementary school (Maktab) teacher who was entirely maintained by the local community by the payment being made in cash or kind. He was provided free meals by the parents and received gifts and presents on festivals.

In some cases the townspeople subscribed to the salary of a college professor also. Marwzi, the Traditionist who founded a study circle in his native province of Khurasan received annually four hundred dirhams from the governor of Khurasan, four thousand from his brother and an equal amount was contributed by the townspeople of Samarkand.

A trader relates how he came across Imam Fakhruddin Razi in one of the lesser known colleges of Bukhara and he was not keeping good health. The savant sought from him monetary help and he collected for him some money from the Arab traders in the town who contributed their tithe to the help of the indigent scholar.

The establishment of a regular system of colleges provided facilities of professional work for those teachers who were retiring in nature and not so well-known. According to Wakhshi 'After an arduous educational career I returned to my native village and nobody had any idea of my worth and no conception of the rich treasure of learning which I had amassed in the course of my travels. I feared that I would fade away in oblivion and none would invoke blessing on me after my death. But God made Nizam-ul-Mulk lay the foundation of this College of Balkh and he got me appointed as the professor of traditions.'

The establishment of colleges provided the additional facility of relieving financial worries of the teachers. Wakhshi for instance had seen terrible times in his educational career. There were days when he was too poor to purchase bread and he would often seat himself beside the baker's shop and inhale the flavour of the steaming bread in order to give a momentary satisfaction to the pangs of hunger.

Pension in Oldage

Sometimes the savants retired from college service and stayed permanently at home where they continued their professional work. Generally they had a chamber for study attached to their residence. Under the Osmanides, the teachers were granted a pension in some cases. Usually there was no appreciable reduction in pay and the savant continued to enjoy the same salary which he received when he was at the college.

Retirement did not depend so much on reasons of age or efficiency. It was left in most cases to the choice of the teacher. He could be dismissed or forced to retire earlier only because of serious defalcations or sometimes on account of the vagaries of royal temperament.

There are instances when the progeny of the savant also benefited through the generosity of the ruler specially in the case of a family which was reputed for its traditions of learning. Muhammad, the Osmanide was told that his kingdom would last as long as a single descendant of Maula Fanari stayed in the realm. The sultan thereupon granted an allowance of fifty dirhams daily for Maula Alauddin, the grandson of Maula Fanari, fifty dirhams for his elder and forty for his younger son. He issued orders that the post of the judge at Ibnah Kol was to be held permanently by a descendent of the savant. Another member of the family was granted an allowance of thirty dirhams daily from his very birthday.

The grants of land made to the scholarly class usually passed from father to son. On the Indo-Pakistan subcontinent Madad-e-Maash, or stipends were granted to individuals on a personal basis while *jagirs* and *Muafies* became a part of the family inheritance.

Some of the more distinguished savants of the Osmanides received annual grants in addition to the daily allowances. Maula Alauddin the grandson of Maula Fanari received fifty dirhams daily and 10,000 dirhams annually under Muhammad which was raised to 70 dirhams daily and 12,000 dirhams annually under Sultan Rayazid.

Agreement for Service

In the teachers agreements common in Spain one comes across the first example of an attempt to emancipate education from its bondage to religion and its establishment on a comparatively secular basis. This great achievement of Spanish teachers must have gone a long way in bringing financial security to a class of teachers who were not attached to a well established institution and who earned their livelihood by means of running private schools.

In Spain teachers entered into agreement with another member of the profession for opening a school on a cooperative basis, sharing the fees and taking turns at teaching. Each partner would hold office for a month by turns.

Agreements were also drawn up between parents and teachers specifying clearly the subject to be taught and the payment to be made to the teacher.

The payment was to be made monthly or annually, as specified in the deed. In some cases the teacher was to receive a specified amount of flour, oil, fresh water. He could demand gifts on the two festivals of Eid and presents on the completion of education if they were included in the terms of agreement.

Authorities disagree on the legality of specifying a period within which the pupil was to complete the reading of the Quran, because it did not conform to the spirit of genuine educational principles.

The teacher was to receive payment for the free day of the week which was Friday and he could enjoy leave within reasonable limits. He continued to enjoy his payment in case the pupil did not attend on account of a brief spell of illness or if his father or guardian withdrew the child from the school for reasons of their own.

These agreements form part of a book on legal documents and such transactions seem to be a normal feature of professional life in Spain. The usage was fairly widespread and master artisans took over apprentices on agreements of a similar nature.

These business relations between the teacher and the taught hardly detracted from the quality of the work. According to the observation of Ibn Khaldun, the standard of teaching in Spain was higher as compared with that obtaining in North Africa. Teachers agreements were all the more necessitated on account of the absence of a well organised system of colleges in Spain, a country where educational system was maintained mostly by individual teachers holding classgroups on a personal and private basis.

Low Economic Return : The teaching profession was not so lucrative as others and Khaldun gives more than one reason for its low economic returns. In the first place, the common people did not count education and learning as something indispensable. Only those occupations which met more universal and immediate demands yielded good returns. Again self-abasement and adulation was the very secret of success in life and men of learning and religion did not approve of these methods. Another reason for their economic failure in life was their preoccupation with Intellectual pursuits which permitted them hardly any leisure for waiting upon kings and nobles.

In his opinion the learned class is compensated to some extent by the honour and consideration which they receive from the people and their states and dignity prevents them from stooping to means adopted by others.

Elsewhere Khaldun rightly emphasizes that the teachers prove signal failures in life because they are so much engrossed in theoretical studies that they are unsuccessful in correlating their knowledge to the needs of practical life.

This affects their economic prospects in an adverse manner.

Sources of Income

Handicraft provided some teachers with a precarious means of livelihood and it would be intriguing to know how they could adjust their teaching hours in case of such occupations. The specialised nature of work, in which a teacher taught only a particular book or subject and the common usage of the pupils attending in person at the teacher's residence might have provided facilities for time table adjustments in such cases.

It is related about Abdul Wahid-al-Baji that he worked as a watchman in Baghdad and on his return to Spain he became a gold beater in the bazar. He used to copy documents, also his pupils related that he came to teach them with the marks of working with a hammer still visible on his hands.

There were scholars who worked as cabinet makers. Abul Fazl the engineer of Damascus was extremely skilful in the art, some of the gateways of the Kabir-Shahi hospital have been prepared by him. He was incharge of the clock-tower of the Friday mosque in Damascus and used to receive a regular allowance for this service.

As most of the teachers carried on some kind of art or craft for earning a livelihood, the authorities on education realised the necessity of laying down certain regulations about the selection of vocations. The teachers were expected to maintain their status by abstaining from vocations which were not considered worthy of their status and dignity.

According to Ibn Jamaah the unsuitable vocations included hair dressing, tannery, money exchange, dyeing etc.

Teachers in the Judiciary : When Imam Abu Hanifa refused to be appointed a judge, Ibn Hubairah the minister gave him ten lashes daily for eleven days but he could not force him to revise his opinion. The Imam was again invited to be a judge by the Abbaside Caliph Al-Mansur who swore a royal oath to appoint him a judge while the savant took an equally determined oath not to succumb to the temptation. He persisted in his refusal after repeated requests and was ultimately sent to the prison cell where he met his end in 150 A.H.

And when Ibn Idris refused the offer, Harun said in anger, "I wish I had never seen your face." The savant replied with quiet dignity, "And so was my desire."

When a savant of the Osmanide period refused to accept the post of a judge at Damascus, his friends mustered strong to persuade him to accept the offer. They found him adamant in his resolution, but they were not discouraged. They were determined not to be defeated. The savant owed money to some of his friends and they declared that if he did not accede to their request he must clear all the debt to the last penny. According to some doctors of law, a person in debt could not occupy the post of a judge.

The poor scholar preferred the judge's chair to the debtor's cell, but not without a passing taunt flung at his friends, " I am only exchanging known debts for the unknown", said he, implying the account of his record as a Qadi which he shall have to render to his Creator after death.

But the fear of pronouncing incorrect decisions was not the only obstacle in accepting the post. There were savants who considered salary for state service to be illegal.

When the Abbaside Caliph Mansur expressed a wish to appoint a person, a governor, he told him that his family people had declared that if he became a governor they wont accept from him even a paltry gift costing two dirhams. So he besought the Caliph not to appoint him to the post.

Function of a Mufti : Besides working as a judge, the teachers very often performed a number of other functions which were closely allied to the legal profession, for instance every teacher of Fiqh was expected to perform the duties of a Mufti. They issued decrees on the legal aspect of everyday problems with which the average citizen was confronted in his daily transactions. Only the teachers who had received an Ijazah (Certificate) for issuing decrees were permitted to function as a Mufti.

As the function of issuing legal decrees was an important duty of the teachers, the writers on education have contributed special chapters on the subject.

The Mufti had to fulfill certain stringent conditions as regards character and knowledge. According to Imam Malik, he did not begin to perform the function of a Mufti until seventy persons testified that he was suitable for the job.

The teachers took a great care in issuing their verdict and would make a frank avowal of their ignorance when they were not sure about it. Once a woman questioned a teacher in the Shahid College at Mardin on religious injunctions concerning menses and the teacher pleaded ignorance. The woman fired up and said, "You flourish the tasselled end of your turban up to your waist and you cannot reply the query of a woman." The teacher retorted with quiet dignity, " If I could answer every question the length of my turban's loose end would have equalled the horn of a bull."

The functions of the Mufti, sometimes interrupted the educational activities of the teachers and they invented interesting devices in order to secure themselves from such distractions. A teacher who stayed in the upper storey of a building received the slip of paper on which was inscribed the debatable point for opinion, in a bucket and draw it up to him and he send back the reply in writing in the same way.

There were a number of other vocations which were closely allied to the above. Some professors acted as witnesses to law papers.

One of the teachers of Ibn Khallikan who lectured in a College used to act in this capacity. This teacher had a pleasant sense of humour which found its expression in his daily contacts with persons who came to him for witnessing the law-papers.

The chancery and the correspondence office provided work for many a teacher. Persons employed in these departments were expected to be good stylists and calligraphists. A good linguist with a flare of literary style had excellent chances for a rise in this line. Ibn Khallikan mentions a scholar Ibn Bari by name from whose pupils he had procured certificates of license. He was a supervisor of chancery and he used to revise the state correspondence despatched to the rulers of foreign states.

Although the job of the secretary was a lucrative one it was not popular with the teachers and it was rare to find a person who carried the functions of the secretary and the teacher side by side.

Art of Copying : Some teachers did an incredible amount of copying. Ibn Jawzi had been preserving the savings of his red pen whenever he was engaged in the writing of the Prophet's traditions and he left instructions that they should be used for warming the water for washing his body after his death. It is amazing to learn that they sufficed for the purpose.

When the total amount of writing work by Tabari, the historian was estimated after his death, it worked out at the rate of fourteen folios daily in his hand and forty folios daily in common type.

For some teachers copying formed a normal feature of their daily programme. It is related of Ahmad bin Abu Daim that he copied manuscripts both for personal use and for payment. When free he could strike away nine Kurasas or more daily, but if otherwise busy he would copy out two or three Kurasas in twenty four hours. It is said that he used to copy out the whole of Al-Qaduri in a single night, but Safdi very much doubts it.

Another savant Abu Said Nahwi used to copy out ten folios before proceeding to the court where he acted as a judge in an honorary capacity. He used to maintain himself entirely by copying manuscripts. Some teachers spread their copying programme over an year and copy one important work or more annually which they would send to a prince or a noble for sale.

The reputation, the scholarship and the aesthetic skill of the copyist determined the price of a manuscript.

In the case of distinguished scholars, the manuscripts copied by them were highly prized for the accuracy of the text.

Copying was adopted as a leisure time occupation on account of sheer economic necessity in most cases, but in certain instances it provided the teachers with spare money for innocent pleasures which they shared with their pupils. The author of Shaqaiq remarks how a scholar used to copy out manuscripts and from the proceeds of the sale they gave feasts to their students during the month of Ramadan.

Looks and Robes

Authorities on education often lay down rules and regulations concerning the dress of the teachers. In a society which observed great punctiliousness in matters of costume because of its vital and symbolic relationship with the social status of the person, the teachers had to maintain certain decorum in dress, speech and general behaviour. The formality of court life might have influenced the teachers also to some extent in this case, but their primary motive in keeping a good standard in sartorial matters was to maintain the dignity of the profession.

Imam Abu Hanifa used to say, "Make your turbans more imposing, your sleeves more ample so that learning and those who profess it might not be looked down upon."

Hammad, the son of Imam Abu Hanifa relates that his father was fond of using scent. When he proceeded on his way he was known by the fragrance which preceded him. He uses a costly cheddar which was once priced at thirty dinars.

Shaikhul Islam Harwi used to issue forth from his house clad in splendid remnants and mounted on a noble steed and he used to say that he did all this in order to maintain the prestige of religion.

In fact teachers whose assemblies were visited by the ruling princes and the nobility must have devoted some attention to their dress and general arrangement of their assembly. Such was the case with Imam Malik whose class had been attended by two Abbaside Caliphs who had travelled from Baghdad with the express desire to study his great collection of Traditions with him.

Imam Malik maintained the dignity of his high status by keeping an impressive assembly and richly equipment. Once a savant criticised his practice of employing a door keeper. Malik quoted in reply the following verse of the Quran, "Tell O Prophet, who has the authority to make unlawful what God has bestowed on his creation and fragrant delicacies" implying thereby that there was no religious injunction against the use of fine raiment and enjoying a good meal.

Tilsan which is considered by some writers to be the precursor of the academic gown was not the distinctive mark of the scholarly class in all parts of the islamic world. In Iraq and Spain, it was a popular style of dress for the common people, only in Spain the styles in which it was worn by the savants and the laity were different.

According to Ibn Khallikan, Qadi Abu Yusuf, the chief judge of Harun-al-Rashid was the first savant to order a special kind of dress for the scholarly class, and this dress has been the hallmark of this class since those days. It included a cloak in addition to a Tilsan.

It appears that this additional cloak was a special contribution of the great Qadi to the fashion of the scholarly world otherwise Tilsan was the usual robe of honour with which the scholars were invested by princes and the nobility in those days. It was also the usual dress of a scholar in the days of early Abbasides.

Asmai for instance used to visit the nobility in his old Tilsan and he relates how he received it as a gift from an Abbaside noble.

It appears that while Tilsan or a cloak was worn by one and all, the rank of a scholar was often known by the cut of his cloak, its colour, his head veil and sometimes by the accoutrement of his ride.

The common dress of scholars and judges in Egypt according tó Sayuti was a loose longish cloak opening on the shoulders and a shash or piece of cloth with its teaselled end between the shoulders and in the direction of the left shoulder, others wore a Farjiah while some used a Tilsan. The Khatib's cloak was black in colour with a black Shash and a black head-veil. They used a cloak round in form.

The robes of honour conferred on the scholars and judges were made of wool and were without any Taraz (ornamentation). They were invested with a head-veil also.

The chief judge of the Shafite sect was distinguished by his Tarhah (head gear).

Although the Ijazah ceremony was a private business between the teacher and the taught and it was not accompanied by any investiture function like the convocation in a modern university, it appears ,that the teacher authorised the pupil to wear the Tilsan, the distinguishing mark of a scholar. It was a rather unusual sight to come across a person with a Tilsan attending lectures because he was considered to have completed his education.

Ibn Khallikan remarks that four hundred persons with Tilsan used to attend the lectures of Imam Baud Zahiri. It implies the universal esteem in which he was held even by those who had already graduated and received their academic gown.

Headgear : The teachers used a simple and light turban for every day use while a more imposing one for ceremonial occasions. But different usages were observed in various parts of the Islamic world. Al-Maqarri saw a savant of Mereia, in Spain appearing bare headed before the king.

Social etiquette demanded that the ministers and the king should be visited in proper uniform and the small turban (Shamlah) which most of the teachers usually wore was not the proper dress for such ceremonial occasions ; nevertheless there were savants who would visit the ministers with the little turban on. When once Maula Yusuf bin Hussain-al-Karmasani was asked by the minister to see him immediately when the Maula issued forth from the mosque after offering prayers, he went straight to him without changing his little turban for another more worthy of the occasion and when the minister objected to it, he replied brusquely that he had presented himself to his Creator in the same dress and did not consider it undignified if he appeared before the minister in the same.

There were teachers who wore a crown on their head which was capped by a small turban. The savants borrowed the fashion most probably from the mystics who very often gave evidence of remarkable ingenuity and taste in inventing various styles of headgear, it being an essential part of the dress of mystical orders.

Academic Phase: The scholarly class, both teachers and students had their academic uniform with the distinction that the graduate's dress was the same as that of the teacher's uniform. Ibn Khallikan has mentioned Thiabah Ahi-ul-ilm (the uniform of the learned) and he ascribes the fashion to Qadi Abu Yusuf, the famous courtier and judge of Harun.'

As a rule teachers and pupils were expected to maintain the professional dignity by dressing themselves in a suitable manner. Imposing turbans, long flowing garments and loose sleeves were the hallmark of the scholarly class in those days.

It is not known whether the academic uniform was supplied by the college although there was a rich abundant of endowments for specific purposes, but there is evidence to show that vestments suitable for the dignity of a scholar were given to him in case of special merit.

When Shahabuddin Suhrawardi went to Allepo, he stayed in the Halawiyyah College. He was clad in coarse garments, but when the Head of the institution discovered his pre-eminence among the scholars he ordered for him the '*anabiyyah*' over garment, an undercloth and a bodice without sleeves. It seems that the anabiyyah was a special mark of the scholars in those days.

The colleges did not hold a convocation for investing the pupils with the academic dress but the mystics used to celebrate an investiture ceremony and every disciple received a Khirqa or Dalq (cloak) of a form and colour befitting his attainments in the spiritual and moral sense.

According to Shahabuddin Suhrawardi, 'The Khirqa is presented to one who has a good report with the Sheikh'.

The choice of the colour and form of the disciple's garments depended upon Sheikh's vision, 'If he sees that his inclination is for splendid and soft remnants he awards him the coarse variety of Khirqa, but if he sees that his inclination is for the coarse by way of hypocrisy and pretension, he clothes him in soft silk.'

According to Haneburg the Western Universities have borrowed their academic gown from the Islamic world. His opinion has been criticised, but there is no doubt that the academic costume in the Islamic world had been established long before the beginning of the first universities in Europe. It cannot be laid down with certainty how far the colleges influenced the West in this respect, but it is possible that the costume and the investiture rituals of the mystics might have set the vogue in this direction.

These fads and fashions were equally popular in the East and the West and everywhere they carried a prestige characteristic of the particular form of dress.

When a Christian doctor came to see Ibn Mitran of Damascus (died 587 A.H.) a Christian convert and personal physician to Sultan Salahuddin, the visitor had on him a tightly fitting suit of brocade, blue in colour with wrapper for the head. Ibn Mitran told him not to move about so often in the dress of a European doctor; he advised him to change it for one more acceptable to the Muslims as he was not following the fashion of the Muslim physicians and forthwith he ordered for him a long flowing anabiyya cloak and a bodice without sleeves.

13

Various Techniques

Competent authorities on Educational Method like Zarnuji quote a well known Tradition in support of maintaining a harmonious balance between work and play and keeping a healthy control on over-work and strenuous efforts which may cause a heavy strain for the pupil. The Tradition runs, "Verily you should act with kindness and restraint in matters of religion and don't be too hard on your Nafs (Baser Self) in the course of devotion and prayer. It is your beast of burden and if you ride it to death in the course of the journey, it will not arrive at the journey's end."

A recognition of the principles of attention and the need of a variety of occupations after continuous application to a specialised form of intellectual activity is borne out by a Tradition in Bukhari, "Read out the Quran as long as your hearts are in it; when tired of recitation, you should stop reading and postpone it for some other occasion."

A change over to other subjects of study and a variety of intellectual occupations was an accepted usage of the companions. Ibn Aqbas would send for poetical works when he got tired of Kalam (Scholastic Philosophy).

The principle was not only observed by the Prophet for the reading of the Quran but he always kept it in view when preparing the programme of his addresses and preaching. According to Abdullah bin Masud, he was not a solemn-looking, an inspiring figure on the pulpit; he would often indulge in pleasantries in the middle of an edifying discourse and would make attempt to tickle the human side of their nature, so that they may not feel tired and lose interest in the subject.

Regular Sessions : For this purpose, he appointed particular days in the week for addressing the assembly and Ibn Masud also followed his example in giving only weekly discourses to his audience. When a member of the audience insisted that he should hold a discourse every day, Ibn Masud protested that he did not hold it desirable to make his lectures burdensome and that he made an allowance for his listeners just as the Prophet did. According to Ibn Masud, the Prophet took into consideration the problem of time and always held the disaffection of the audience as undesirable.

Sowing in Rich Soil : And he always took the greatest care that the seed of truth which he was sowing broadcast should fall into the rich soil where it should blossom forth in full bloom. He enjoins that the teacher should discover the capacity of his pupil and find out how far he is spectible to moral and intellectual influences. But once he is convinced of the genuine enthusiasm of the pupil for knowledge and moral progress, he is prepared to provide all kinds of facilities for him. The copying out of Traditions was banned in the earliest stage in order to safeguard the authenticity of the Quranic Text which might not be confused with the Traditions, but considerable concession was made in this respect later on and on the representation of a visitor who complained of bad memory, the Prophet advised him to avail of his right hand and made a sign implying the art of writing.

A number of Traditions deal with one of the most fundamental problem of class instruction, viz the adaptation of the teaching material to the intellectual capacity of the pupil.

According to a Tradition, "I belong to the group of Prophets and I have been commanded by the Lord to treat people according to their ranks and talk to them according to their intellectual capacity." It is further confirmed by the verse of the Quran, "Don't give away your property to the fools. A tradition of the Prophet is strongly reminiscent of the parable of Bible on casting pearls before the swine and seems to be a further amplification of the same." "Don't put a diamond necklace on the swine because wisdom is better than diamonds and the person who thinks low of wisdom is worse than the swine."

Another Tradition that lays strictures on imparting knowledge to the undeserving has a rather poignant significance for the great tragedy of Jesus Christ.

"Whenever a person says something to a people which is beyond their understanding, it results in Fitna or a period of trial and travail for a part of these people."

It is interesting to discover that while Jesus has emphasised upon knowledge and its benefit for the individual, Muhammad (PBUH) has referred pointedly to the social purpose for which knowledge is to be utilized and it influences on men in general.

Bridle-bit of Hell-fire : The above Tradition which emphasizes the imparting of knowledge to the deserving seems to be apparently in contradiction with another where he condemned a scholar with the bridle-bit of hell-fire if he kept his knowledge a secret. This seeming contradiction is resolved by the remarks of a scholar who was approached for enlightenment by a person of some intellectual limitations. When the savant kept silent on his query, his interlocutor reminded him of the Tradition about the bridle-bit. The savant retorted that he should move off with his bridle of fire because this function of briding him up would be performed more properly by a person who had the capacity to understand and had approached a scholar for the receiving of knowledge.

The Prophet was always keenly conscious of the limitations of his audience and he would always adapt his style of address and even its vocabulary and idiomatic phraseology to the capacity and the cultural background of the person whom he addressed.

Knowledge of Dialects : It is interesting to learn that he had a knowledge of the finer shades of differences in grammatical usage and vocabulary as regards different dialects spoken by various tribes in the Peninsula and would address them accordingly.

For instance, in the Tradition of Amiri he said, "Sal Anka," while in accordance with the correct grammatical usage he should have said Sal Anma Shita. In this case, he used the dialectal usage of the tribe of Banu Amir.

According to Atbah bin Saad, he used and in place of — and introduced the nunnation of 'ayn' according to the usage of his tribe. He seemed to have some knowledge of the Abysinian language. During the Meccan period, two groups of Muslims migrated to Abysinian on two occasions and there was a fair sprinkling of Abysinian slaves in Hijaz. As a downtrodden section of the community, they had a special claim on the Prophet and there is evidence to show that he knew a few words of their language. In one case he used the word (beautiful in Abysinian), when he was showing an embroidered sheet of Yemen to Amamah, an infant granddaughter who had seen the light of the day in Abyssinia. In another case he used the term for 'murder' a word which is of Abysinian origin. According to Abu Hurayrah he is said to have used a Persian phrase also.

Style of Epistles : When dictating his epistles to his correspondence secretaries, the language and style were adapted to the cultural and literary background of the addressee. According to Qadi Ayaz there is a remarkable difference between the style of epistles addressed to the higher classes and to the masses.

Qadi Ayaz gives extracts from his letters to Zi-al-Shaar al-Hamadani, Wail bin Hajr-al-Kindi and others, the rulers of Hadrmut and Yemen and they are a fine specimen of literary expression in rhythmic prose. The style of these letters is in a sharp contrast with the document which he ordered to be drawn up on the subject of Sadaqa (charity).

Learning as an Art

The main aim was not to parade his knowledge of these linguistic curiosities but to bring home to the people he addressed, the great message and spoke to them in a language which would open windows into their hearts. On certain occasions the Companions would ask him to explain the unfamiliar phrases and expressions which he used in his interviews on such occasions.

He had acquired this wonderful adaptability on account of his early training both in the language and idiom of the town and the countryside. When the companions expressed their admiration of his style he told with legitimate pride that he belonged to the Quraish (who were townspeople) and was brought up among the Bani Saad a tribe living in the countryside.

Value of Spoken Word : The addresses which the Prophet delivered on various occasions from the pulpit or outside are couched in a simple, direct and forceful language. They are a pleasant combination of high idealism, universal truths and hard realities of concrete situations. There are no flourishes of oratory, none of its frills and furbelows, they throb all along with suppressed spiritual fervour and restraint. As for effect and inspiration, none could wield this powerful weapon to greater advantage. He personally claimed to be the most eloquent of all the Arabs, one who was sent with the most comprehensive of Word, and his claim had abundant justification. He was a scion of the Quraish and had received his early training among Banu Saad, the two people famous for their mastery of the language throughout the country.

Address Techniques : The style and the technique of his addresses require a careful study not only because they are literary masterpieces but because they functioned as potent force in moulding the style of whole generations of teachers and preachers. One of the most important problem for the teacher and orator is to attract the attention of the audience and the Prophet would arouse them by a word of exclamation or by positing a question. He initiated his soul stirring address on the Mountain of Safa with the call "Ya Sabahah", an exclamation used when a tribe is unexpectedly raided early in the morning. And in fact the whole of the Peninsula was being stormed at that period by the forces of evil and ignorance, an affliction which was certainly more disastrous than the raid of a neighbouring tribe. Their curiosity aroused, the Prophet asked whether he should inform them of an enemy which assailed them every morning and evening.

Goals and Purposes

These addresses were extremely powerful and dynamic weapons for the moulding of public opinion, and proved useful during that critical stage of society when great changes spiritual, social and cultural were on the horizon.

While the ancient addresses of Jahiliyyah were mainly directed for inciting people to war, the Prophet utilised this dynamic weapon for a variety of purposes. They were used for spiritual counselling, warnings and blessings proclamations and announcements. Through these orations he called people to religion, self-surrender and self-sacrifice. The address of Hajjat ul- Wida is a supreme example of an inspired oration on individual rights, that of the Mount of Safa on spiritual bearings delivered in the language and the style of a harbinger of fateful news.

A Challenging Question : Sometimes his address opened with a challenging question and his address on the battlefield of Hunayn is strongly reminiscent of the beautiful trilogy of questions posited in the Sura Wadhdhuha. "O People of the Ansar," he began, "Didn't I find you stragglers from the Path and God blessed you through me." And the audience replied, "Verily the Prophet of God is the custodian of truth." He continued positing a chain of questions in the same vein and every time the audience hailed him with an 'aye'. But after the climax came the anti-climax, the positive interrogation was followed by the negative. In an outburst of enthusiasm for their dignified acquiescence he declaimed passionately, "But why do not you say that you came to us as a fugitive from home and we gave you shelter; you were in want and we lavished our sympathy on you; you were friendless and we befriended you."

Then came the summing up of this grand oration with an appeal to those members of the audience who were dissatisfied with the division of the spoils. Once more he put them a concluding question which clinched the whole issue. "Won't you prefer," he says," that others' share should be camels and goats while yours the Prophet of God himself."

Rhythm of Repetition : A formidable weapon in the hands of a speaker is the judicious repetition of certain words or phrases and the Prophet could use this device with tremendous effect. His address on the occasion of the last pilgrimage is a supreme example of this technique as harmonised with the device of interrogation. They are not the frills and flounces of forced rhetorics but the blossoming up of an inner urge for rhythm of thought and expression. It synchronises with the tone of the audience which pulsates with that of the speaker. This progressive repetition and questioning raises the whole process to the level of a shared experience between the speaker and the audience. The well-timed question, with its reply echoed back from the audience weaves constantly a meshwork of emotional and spiritual ties which helps in the growth of an atmosphere of sympathy and understanding.

Some of his remarks are unrivalled in sustained emotion and simple and dignified beauty of expression. One would have expected a funeral address on the death of his son Ibrahim but it was too great a sorrow for an address. When a Companion made some remark on his bursting into tears, he said, "The eye sheds tears and the heart is full of sorrow and we don't say anything except that we have surrendered ourselves to the Will of the Lord and O Ibrahim, we are certainly heart-striken by thy bereavement."

Rhythm of the Entire Personality : In his method of delivery he appears to have expressed himself not merely by his word of mouth but by his entire personality. According to 'Abdullah bin Umar,' he was discoursing on how God would hold heaven and earth in his mighty grip. He closed his fist and then unclosed it while his whole body swayed from one side to another and the pulpit shook under him. Sometimes he was so moved by the rising upsurge of spiritual fervour that he would repeat a phrase more than once and then make an eloquent pause in his speech. It was no more oratorial gesture, rather it was an expression of the rhythm which regulated his inner life.

Dramatic Air : One of his early addresses which he gave on the Mount of Safa has a dramatic air of extreme realism. He has used in this oration the technique of a vitalised dialogue between the speaker and the audience with great effect. The great queries and the rejoinder echoed from a thousand lips covers up the gulf between the two and merges the divergent tendencies of thought into one big unified current.

When the verse "*Wa anzar Ashiratika al aqrabin*" (Warn thy relations the nearest ones) was revealed to him, he got up the Mount of Safa and spoke out, "O people of the Quraish' and the Quraish who were obviously surprised to hear his ringing tones from the top of a hill said, "Come along, Muhammad is calling you from the heights of the hill." Then they collected round him and said, "What is the matter with you." Thereupon he said, "Would you believe me if I warn you that there is an army under the foot of this hill." They said, "Yes, you have never been charged with falsehood and we have never experienced anything untrue from thee". Thereupon he said, "I am going to forewarn you about a terrible punishment;" and then he called out the various branches of Quraish one by one by name and said, "God has ordained that I should warn my kith and kin and I have no authority to benefit you in this world or the next except that you say the formula "There is no God but Allah."

Pauses as Pointers : The principle of carefully planned pauses and the introduction of small intervals for cogitation and the searching of hearts, the principle of gradation rising by degrees to a certain climax of words and moral fervour, the principle of recurrence and repetition, all are evidenced in his well known address on Hajjat-ul-Wida.

He delivered this address while seated on a red-coloured camel, and the mastication suds flowed down on the spectators below; a boy among the audience could picture clearly the impressive spectacle when he listened to the address while standing on the shoulders of his father who was seated on a camel.

The address opened with a pathetic note in which he declared, "O men, listen to my words because I don't know whether I would ever meet you again after this year, at this place."

These fateful words must have quickened the whole gathering into an attitude of great expectancy. The last words of a Prophet must be worth listening and remembering. Then he posited a query and said, "What day is this," and the audience replied, "God and his Prophet know better." Thereupon came an extremely eloquent pause. He paused so long that the audience thought that perhaps he was going to rename the day. Then he spoke out: "Is it not the day of sacrifice!. And they replied, "It is so."

Then he asked, "And what month is it?" And again came the same reply followed by a long pause and the people began to think that he was about to give it another name. Then he asked, "Is not it the month of Zil Hijj?

Then he asked, "What town is this?"

This series of questions following by three intervals, crowded with furious thinking and expectancy on the part of the audience was the most appropriate introduction for what was to follow.

According to another version he had asked, "What day was the most auspicious?" And the people said, 'This day, "and what month, and what town," were the next two questions.

After this came the climax when he declared.

"Your blood and your properties are as sacred as trust as the sanctity of this day of yours, in this month of yours, in this town of yours."

Then he gave them his parting words of counsel with the tragic air created by the spell of his opening words about the approaching end.

"Beware! don't be led astray from the path and kill each other. Beware, have I brought home to you the Truth?"

"Beware, one who is present may carry my words to him who is not present because some of those who are absent may preserve my words more faithfully than those who are present. Beware haven't I propagated the Truth," and according to a version, at the end of this grand oration he turned towards Heaven and said, "O God I have brought Thy words home, O God be these my witness."

When the Prophet addressed people his eyes became red, his voice would grow high and his emotions were aroused. He looked very much like one who delivered the warning about the impending attack of the enemy who would come down in the morning or evening.

On such occasions he would say, "I and the Day of judgement have been sent like this," and with this he would join the forefingers and the middle one together."

Address on a Battlefield : The address given after the Battle of Hunayn was delivered in an extremely delicate situation. The spoils of war obtained during the campaign seemed to have surpassed all expectations and some ill-feeling was created in the course of distribution, the disaffected parties being the Ansar of Medina and Arabs of the desert.

The address is a noble attempt to resolve the situation by a heart moving appeal to the Ansars. The Prophet recounts in his deeply emotional style the spiritual blessings which he had brought to the Ansars and when the climax had been reached, he unfolds the anticlimax by describing the support and help which the Ansars brought to him and after a survey of the credit and the debit sides of this grand human change, he makes them realise the great union of the soul with which they are wedded together. He sums up with the convincing note "Let others take worldly wealth, because for you is the Prophet."

His dramatic entry into Mecca and his short cryptic speech in the serene setting of the Holy sanctuary of Mecca had all the impressive grandeur of a Greek play.

He entered Mecca on a dromedary and made seven circumambulation of the Holy sanctuary. Then he took the keys of the Kaaba from Uthman bin Talhah, its keeper and stood in silent dignity at the gate of the Kaaba. He broke the solemn spell of silence with these words.

"There is no God but Allah. He is without compeer. Honoured is His promise (Waadu-hu), supported was His Believer (Abdu-hu), routed were the rival groups by the One (Wahdu-hu). Beware that all matters of pride, whether blood money or wealth, are under these feet of mine except the service of the Holy sanctuary or provision of water to the pilgrims."

Then he called out, "O tribe of the Quraish, verily God has taken away from you, the arrogance of Jahiliyyah and the pride of lineage."

"Man derives their origin from Adam and Adam was created out of clay."

Then he said, "O tribe of the Quraish, what do you think I am going to do with you!" They said, "Beneficence—thou art a beneficent brother and the son of a beneficent brother" and he declared, "Well go off, you are all free."

Spiritual Counselling : The above oration had a dominantly political air about it but most of his addresses were devoted to spiritual counselling, the vanity of man and his ambitions and its baneful influence on his sense of social responsibilities.

In one of his addresses he has made a scathing criticism of the self-complacency and the egoistic nonchalance of man and how blindly he persists in his course of evil. "O men, it seems to us as if death has been ordained to all except ourselves and the duties are imposed on all except on us, and we accompany the dead on their funerals with the knowledge that we are sending them on a journey whence few return to us. We put them in the graves and enjoy their inheritance as if we will continue for ever after them.

"We have been oblivious of all counsel and we feel secure from all calamities. Blessed is one whose sins have occupied him from sinning against others and who gives in charity from what he has earned in an honest way."

The note of warning which he often struck in his speeches gave him the air of the guardian angel or the watchman of the tribe.

In one of his addresses he compares himself to a Raid or the person who is sent by the tribe to search for a water hole or pasture ground in the desert.

He says, "I am unto you as a Raid is for his tribe and a Raid never tells lies to his people."

"And By God you will die (as surely) as you sleep, you will be resuscitated as surely as you awake. You will have to render account for all what you have done. You will be rewarded for your good with good and you will be repaid for your evil with evil and verily heaven is eternal and hell is also eternal and those of you who have been warned first are nearest to the Judgement Day."

Historic Orations : His addresses were both long and short and their length was intuitively adapted to the needs of the situation. Generally, the Prophet did not like to deliver lengthy addresses and he approved of a person who shortened his address and lengthened his prayer on Fridays. According to Ibn Masud, "he would cut short his address in order to save us from inconvenience."

But when needed, he would give long orations. The text of one of his addresses which he delivered in the course of an afternoon was "Verily the world is a verdant fruit. Beware and God hath made you his vicegerent in it in order to test how you perform your duties."'

He opened his address after the afternoon prayer and continued with it till there was left nothing of the sunlight except its rosy reflection on the fringes of the palm boughs.

But sometimes these addresses were gems of artistic brevity and his successors often followed his example in this respect. For instance, the first address which Umar Ibn Khattab delivered after his election as the Caliph comprised one single cryptic announcement on the duties of the ruler and the rights of the ruled.

He said, "O men, verily by God the weakest is the strongest with me until I acquire his right for him and the strongest is the weakest with me until I wrest the rights of others from him." And after this brief and cryptic statement he descended from the pulpit. The simple and direct way in which he summed up the political rights and obligations of the ruler and ruled on the day of his election was as neat and perfect as a crystal. He said on another occasion:

> "Verily people are like a docile camel which follows its guide, and it is for the guide to see where he leads it to and by the God of Kaaba I will certainly guide you along the right path."

Literary Flavour : The Companions who had passed their whole lives in the closest association with the Prophet would sometimes marvel at this unexpected manifestation of literary florescence.

Abu Bakr had a fine taste for poetry and had the opportunity of listening to some of the greatest orators. He had a knowledge of the literary styles of various tribes. Once he was so much impressed by the expressive language of the Prophet that he could not help asking him, "Who taught thee?" and the answer was, "My God, and what an excellent training He has imparted to me."

His closest Companions would often marvel when he conversed freely in the dialect of the tribal groups who visited him from all parts of Arabia. When Ali saw him talking with the deputation from Banu Nahd he said, "O Prophet of God, we are the descendants of the same ancestor but we observe you talking to the Arab deputations in a language which we don't understand."

An eloquent example of the Prophet's knowledge of different

dialects spoken or written in Arabia is his letter which he had dictated to Wail bin Hajr al-Kindi, one of the princes of Hadramut.

The letter is notable for the choice of vocabulary and the selection of words and phrases which has been carefully chosen to impress a grandiloquent prince of a high lineage. The words have a phonic, rhythmic and picturesque value of their own which accords with the intellectual and social background of the person to whom the letter had been addressed.

For instance, the words ' Ya taraffla' meaning, Wail bin Hajr 'trails his skirts' over the rest of the princes, brings forcefully to the mind a picturesque image which cannot be so graphically represented by the words 'Yatrasa'.

Other words which describe punishments laid down for various crimes echo the sense by their harsh, crisp and impressive notes.

Tete-a-Tete Discussions : But his method of tete-a-tete discussion and everyday conversation with persons whom he buttonholed on the wayside or in the mosque has a far more educative value for the teacher than his ceremonial orations. He was most epigrammatic in his sayings and had an unparalleled mastery over a happy and graceful turn of word and phrase. The rhyming of words and phrases, the rhythm of thought and idea, the use of contrasts and comparisons were some of the devices which made his words stay in memory like a haunting music, and his way of expressing them left a lasting impression on the mind. Years after, the Companions could visualise the exact pose and manner in which the Prophet had related a particular Tradition.

Eloquent Fingers : Once he was relating a story out of the history of Israelites and described a mother suckling her babe. While narrating the Tradition later on, Abu Hurayrah added that he could even now picture before his mind the Prophet sucking his finger to show the movements of the child. He had an intuitive knowledge of teaching technique and would explain the abstract through the concrete, the complex by means of the simple. He would often use his hands and fingers in impressing an idea on his audience, the latter playing a specially expressive role in the process. He would indicate close proximity by referring to the closeness of the middle finger with the finger next to the thumb.

Once he compared the Muslims to the foundation stones of an edifice which re-inforce one another and he illustrated it by placing the fingers of one hand in between the fingers of the other.

Most of the Traditions which involved an action which could be demonstrated with the help of the movement of the fingers of the hand describe also the actual movement made by the Prophet on that occasion.

He has described the miser and the generous in an extremely apt simile. They are both like those persons who have coats of mails on them. They are so close fitting that their arms appear to have stuck fast to their chests and their necks and when the generous person desires to give away, his coat of mail becomes wider and longer till it is so ample that it reaches his finger tips and trails over his footsteps and obliterates the foot-prints. As for the miser, his coat of mail shrinks up and every link of it refuses to be flexible and refuses to yield.

The Tradition has been narrated by Abu Hurayrah who tells that when the Prophet described the shrunken coat of mail, he pointed with his fingers towards his neck and made as if he desired to stretch it further but was not able to do so.

He would avail of every day situations for the purpose of moralising. The simple and direct reasoning associated with concrete situation went home and had the desired effect. Once when he was passing by the corpse of a kid he asked whether anyone would buy it for any price. On receiving a reply in the negative he told that the worldly riches were more contemptible in the eyes of the Lord than the dead body of this kid. On another occasion a captive woman was brought into the presence of the Prophet and her breast was laden with milk. From time to time she would catch hold of any babe in the assembly, clap him to her breast and give him a suck. The Prophet was moved and asked the Companions whether that woman would consign her child to the flames, "Never", came the reply. "Verily", said the Prophet, "God is more compassionate on his Creation than this mother on the child."

Historic Doctrine : Sometimes he would impress a lesson by what may be described as a practical demonstration of the Doctrine of Natural Consequences. The Prophet had emphasized more than once the putting out of light or fire before retiring for the night. Once he was sitting on a mattress, when a rat crept along and carried away the wick of the earthen lamp burning in the room. The servant maid raised hue and cry but he asked her to keep quiet and observe the consequences. The rat left the wick on the mattress on which he was seated and a part of it was burnt. It was after this practical demonstration that he advised that lamps should be put out before retiring.

Method of Demonstration : Once Janadah brought some camels to the Prophet One of the animals had been branded on the nose. He said, "O Janadah could not you find any other place to brand the animal. You shall have to compensate for it."

Thereupon he pointed out the proper place on which the animal should be branded and made him brand the animal in his presence.

At first Janadah kept the branding instrument against the neck but the Prophet asked him to move on to the rear. He went on repeating the instruction till the instrument was against the thigh of the animal. Then he said, "Now, with the blessing of the God" implying that it was the most proper place for branding.

Teaching Approaches

An interesting feature of his education in morals was that it was extremely concrete and realistic. It was colourfully illustrated by similes and metaphors which were culled from everyday experience and which brought the light of his concrete objective realism to play about the point. The study of his verbal illustrations of moral precepts would prove a subject of immense interest for the teacher of method.

Sometimes he would proceed beyond the limits of verbal illustrations and present for his moral teachings illustrative material in concrete

According to a Tradition by Abdullah bin Masud one day the Prophet drew a straight line in his presence and told that it represented the Path of the Lord. Later on he drew a number of lines to its left and right and added that they were other paths (besides the True one) and they were all guarded by a Satan who calls (people) to himself. Then he recited the Quranic verse, "Verily my Path is the straight one, so follow it."

Once he drew a figure illustrating concretely the destiny of man on earth.

He drew a square and inscribed a line in the middle of the square. He drew another line which went outside the square. After that he drew a number of short lines which projected outward from the four sides of the square towards the line which he had drawn in the centre. Then he explained that the line drawn in the centre of the square represented man and that the square symbolised his destiny. He was hemmed in from all direction by it, and the solitary line going out of the square is the line of hope while the shorter lines are the calamities. If he escapes one, he will be destroyed by another.

"The true Path is the straightest path. It had no deviations or dangerous turnings. It was bright as the day and it could be traversed easily by the Arab of the desert or the children at school alike. But nevertheless it has its 'catches' and its 'danger points'."

The point has been brought out through a variety of expressive similes. According to another Tradition, the True path leads between the walls which are broken in by a number of doors closely draped with curtains and there is a 'Caller' who stands on the head of the path (nearer end) and another who stands above (the farther end) while God calls man towards the Dar-ul-Islam (House of Peace) and leads all whom he desires on the Straight Path. Now the doors opening on both the sides are Hudud Allah (punishments prescribed for sins) and none lapses into them unless the curtain is raised and one who calls from above is the preacher of God.

According to Ibn Masud, the (Sirat) on the straight Path represents Islam, the doors are the Muharim (prohibitive commandments) and the curtains are the Hudud (punishments). The caller who stands at the head of the Path is the Quran and one above him is the Preacher of God who has a place in the heart of every Believer.

The entire simile represents in a colourful and realistic manner the progress of the Faithful towards the Kingdom of the Blessed. The great call which is ringing into his ears from the Olympian heights towering above and the immediate dangers which beset his path at every footstep lend the entire scene the charm of a romantic adventure on the path of Allah.

Teaching by means of parables has proved a highly effective instrument of moral instruction in the hands of great masters and the method has been equally effective both in the case of children and unsophisticated adults. The children are attracted by the story element and the adults by the moral tone of the parable. This kind of literature provides a simple and naive form of illustrating some moral principle. While a simile or a metaphor stands for an isolated idea and is used for embellishment or clarity, the parable illustrates a principle of moral life in a more developed form and has the additional quality of clothing the idea with substance and reality. It is simple and direct and has a greater appeal for the uninitiated humanity.

The parables occurring in the Traditions are longer and fuller as compared with those in the Bible and add something immediately human to the moral fibre of the story. There is the well known parable of the blind, the bald and the leper; Two of whom were cured of their physical ailment through the mercy of God and were blessed with plenty and pelf but they could not recover from their moral afflictions. The blind man in the Tradition symbolises one who had his inner sight restored. Another beautifully simple parable describes the three religions as three groups of farm labourers. While the first two groups left the task unfinished and retired unremunerated, the third group which represents Islam and had joined late in the afternoon, received the fullest reward for the day's labour because it had fulfilled the Will of the Master. Another parable is that of the three travellers who were entrapped in a cave by a falling boulder.

This parable originates like a few others from the Old and New Testament. In this parable the three groups were employed by the same master. The Jews worked from morning till noon and received one Karat each; the Christians from noon till the time for the afternoon prayers and they also received the same wages. The Muslims who worked from the afternoon to the evening prayer received double the wages and when the first two groups objected that they had worked more and received less, the Lord said "Have I been unfair to you. Verily this is my beneficence and I grant to whom I please."

The simile of casting pearls before swine was further amplified by the Prophet who described the person who brings knowledge to the undeserving as one who adorns the neck of the swine with a necklace made of jewels, pearls and gold.

Figures of Speech : The similes and other figures of speech which he used did not belong to the domain of rhetorics; they were an essential device for making his meaning clear and were accordingly adapted to the intellectual level of the audience. While the poet uses them for their wealth of imagery and emotional associations, they are used in the Traditions for emphasizing the qualitative and sometimes the quantitative value of an abstract quality. For instance he claimed to be the Last of the Hierarchy of Prophets and he compared himself to the capping stone of a noble edifice without which the whole plan could not be brought to completion; on another occasion he compared four classes of people to four kinds of fruit. There was the Believer who read the Quran and acted upon it, he was to be likened to the orange, fragrant to smell and delightful in taste. The Believer who acted upon the word of the Holy Book but did not read it was like the date which though delicious in taste had no smell; the hypocrite who read the Quran but did not act upon it was like the fruit of the sweet balsam, sweet in smell but bitter in taste while the hypocrite who did not recite the Holy Book nor did he act upon it was the colocynth, bitter in taste and foul of smell.

Sources of Illustrations : One of the most frequent sources from which quite a repertory of illustrative material has been derived is the phenomena of nature and the Quran provides a number of elaborate similes from the world of physical nature with which the desert Arab was familiar.

The date-palm, the pasture grounds, the arable lands in the oasis, the heavens above and the earth below all appear to provide him with a rich source of material for illustrative purposes.

He compares the Believer with the date-palm, an evergreen

plant which always bears fruit and foliage. Elsewhere he is compared to a tender plant that is bent by the gust of the wind and another time is straightened up, showing that he has the flexibility to bend himself to the Lord of the storms, while the Munafiq (doubter) is akin to the cypress which never bends but is uprooted all of a sudden. The Quran also compares faith to a growing sapling that brings happiness unto the heart of the grower.

Three Tracts of Land : He compares his influence to the abundant rains from above that fall on land and compares people to three kinds of soil. The first kind imbibes the genial influence of the kindly rains and is covered with a luxuriant growth of green grass and verdure. The second tract with a rocky bed withheld the moisture and provided water for drinking and agricultural purposes. The third kind did not absorb moisture or store it because it was a flat and barren waste.

Figures of Speech from the Sea : The Quran and the Traditions reveal a fairly intimate knowledge of the sea. The Quran speaks of the storms and the silent seas, the boats, the pearls and the corals. In the Traditions the sea is used as a symbol for vastness. "The riches of this world are nothing as compared with those of the next world (eternity). One who loves lucre is like one who dips his finger into the sea and awaits what it brings back to him."

It appears that he was familiar with the double deck boats that plied on the sea and carried passengers. There is the highly instructive parable of the person who neglects Hududullah or prohibitive commandments. He is likened to a person travelling on the lower deck of a boat and how he tries to bore a hole into the bottom for obtaining water. His action means destruction for all of them.

The spirit of the Hudud was not the protection of the rights of a particular class or individual but that of the society as a whole.

In the well-known Tradition related by um-Haram he described how man sat in the boats as kings on their thrones.

Animal Kingdom : The animal kingdom provided him with some extremely instructive analogies. Once he compared men to the moth who would rush upon fire in an insane urge for self-destruction. The Prophet likened himself to the man who tried to extract them from fire (of hell) but they seemed to overwhelm the fire. Again he compared the unbeliever to a goat that stood indecisively between two flocks, sometimes tending towards one and then towards the other.

For him faith is like a powerful binding chain or the peg which provides the Believer with some principles that give moral stability in spite of slight aberrations or moral defalcations he may be prone to. He compared the Believer to a horse tied to a peg who moves round the peg but ultimately reverts to it. Likewise the Believer commits a fault (sahw) but ultimately returns to the fold of faith.

The Prophet had himself looked after the grazing animals when in Mecca and some of the most striking similes come out of his experiences. He has compared himself to a shepherd and the Satan to a wolf for humanity who pounces on the goat that strays away in stubbornness or saunters away in search of grass and is lost. He warns them of the vales (and their attractions) and exhorts them to be one with the Jamaat and the common people.

According to him every tribe or important person had his Hima or the reserves for grazing purposes. Every ruler had his Hima and God's preserve were his Muharim (forbidden things).

Somewhere else he speaks of a person who reports only the wicked things out of what he hears from a friend. He is like unto a person who has been allowed as a shepherd to make his choice of the whole flock to slaughter an animal for himself and he finally catches hold of the shepherd's dog by the ear.

The Camel : In most cases the Prophet would carry an edifying discourse on the back of a camel and the animal came extremely handy by way of illustration. When a desert Arab put him an irrelevant question while seated on his camel he said, "I don't know who's more lost, the rider or the ride." Once while proceeding for Hajj, his followers recited the holy formula (Tahiti) and raised their voices to an inordinate pitch, he said, "God is not devoid of the power of hearing. He is nearer to you than the neck of the camel (you are riding.)"

In his well-known Tradition that every child is born according to nature and it is his parents that make a Christian or a Jew of him, he refers to the inner Good that lay in man. The statement was further amplified by a reference to the calves born of an animal. There is none born with a split ear. According to him all these deformations arise out of postnatal causes and not out of innate nature.

Smaller Fry : The Quran refers occasionally to the most insignificant of living beings by way of metaphor and the bee, the mosquito and the fly are included in the list. Quran mentions specifically that God is not ashamed of quoting the simile of a mosquito. The Traditional literature uses "the wing of a mosquito" for indicating something extremely insignificant. "If the worldly riches had been worth a mosquito's wing in the eyes of the Lord, he would not have granted to the unbeliever even a drink of water out of it."

Again one who takes back what has been given as a gift is likened to the dog that licks up its own vomiting.

Naked Runner : The tribal life and its Traditions of eternal warfare provided a fruitful source of illustrations. He would compare himself to a Raid or the Guide who is sent in advance in search of new pastures. His people repose an implicit confidence in his integrity and he asked with vehemence how could such a trusted person tell them anything but the truth. Elsewhere he compares himself to the 'naked' runner, a usage of the Jahiliyah when an unclad messenger would go from tent to tent warning them of the impending attack by a hostile tribe. In a rather elaborate Tradition he describes the parable of a guide who came upon a caravan stranded in the desert and how he leads them to an oasis with running rivulets and green orchards and when he proposes to lead them on to yet more green fields and pastures now they are adamant in their refusal to move onwards.

Significant Allegories : There is another class of Traditions which have an impressive fascination of their own and are awe-inspiring in nature. They have been the precursor of a new class of literature in Arabic and other languages and have inspired the imagination of generations of poets and writers, finally culminating in that graceful specimen of this class of literature, the Javed Nama of Dr. Iqbal. According to Asin, the Comedia Divina of Dante was directly inspired by this class of Traditions.

These Traditions have a fiery grandeur of their own and must have proved a powerful check on the antisocial propensities of the wild Arab whose passions often blazed like the simoom which sweeps across the vast barrenness of the desert. These Traditions have an air of classical restraint and have a deep undercurrent of suppressed sympathy for the condemned. But nevertheless they reveal a fine sense of justice and the closest correlation between sin and punishment. Among a people who had cherished for so long the rule of "an eye for an eye and a tooth for a tooth", these Traditions must have exercised a considerable moral influence. They are fine examples of the Doctrine of Moral consequences.

In the course of the morning assembly he would describe his experiences in a dream and invite others to narrate theirs. Once he told how he saw the liar being tormented by having his mouth ripped open; how the scholar who taught the Quran to others but neglected it himself was punished by having his head crushed.

In one of his allegorical dreams, the Prophet saw a man swimming in a river of blood while another stood on the bank with a stone in his hand. When the first person tried to approach the bank, the person standing on the bank struck him with the stone; his mouth opened and the stone made its way down his throat. He collapsed once again into the current and the same tragedy was repeated again. According to the Prophet the man swimming in the river of blood was an usurer.

The Traditions on the Ascension or the Miraj contain some hair raising details of the punishments meted out to the sinners who were condemned to hell and in all cases, a principle of poetic justice appears to determine the nature and the intensity of punishment. A scholar who did not accost a seeker after knowledge with a reply will have a bridle-bit made of hell fire in his mouth and the man who learning and did not benefit others by his scholarship will burst his belly and carry his entrails like the mule which drives the flour mill.

According to a Tradition the hoard guarded by a person in the world would change into a python on the day of Judgment and would chase the hoarder. And he would munch his head with his jaws like a camel. The interpretation of dreams has transformed itself into a respectable science in the hands of psychologists like Freud who has made a remarkable study of the dreams of the

Leonardo da Vinci. But the Freudian School works within very great limitations and it is hoped that the psychologist of the future will present a deeper and more meaningful analysis of the subject in the light of a broader and higher conception of the main springs of human action and thought.

Historic Style : The Prophet's style of speech and manner of addressing others profoundly affected the method of work in the schools of the Islamic world. Qadi Abu Jamaa recommends the repetition of a sentence three times after the manner of the Prophet who used to repeat his sentences thrice. He never burried, but expressed himself always with great deliberation and case. We have it from Aishah how once she was visited by Abu Hurayrah when she was offering the night prayers. Abu Hurayrah seated himself on one side of the room, related to her hurriedly a Tradition and she had hardly finished her prayers before he departed. Upon this Aishah told that if she could catch hold of Abu Hurayrah she would have informed him that the Prophet was never so hurried and indistinct in speech as Abu Hurayrah.

Tartil, not Tarsil : According to Bukhari, the Prophet spoke word by word so that one could count them if he desired. Tartil instead of Tarsil was the running note of his speech. He did not approve of any interruption in the course of his speech and they were not infrequent in a society which was composed of a large section of members living an individual life of their own in the desert. But such strangers to the ways and life of an organized group life very seldom put him out of temper and he would reply to such intruders after he had finished with the topic on which he was discoursing at that time. Irrelevant queries were positively discouraged by him.

Principles for Audience : In a chapter on the manner of listening to a Tradition, Tirmidhi gives that the Prophet had enjoined that it should not be listened to in a posture when one is reposing or reclining against a support, implying thereby that the listening posture requires alertness, physical as well mental. The teacher, of course, had the right to recline against a column or to sit on a raised seat after the usage of the Prophet.

The Prophet always had a word of warm welcome for every visitor, and advised his people to extend such cordiality to all. He prophesied a future for his followers when people would flock to them from far and near and he advised them to welcome these seekers after knowledge with a Marhaba (welcome). "When people flock to you from the four quarters of the globe, advise them well and receive them with soft and loving words."

The time appointed for addressing the people was usually after the morning and the afternoon prayers.

After every prayer in general and the morning prayer in particular, there was always a gathering which had been already motivated for such knowledge. These addresses which were declaimed with moral earnestness moved the hearts to their very foundations and some of the audience would burst into tears on such occasions.

He had appointed a special day in the week for addressing women and this arrangement had been made on the express desire of women.

Recitation and Inscription : Among ancient peoples and old societies, power of forceful expression and declamation was highly prized and among the old Greeks and Romans, oratory formed a prominent feature of the school curriculum. Among the Arabs, political addresses or literary declarations have played an unprecedented role in history and have directed and sometimes diverted the course of historical events.

Almighty's Name

The Divine Education of the Prophet originates with the revelation of the Sura Iqra, "Read in the name of the Lord who has created Man from congealed blood. Read, Great and High is thy Lord in His Beneficence." Reading is to be interpreted here not in the sense of the reading aloud lesson in the classroom but as a piece of inspired recitation expressing the glowing enthusiasm of an entire personality, emotionally and intellectually.

Again and again, the Prophet has enjoined on his people the reading of the Holy Book. "The highest form of prayer for my people is the reading of the Holy Book." Again, "The most virtuous amongst you are those who learn the Quran and teach it and the entire group which comes together for reciting the Holy Book and learning it are blessed with peace and tranquillity." According to a savant, "Every verse of the Quran is a stage of paradise and an illuminant for your houses."

Reading and Writing

As the recitation of the Quran played such an all pervading part in the social and cultural life of the period, it gave rise to a class of readers (Qura) who later on developed into several specialist schools of reading. It appears that the reading of the Quran formed the main item of education in those days and the Companions often indulged inordinately in their enthusiasm for its recitation. The Prophet had to issue instructions that the reading of the Holy Book may be stopped for a while when one gets tired of it. The style of expression and pronouncing words was deeply influenced by the Traditions of the Prophet, whose reading is described as Tartil (distinct and deliberate), pronouncing each word clearly and with the proper accent. When a child learnt for the first time to stumble into speech, the Prophet advised that he should be made to repeat *'La Ilaha Illallah'*, a combination of sound, rhythmic in cadence and facile to pronounce.

Ornamenting the Quran : The Prophet had a keen ear for rhythm and several Traditions reveal the emphasis which he placed on sweet and rhythmic recitation of the Holy Book. According to a Tradition, "God has never enjoined anything so much on the Prophet as the rhythmic recitation of the Quran." "One who does not read the Quran melodiously does not belong to us." "Ornament the Quran by your voices." Again, "Verily God listens to the Reciter of the Quran better than the master of a singing girl listens to her music." According to Abu Hurayrah, "God has not given any command to the Prophet similar to that which appertains to the melodious voice for reciting the Quran."

The Companions were vividly alive to the aesthetic aspect of Quranic recitation and when the Prophet recited a verse to them, one of them told that it was as refreshing as the rain from within and fruitful from without."

Gift of David : The taste for rhythmic recitation was widespread and when once the Prophet overheard a slave reading in a melodious tone, he thanked God who had blessed his people with such a good person.

Abu Musa al-Ashaari was noted for his good voice and the Prophet was often so enchanted by his recitation that he would forget everything else and when the company called out that it was high time for prayers, he would remark, "Are we not already in the midst of our devotions?" He often told that Abu Musa had the gift of David's music.

Holy Recitations : The remarks of the Prophet on the subject of recitation (Qirat) were made with reference to the Quran and he has emphasized its recitation for the blessings which it brings to the individual and to the society. But in all his behests in matters of religion and education he is always inspired more by its social significance than the benefit which it brings to a particular individual. This viewpoint has been brought home by a number of beautiful and expressive similes with specific reference to recitation.

"One who learns the Quran and does not recite it is like a person who has preserved musk in a bag and holds its mouth tightly closed. While the other who recites it has loosened the strings of his bag and its fragrance is wafted all around. In this case, his learning has a social utility, beneficial for himself and for others.

Orange and the Aloe : There is another Tradition which has been narrated by Abu Musa al-Ashaari, that melodious reader of the Quran is he whose recitation was so much appreciated by the Prophet. According to Abu Musa, the Prophet had said, "The Believer who recites the Quran is like the orange that has a good taste and a delightful flavour. And the Believer who does not recite is like the date which is delicious in taste but has no flavour. The Munafiq who recites the Quran is like the Rayhan which has a good fragrance but is bitter in taste and the Munafiq who does not recite it is like the aloe which is bitter in taste as well in flavour." Hence faith in the holy word and its propagation both have equal importance.

The above simile throws light on the social and the individual benefit which accrues from the recitation of the Holy Book and it can be generalised and applied to the educative process as a whole. The social aspect of the process being so important, the

Prophet preferred to hear the recitation in company and would often request one of the company to recite.

Good reciters of the Quran were very much prized in the early days and an emancipated slave (Mawla) was made the head of his tribe among the people of the valley during the period of Umar Ibn Khattab, because he was a Qari (Reciter).

Style of the Prophet : The Prophet's style of recitation was that of Tartil. It was neither quick nor hasty. Rather he would pronounce one letter after another separately and distinctly and would introduce pauses after every verse (Ayat). He would enunciate lucidly the long accented sound (Mad) in al-Rahman and al-Rahim)

He would recite the Quran both in a loud (Jahr) or low (Khafi) voice. But the distinguishing feature of his recitation was not so much its pitch, speed or volume; it was lucidity and clear intonation. According to Ibn Abbas when he recited in the courtyard a person sitting in-doors could clearly hear his recitation. According to Umm-e-Hani she used to hear his recitation clearly when she (had retired for the night and) was on the roof.

Musical Rhythm : There is evidence to prove that the Prophet himself recited the Quran with musical rhythm specially in moments when he was emotionally aroused. When on the day of the Victory (Yawm-ul-Fath) he entered Mecca on a camel, he was reciting according to Abdullah bin Maghfal, the verse, "*Inna Fatahna laka Fathan Mubina,*" and he repeated the letter alif three times. According to Ibn al-Qayyam Ibn Jawzi, this Tarje or repetition did not arise out of the movements of the dromedary on which he was seated but it was a voluntary expression. Abdullah continues that had he not feared that the people would gather round to listen (to him, disturbing thereby the order of the victorious march) he would have followed the example of the Prophet.

It has been remarked elsewhere that the Prophet liked immensely the recitation of Abu Musa al-Ashaari and once the Prophet heard him reading the Quran, and when Abu Musa was informed of it he told that he would have made the Quran more beautiful and would have embellished it with his voice had he known it.

Melancholic and the Ecstatic Note : Umar Ibn Khattab who was a man of extremely puritanic temperament liked immensely the recitation of the Quran by Abu Musa al-Ashaari and would often exhort him to recite by saying "*Zakkarna Rabbana*" (Make us remember God).

Then Abu Musa would make a recitation and read it with melody (Lahn). Thereupon Umar could say, "One who desires to introduce music (Ghina) in the Quran should do it in the style of Abu Musa al-Ashaari." The chief note of Abu Musa Ashaari's recitation was melancholic (Huzn) and not ecstatic (Tarab). When Aqbah bin Amir who had a beautiful voice was requested by Umar Ibn Khattab to recite, he read a verse with such effect that Umar Ibn Khattab wept profusely and said, "I could never conceive that this verse was of the revealed ones."

It is interesting to note that an authority like Ibn Qayyim Jawzi who was a very close disciple of Ibn Taymiyyah and who is the main exponent of the orthodox school sums up the discussion by saying that although recitation with musical notes is not permissible but it can be done in the style of the ancients who embellished their voices while reading the Quran and read it with the fullest emotional expression, melancholic or ecstatic.

Symbols of Vocalisation : The genius of the Arabic language and the great solicitude which the Muslims showed in the preservation of the Word of the Holy Writ and the Traditions gave rise to the need of formulating rules of Grammar and vocalisation. By the time of 'Umar the Muslim armies had crossed the confines of the Arabian Peninsula and had annexed many a non-Arab countries to the Islamic State. The process of political domination went along with that of moral and religious conquest and the need for presenting the sources of Islamic inspiration in a correct form to these people became insistent in the days of the early Caliphs. Even the Beduin who lived a life of his own in the heart of the desert found difficulties in vocalising the text but for the non-Arabs it presented a more formidable problem.

It is related on the authority of Abi-al Aswad-ud-Dawali that one day he visited Ali. He looked disconsolate and out of spirits. Ali was feeling very much perturbed because he had heard some one reciting the Quran with wrong vocalisation. He told Abi- al Aswad that he had decided to compose a book on the principles of Arabic grammar. Abi-al Aswad welcomed the idea and told that he would give a fresh lease of life to the language and preserve its vocabulary through this action. When he visited him again after three days, Ali showed him a book wherein he had defined Ism, Fel and Harf (noun, verb and preposition). He instructed Abi-al Aswad to proceed with the work who added Huruf-an-Nasb to it. According to another source, Ali was the first scholar to devise the symbols for vocalisation.

Moderation in Recitation : The Quran enjoins upon the Prophet to be moderate in the reading of the Quran. The injunction laid down that the self-imposed rigorous discipline should in no way tax the energies of the Prophet and the Faithful. Whenever he heard of cases where a person kept longsome nightly vigils for recitation, he prohibited him from doing so. A prominent case was that of the young enthusiast, Abdullah bin Amr bin al-Ath.

The Prophet followed the spirit of the Quran by permitting such individual variations in reading which did not interfere with the meaning of the Holy Writ. Once Umar Ibn Khattab heard Hisham bin Hakim bin Hizam reciting the Quran which in his opinion was not after the style of the Prophet. He was so much aroused that he was about to pounce upon him for this sacrilege when Hisham finished his prayers, Umar caught hold of his sheet and took him straight to the Prophet. The Prophet heard both of them reciting the same verse and approved both the recitations. He concluded his remarks with the words "Verily Quran was revealed in seven letters. Read out of it which is more feasible for you."

Place in the Syllabus : The Problem of the placement of reading in the syllabus received a good deal of attention on the part of Muslim educators and Ibn Khaldun devoted a chapter to the critical study of the problem in his Prolegomena. His illuminating analysis of the contemporary methods of teaching reading in different countries reveals a thorough grasp of educational principles and the capacity to study problems from a scientific and detached viewpoint; under such genial influences the Islamic institutions developed a noble tradition of the art of oral expression.

Unfortunately, the present schools of the community, whether indigenous or imparting Western education, have lost the art and it is high time to recover once more the spontaneous and joyful expression of personality through the spoken world which will always maintain a social and political significance peculiarly its own in any democratic society and opens out a channel for the building up of a well integrated personality.

Implications for the Present Day System : The Prophet and his Companions have endowed their people with a rich legacy in the form of the Quran, the Traditions and their addresses. They vibrate with an inspired style, simple and direct, illumined with moral fervour and emotional restraint; the present-day textbook writer will discover therein a rich field of literature which is nearer to the elemental make-up of the child than the sophisticated literature of the later times.

For centuries, the Muslim child has opened his school career with a chapter of the Quran but often the veneration in which the Holy Text was held by the Muslims worked adversely against a harmonious education of the child when the Holy Book and specially its last chapter which is a miracle of elegance, brevity and pointedness was chosen as the chief content of education for the earlier years. Educators like Qadi Abu Bakr Ibn al-Arabi boldly criticised the practice on pedagogic grounds and recommended priority to subjects which claimed a direct and closer appeal to the innate interests of the child and which may have a higher utility value for him. The Quran was removed by him to the third stage of Education, the two preliminary stages being devoted mainly to mother tongue and arithmetic.

Great Challenge : It would be interesting to make a comparative study of our efforts for a more efficient teaching of the Arabic language as compared with the solicitude of the Muslims in the first century of the Islamic era. The problem is beset with peculiar difficulties in this country and is all the more complicated by the variety of cultural and linguistic groups who take to the learning of the Arabic language. When one comes across the pathetic spectacle of the Manipuri or the Bengali Muslims struggling with the Arabic syntax in the Persian-cum-Urdu medium of instruction, he feels that the scholarly class of this country has yet to perform the impossible and write a suitable Grammar of the Arabic language in Urdu and other Provincial languages of the country for the benefit of the learner of the language.

We may be legitimately proud of the contributions of our scholarly class to the study of Islamic law, dialectics and literature but we must see whether we have been successful in making it a spiritual heritage of the masses or how far we have helped the average learner in surmounting the preliminary, yet impregnable difficulties in mastering the language, thereby transforming him into a genuine and effective missionary of its spiritual heritage.

Writing : The art of writing and penmanship has a glorious record in the history of Islamic education. The word 'pen' has a strange fascination for the historian and beautiful legends are related about its origin and the priority of its creation. According to a Tradition, the Pen was one of the earliest of creation; and in the Quran, there occurs a verse which runs as follows: "Read in the name of the Lord who created Man from a drop of congealed blood. Read and thy Lord is highly Benevolent; verily He is thy Lord who taught thee with the Pen and taught man what he did not know." Implying the sanction and approval of the art of writing by the Divine Power and commending its use for Men.

Pen, a Hallowed Name : Kalam is a hallowed name in Muslim doxology because it occurs as an oath in the Holy Book and one of the most glorious rhapsodies in the praise of God states that if all the vegetation on the earth's surface provides the quills and water of all the oceans, the ink, they would dry up before the Praise of thy Lord comes to an end. In another place, we come across a verse "By the ink-hom and by all that you write."

The Islamic Tradition traces the significance of the art from primitive times and there is the legend of an Evil Spirit enquiring from Solomon about the nature of speech. He replied that it was like the breath of the wind and when asked how it could be preserved, the reply was, "Through writing."

In the beginning it was considered advisable to preserve only the Quranic text in the form of writing partly on account of the scarcity of parchment and partly from fear that other kind of literature like the Traditions might not be confused with the text of the Quran. But when experience proved all such fears to be baseless, the writing of the Traditions also received the approval of the Prophet. When he delivered his address of victory after the fall of Mecca, he allowed the preparation of a written text for the benefit of a person called Abu Shah, apparently of non-Arab extraction, who hailed from Yemen. The Prophet established the Tradition of teaching the art and encouraged it by all possible means.

A Tribe with a Single Literate : Very few persons knew how to read and write in the days of Jahiliyah. The skill of writing was rarer than that of reading and Ibn Saad the author of Tabaqat makes a specific mention in case of those who knew the art of writing as a noteworthy qualification that was conspicuous by its rarity. It was more or less the same case with the skill of reading.

When the Prophet sent his epistle to Bakr bin Wail after a deputation from the tribe had visited Medina, it was a problem for them to discover a person who could read it as there was only one man, in the whole of Yamamah who knew the art of reading. The progeny of this man was known henceforth as Banu Qari (the progeny of the Reader) because he had read out the epistle of the Prophet.

Captives, Turned Teachers : Medina was a settlement of an agricultural community who were moré backward in three R's than the Meccans who were businessmen and had their trade relations with Yemen and Syria. There was a scarcity of persons who knew the art of writing. Hence the Prophet did not like to lose any opportunity for the propagation of this art and when seventy Meccans were made captives in the Battle of Badar they were asked to teach the skill to ten children or adults as a compensation for their ransom money which was forty Awqiyah for each captive. Those who had no ransom money to pay readily agreed to the arrangement and took to the work in right earnest. Zayd bin Thabit was one of those who learnt the art from these captives.

The Prophet was keenly interested in the propagation of the skill of writing among his people. He had once requested Shifa bint Abdullah, a scholarly lady of the period, to teach writing to Hafdhah, the wife of the Prophet who was the daughter of Umayr.

When the Prophet Wrote : The Prophet had no knowledge of reading or writing and this fact has been advanced in the Quran as a forceful argument in favour of the claim that Quran is a revealed book. "Before this we never made you learn how to read or write," says a verse of the Quran.

The words "The Prophet wrote" which occurs in some Traditions are advanced by some as a proof of the Prophet's knowledge of the art of writing but obviously it does not-imply actual writing by the Prophet but only dictation. It appears that once he wrote his name. According to the Tradition of Al-Qaziyyah, the Prophet took the paper and as he could not write well so he wrote in place of Rasul-ul-lah' the word 'Muhammad. It is narrated that he wrote Muhammad in his own hand on the Day of Hudaybiah.

Although the Prophet did not write himself he seems to be acquainted with the form of letters and art of calligraphy. There is a Tradition which according to Muawiyyah, throws light on his taste for artistic expression: Something was being written in the presence of the Prophet when he said, "Take care of your ink-pot, mend your pen in a slanting direction, straighten up the' Ya,' indicate clearly the points of 'Sin,' don't make the 'Mim' blind, write the word 'Allah' well, place a 'mad' on Rahman and write the word 'Rahim' well.

Correspondence Secretaries : Literacy was not very common among the Quraish and it is said that no more than seventeen persons knew the art of writing among the Meccans. Some of the more distinguished Companions, knew the art and the Prophet did not find much difficulty for correspondence work.

According to Zad al-Maad, the following Companions functioned as correspondence secretaries (Katib) of the Prophet. They were Abu Bakr, Umar, Uthman, Ali and Zubayr.

But finally this office was entrusted to Zayd bin Thabit who received further training during his stay with the Prophet. Zayd bin Thabit did not know Syriac and the Prophet had to depend mostly in this connection on the Jews. But the Jewish scribes could not be relied on. So he asked Zayd to learn Syriac which he did within a short period of fifteen days. After that the entire correspondence in the language was carried on by Zayd.

Zayd bin Thabit : Zayd bin Thabit did a great service in compiling the Quran under Abu Bakr and Uthman. He was highly respected for his skill and learning. Once Ibn Abbas took hold of his stirrup as a mark of honouring the scholar and when Zayd protested and said "Oh Cousin of the Prophet, leave it off," Ibn Abbas replied, "We have been asked to honour our scholars in this way." Thereupon Zayd kissed his hand and replied, "And we have been asked to respect the family of the Prophet like this."

Zayd bin Thabit was entrusted with the duty of compiling the Quran by Abu Bakr when a large number of readers had been killed in the battle of Yamamah. He compiled it from fragments, leaves of date palm, soft stone and from those who knew it by heart. Zayd was selected by Abu Bakr because he used to copy out the Wahi — the words of God as revealed to the Prophet. The copy prepared by Zayd remained with Abu Bakr and then passed through Umar and Hafdah, his daughter, to Uthman who ordered another copy of it to be made for a fresh compilation. He appointed a committee of three including Zayd bin Thabit for preparing the new compilation.

Growth of Kitabat : The Muslim Law provides facilities for the slaves to work for their liberty by earning the ransom money for their masters. The profession of the Scribe was popular with the slaves who desired to work for liberty and we come across the name of a freedman of Aishah who copied the Quran for her mistress. With the growth of contacts with countries outside Arabia, the drawing up of business deeds became an essential feature of the economic life of the period and all books on Fiqh contain invariably a Chapter on Kitabat. The Deeds of Will were a part of the normal business and we have reliable evidence to prove that the Prophet sent for writing material on his death-bed so that he might leave behind a will in writing for his people. The text of his epistles to some of the contemporary kings and others are extant in the collections of Traditions and treatises on Islamic History.

Savant's Ink and the Martyr's Blood : Zarnuji quotes a tradition on the authority of Hilal bin Yasar who once saw the Prophet discoursing on knowledge and wisdom in the presence of his Companions. He approached him with all promptitude and requested that he might also receive the benefit of his wise words. The Prophet asked whether he had pen and ink and receiving a reply in the negative, he advised him not to discard the inkpot because the inkpot comprised all the good which might be done till the Day of Judgment.

Elsewhere we have made a reference to the comparison which is frequently made in the Traditions between a teacher and a martyr, and according to one of them the ink of the savant will be weighed against the Martyr's blood on Doomsday while, according to Hassan Basari, when these two will be weighed together, the ink will outweigh the blood.

Receiving Education

The Age of the Prophet was the age of human contacts, the age when the oral word dominated the written; when knowledge originated and was published orally; when word divorced from personal associations of a heated declamation or verbal flourishes lost much of its charm. It is surprising that a tradition of the cult of writing sprang so abundantly after the advent of Islam in spite of the great paucity of parchment, persons living in much later periods like that of Imam Shafii and Abu Yusuf using bones and potsherds for writing purposes.

This got certainly some impetus from the Tradition enjoining the Faithful to captivate knowledge through writing, and some of the Companions did captivate it in an admirable manner. We learn from the frank avowal of Abu Hurrayrah that 'Abdullah bin Umar who preserved the Traditions in writing had a richer knowledge of them than himself who retained them by memory. The Prophet allowed a Companion to take down everything on which he discoursed, a duty more or less similar to a stenographer and he waived off all objections raised by others in this connection. According to a savant one who does not preserve knowledge in writing should not be counted among scholars. Again according to Khalil bin Ahmad, he never heard anything but he put it in black and white; and never wrote anything but he memorised it and he never memorised anything but he got some benefit out of it.

Hisham bin 'Urwah's manuscripts were destroyed on the

Day of Conflagration and when he was apprised of the tragedy, he exclaimed, "I wish I had perished with them along with my progeny and property." By the time of 'Umar bin Abdul 'Aziz, the art had become so popular and the material preserved in writing so abundant that whole volumes of religious lore were copied out and manuscripts despatched to the various parts of the Dominions. There are good many injunctions emphasizing the importance of a clear, bold and graceful style in writing. Ali summarises it in one of his most illuminating aphorisms, "Illumine the pen as it was illumined by God." On another occasion he had told that writing represents symbols and hence the more expressive it is, the more appropriate it would be. He prized grace and beauty in writing because it contributed something additional to its inherent function of expression.

The instructions laid down by Ali on the art of writing not merely reveal his great love for learning but also his passionate desire to propagate the art in a correct and beautiful form. The minutest details which he adds to his instructions would do credit to any modern educationist and would prove as useful to the novice today as thirteen centuries ago. He would like the cut of the pen to be elongated and broadened with its angle inclining towards the right. His instructions on the writing of the alphabet are a delightful combination of the harmony of form, sound and movement. For instance, it was a delight for him to hear the vibrating note of the pen when the pen completed the finishing stroke of the letter 'Nun', the slower movement in rounding up the 'lam', the firm and steadier hand in writing 'Ba', 'ta' 'tha', and so on.

In the opinion of a savant, writing is that characteristic function of a man by dint of which his innate capacities find channel of expression through activity. This symbolic instrument for business transactions and social life became a medium of expression for that love of beauty and rhythm in form which has contributed to the artistic heritage of humanity, those glorious masterpieces of calligraphy which harmonise so delightfully the utilitarian and the aesthetic aspect of Art. The Kufic script of the Prophet's time with its straight lines and rigid curves did not provide ample scope for artistic expression but the later masters founded those Great Schools of Calligraphy which supplied a new and comparatively easy outlet of expression for the school child and which later on developed into a preliminary stage for artistic expression in other media.

14

Basis of System

The primary aim of this brief study of the Prophet's Traditions is not to justify his claim to the title of a preceptor and to discover in his teachings all the minutemen of classroom pedagogics. It will be a left handed compliment to style a Guilder of men as a pedagogue and to read into an architect of life the soul of a crack craftsman who worked out a system of classroom technique. He does not provide us with a psychoanalytical method of child study but he discovered with all the vigour of his intuitive powers and the largeness of his heart, the principle of love and sympathy, that wondrous spell which helps in opening magic casements into the heart of a child when other methods break down; which not only helps us in understanding the child but is the only secure foundation for the harmonious development of his personality. He does not posit a theory of discipline but he found out for generations of teachers and savants those genuinely human relations which could be the only bond of moral and intellectual understanding between the teacher and the taught.

He did not lay down any laws for curriculum-making but he transformed the entire social life into a school and the environment into a great educative force. He did not initiate any new fangled system of formal education but he gave a practical demonstration of a method of informal education which vibrated with the spirit of joyous spontaneity, and closest association with the life of the community.

Schools and Education

One of the imminent dangers of the present-day system of formal education in this country and elsewhere is the gradually widening gulf between school and society and the consequent deadening influence on the educative process as a whole. Some of the leading thinkers of the educational world, John Dewey and others have already given a timely warning of the menace which threatens the development and growth of educational systems on account of their gradual dissociation from an intimate and intelligent contact with the needs of the community and the living problems of the day. While the rushing currents of Time march on their inexorable course, they tend boundaries of the school, as barren patches of islands in the stagnant backwaters. The moral and social world is afflicted as relentlessly with the law of inertia as the physical world and our institutions have a tendency to lag behind times unless stimulated by new ideas and hitherto untapped sources of potential energy; some time they flower into a second spring by discovering in their living past, those nascent principles of life and activity which had made them once a dynamic factor of social progress. The new movement in education is making a serious effort to capture once more the spirit of the old informal system of education and introducing it into the formal, straight-jacketed and colourless atmosphere of the present day school.

The system of informal education employs the principle of active sharing of experiences through life-situations and the method of the Prophet as revealed in the Traditions is a shining example of such an education. He participated so joyously and spontaneously in the social life of his people and his contacts with the younger generation of the commonwealth of Islam, including the youngest, were always so rich, abundant and fruitful; therein lies a promise of hope and inspiration for those who are working for the propagation of the new ideals in more than one field of education today.

The method of informal education inherent in the Traditions has an appeal which transcends the educational frontiers of any particular caste, community or race. They are broadbased on such a conception of human association and social cooperation which has a universal application. They lend a refreshing note to the educative process and place the sharing of life-experience on a personally vital basis. This method of education, which is informal and incidental is not symbolic and abstract as in the case of formal education; it is closely linked with the everyday pursuits of life and is a natural outcome of social needs and requirements. The greatest danger of the present day education in Indian and Pakistani schools is its tragic dissociation from the social context, both in contents of education, its method of organising those contents and handling them in the classroom. Public opinion has awakened to the graveness of the educational crisis and there is a general demand for some kind of education which may develop better social attitudes in the pupils; create in them a living sense of civic responsibility and foster a mental outlook which may enable them to repose their faith in a cooperative rather than a competitive mode of life on an intellectual and practical basis.

Social Trends

Our present system of education is rapidly transforming the average pupil into an egoist, a tendency all the more accentuated by the narrowly individualistic outlook of the society at large; it has awakened in him dangerous propensities, which may minister to his personal advancement and prosperity, but function nevertheless as disintegrating and disruptive forces for the society as a whole. If we are desirous of discovering some means of counteracting their influence, we will find in the system of Islamic education, as represented in the Traditions of the Prophet, an example of informal education which provides some indispensable elements for the social development of the citizen's personality. It would release the educative process from the darkening shades of the school room and would transform the business of acquiring knowledge into a vital pursuit of sharing life experiences with the adult and the older members of the society.

Social Atmosphere

If we make a study of the educative value of the social environment today as compared to the period of indigenous system of education in this country, we are convinced that the educative influences in the latter case were more comprehensive, deep and effective. In those days all the social institutions functioned in one way or the other for the education of the younger generation in its limited sense and every adult member of the society felt in an intensively religious way, his responsibility to function as an agent of informal education for the younger people. Western educationists and administrators who have studied this system with sympathy and understanding have appreciated this redeeming feature of the system which ensured for the school and the teacher the cooperation of the entire society. There may be no dearth of socially minded people working for the educational development of the younger generation outside the school these days, but no effective drive for mass education can be initiated through individual efforts. A study of the history of mass education reveals that large scale success has only been achieved either through religion of state. In the case of Islamic education the mainspring of inspiration was religion as represented by the Holy Quran and the Traditions of the Prophet.

The Traditions of the Prophet have been a tremendous formative influence in the growth and development of certain elements of Islamic education. The Prophet was a great builder of men, a radiating centre of influence who constantly moulded and transformed his Companions. Later on he became the inspirer of generations of teachers whose life ideals were illumined by his Teachings and whose classroom methods were coloured by his personal example. The educational conceptions of the great savants of Islam, their aims and objectives, their classroom etiquette and general behaviour in addressing lecture groups are strongly reminiscent of the chapter on social behaviour (Bab-ul-Adab) in the Books of Traditions. The Sayings of the Prophet on this subject are still a living force in the indigenous schools of this country and elsewhere in the Muslim world although they appear to have lost much of their primal vigour and vitality through the passage of time.

Literacy Tradition : The Traditions have a special significance as a literary heritage of the Islamic people, an influence which has been constantly moulding the style of generations of scholarly writers whose medium of expression was the Arabic language, the lingua franca of the Islamic world. In certain cases it helped in the growth and development of the local languages by lending them the charm of its racy, genial and human style. A study of the English and the continental languages reveals how profoundly they have been influenced by the Bible and the author of juvenile literature in Islamiat and Pakistani languages of Indian Subcontinent would do well in drawing more freely on this perennial source of literary inspiration for the Islamic people.

The educational conceptions implied in the Traditions have a special message for the social worker in the field of adult education. They determine for him in broad terms the aims and objectives of the educative process and lay down for him in clearly unambiguous terms that all education dissociated from the masses is a travesty; that all teaching divorced from moral values is hardly worth its name; it provides for him in a practical and realistic manner some highly effective means and devices of informal education for the old and the young.

Various Schemes

A careful analysis of the mainsprings of Islamic education, a survey of its inner forces, moral, social and intellectual is essential before we can appreciate its spirit or foreshadow a new scheme of education for the Muslims. The Traditions may not be able to supply us with an Educational Code or our educational programme for the future but they provide us with something more significant and valuable. They throw light on those hidden life springs which functioned as dynamic factors in the growth of an educational system, conspicuous for its intellectual vigour and socialised outlook, elements which form the only basis for a consistent and efficient system of education. The builder of a scheme of education in future who is gifted with vision and insight would concentrate on the marshalling of the moral and social forces rather than the unravelling of the problems of Individual Psychology or the technique of teaching.

The educational research of the modern period has been mainly directed on lines essentially psychological and technical and the educationist who ought to have been more of a sociologist and moralist has been concentrating on the narrow instructional aspects of education. He has ignored the wider issues, social and human, implied in the educative process and has followed only too often the ignes fatuus of sugar coated methods and soft pedagogy, betraying at one time the misplaced enthusiasm of a specialist and at others the weakness of a publicity-monger. His insistence on his new fangled methods of teaching, apart from any consideration of the social and economic context savours of the propaganda technique of a mountebank who prescribes his patent recipe as a panacea for all human ills. But no amount of patented stuff would do good to the suffering humanity unless it discovers once more those vital principles of social and moral life which can form the only sure foundation for the raising of a better race of men.

Philosophical Foundation

The world political crisis was preceded by a social and educational one and the second world war was a natural outcome of the moral and intellectual confusion which reigned supreme before the forces of destruction burst into a general conflagration. Thinkers in the West are realising the need of a new ideology of education in the moral and spiritual sense which may create harmony between man and man and one nation and another. This tendency would introduce a new orientation in the field of educational research as well. The Islamic education once released tremendous forces for intellectual and cultural cooperation on an international basis and the study of the inner workings of such a movement should be of some interest to all who desire to make a better world out of the old.

Al-Ghazzali has initiated a thought-provoking discussion on the problem of curriculum in the course of his commentary on the well known Tradition that search after knowledge is imposed as an obligation on every good Muslim, man and woman.

Academic Perception

He raises the issue by propounding the question — What is knowledge and who should decide its nature and contents? and he continues how the mystics, scholars, the Traditionists and the *Faqih* (legalist) differ on the fundamentals, each pushing up the claim of his particular branch of learning as the knowledge implied in the sayings of the Prophet. According to Al-Ghazzali, it does not refer to any particular branch, neither does it make obligatory all kinds of knowledge. "Every individual should learn that knowledge which is indispensable for the performance of his particular function in society. Any particular branch is not obligatory on one and all, rather the contents of education vary with the environment, the temporal and other conditions of the individual."

This Tradition is generally interpreted as dealing exclusively with religious studies but we have another Tradition on the subject with a flare of crystal crispness playing about it, and enshrining the glorious usage of distant journeying in quest of knowledge. "Seek knowledge although you may find it in China."— knowledge implied here is not obviously religious lore. China was not known for its moral teaching but for its fine arts, handicrafts and cultural refinement. Naturally the word knowledge here should be construed in the secular rather than in the religious sense.

At this stage it won't be out of place to devote a few lines to the attitude of Al-Ghazzali towards this fundamental problem of education. He has based his conclusions on the Traditions and his observations on the subject are illumined by his wide scholarship, practical experience and that intuitive insight which makes him such a wonderful reconciler of cold reason and warm-blooded sentiments. His evaluation of the contents of education is utilitarian in the main wherein the social and the individualistic aims merge into one another and harmonise in the bosom of religion.

According to him, the knowledge which has been imposed as obligatory on every Muslim is the knowledge of Muamalat (Transactions), a part of experience which is vitally concerned with the relation of the individual with other members of the society. This knowledge may be classified into Farz-e-Ayn, and Farz-e-Kafaya. Farz-e-Ayn is obligatory on all the members of the society without exception; they are the duties which the individual owes to himself and to the social group at large, while Farz-e-Kafaya is obligatory in a partial sense, partial because it is imposed on a part of the society or some of its members but the partial nature of obligation does not lighten in any way its responsibility on those who have been appointed to perform that particular function in the society.

The education of the heart which includes both religious beliefs and the development of the moral sense is obligatory on all (Farz-e-Ayn), because none is free from such moral affections as jealousy, pride, distrust, vengeance, etc., and according to him, these common epidemics which attack the heart cannot be cured unless the individual receives training in their proper treatment.

Functional Dimensions

He has analysed critically the kind of religious information which is imposed as obligatory on an individual. Contrary to the practice of the contemporary teachers of religion who would like to unload the entire burden of religious learning on to the pupil, he advocates a careful adjustment between the needs of the individual and the information to be imparted to him. Its nature and contents must necessarily vary with the conditions and environment of different individuals, and the knowledge becomes obligatory only when the need for such a knowledge arises in an actual life situation. An acquaintance with the religious observances of the pilgrimage, for example, should become compulsory on the eve of its performance and not before, while a familiarity with the religious injunction on marriage should become indispensable after the nuptial ceremonies had been performed. In fact he recognises such a close inter-dependence between knowledge and action that knowledge in vacuum, even religious knowledge with all the halo of sanctity playing about it, carries no significance for him as a telling factor in the educative process.

The part of knowledge styled by him as Farz-e-Kafaya or an optional obligation on a particular section of the society is further subdivided into religious and non-religious.

Under the non-religious branches, he includes medicine, mathematics and vocations like agriculture, weaving, blood-letting, tailoring, etc., and he derives his conclusions from a Tradition of the Prophet which makes a knowledge of Muamalat obligatory on every Muslim. Secular knowledge of such a nature when once imposed as obligatory on a particular member of the society for the furtherance of social good is as essential as Farz-e-Ayn and therefore education which guarantees the maintenance of the society and ensures its continuity is an equally essential part of the scheme of education as studies of religious nature.

According to him, all the branches of learning mentioned under the general title of religious studies, are not essentially religious and he insists upon a critical analysis of the contents of curriculum prescribed for the purpose. He classifies religious studies into fundamental or principal subjects, the subsidiaries and the preliminaries. He differentiates knowledge pursued as an end in itself from that which serves only as an instrument or means for others. Fiqh is, according to him, a subsidiary subject. The third kind of knowledge, the Muqaddamat or preliminaries are language, syntax and the skill of writing.

He had observed with his own eyes the tragedy of uninspiring routine work as carried on in the schools and he was sorely grieved on seeing pupils wasting whole life time on the subtleties of law, syntax and grammar. Evidently they were chasing the *will'-o-the-wisp* of puristic gymnastics instead of setting their course towards those highlights which could illumine the personality with noble thoughts and integrity of character. His analysis was an eye opener for those who followed such a puristic form of learning in the belief of obtaining spiritual benefit and a reward on the life to come. He announced that these instruments or skills should not be confused with real knowledge and should in no way be deified as the chief objective of the educative process as they had no intrinsic value for the individual. The subjects of subsidiary importance could only bask in the reflected glory of the foundational studies and their worth would be determined by the help which they bring to bear upon the principal branches of knowledge.

In learning the Arabic language one should not make a fruitless attempt to master the entire vocabulary—but should discriminate intelligently between the working and the recognition vocabularies of the language. One should learn so much as is essential for clear comprehension and speech, while out of the rarer words one should learn only those which are indispensable for the study of the Quran and the Traditions. That much would be more than sufficient for all practical purposes.

He fought gloriously against the tendency of the scholars who professed different studies and claimed for their particular branch, the annotated sanctity of religious learning and the approval of the Prophet, thereby revelling in the glories of spiritual self-complacency. In the first place, he discredited the idea that secular education was in any way inferior to the religious; one was as essential as the other; while the one sowed the seed and prepared the harvest, the other ripened the fruit and made it luscious. Hence some of the studies which had been raised to the pedestal of religious knowledge were relegated by him to the domain of secular learning and received their right place in a well thought out, carefully graded scheme of education. He had yet a surprise in store for the scholars, so self-complacently incensed within the stronghold of their privileges, the most startling surprise of their life when he declared that Fiqh belonged essentially to the field of secular learning, not only because it was learnt primarily for obtaining lucrative jobs under the State but also because it belonged to the field of legal administration rather than the cultivation of morals of the growth of personality.

Just as the Sultan should make laws for keeping his people in control so the legalist, a master in political administration should be well versed in the art of maintaining justice and equity among them... as a Sultan is necessary for the preservation of a Kingdom or its administration, Fiqh is essential for deciding differences among men. Just as ruling over the people by dint of political supremacy does not conform to the highest conception of religion, knowledge of the ways and means of administration which Fiqh in reality is, cannot be ranked as a religious study of the highest value. Thus Ghazzali not only made an original contribution to the problem of evaluating different branches of learning, he rehabilitated secular knowledge into a respectable place in the scheme of education and established a carefully graded scheme of studies. His work would always be prized as a contribution of the highest value in the field of curriculum reconstruction.

His remarks sparkle with a reflected glory for the devout because they are inspired by a single Tradition of the Prophet; they stand out so sound and rational because of the clarity of his thought and the sincerity of his outlook. In fact our indigenous system and the other schools stand desperately in need of a new birth, a renaissance in aims and ideals, contents and method of education. Once in the olden days, Al-Ghazzali touched the inner springs which constituted the foundations of the Islamic system of Education and released tremendous energy of thoughtful activity. Once through his Great work, the "Resurrection of Knowledge" or the "IHYA", he awakened the forces of the revolutionary thought and action. We hope one day some adventurous successor of his would once more galvanise the stagnant pool of our indigenous education into the rolling waters of a might current. But the original source of such a dynamic power lies hidden in its basic foundations, the Quran and the Traditions.

15

Basic Education

According to the social usage observed among the Muslims, the child started his alphabet on the fourth day of the fourth month in the fourth year of his life. According to the religious injunctions, the boy should be taught how to perform obligatory prayers from the seventh year and such an early training has been enjoined to habituate him to the individual and social discipline of Muslim prayers right from the very beginning.

The Prophet was keenly alive to the significance of education in the early years, the pliability of the young and their marvellous capacity to learn by imitation or otherwise. One who acquires I knowledge in his youth has inscribed it on the granite and one who learnt when he was advanced in age was like a scribe who tried to scribble on the surface of water. According to Hassan, "Learning during childhood is akin to writing in stone."

The history of Islamic education supplies examples of prodigies who gave wonderful demonstration of memory and intelligence in their early years. There is the account of a savant who attended the assembly of a Traditionist at such a tender age that he was actually carried in arms to the spot. Al-Ghazzali states on the evidence of Sahl Tastari how the education of the latter began in the third year and when he grew sick of attending for long periods he was allowed more freedom by teacher and he attended the school only for an hour.

Important Factors

The importance of educating children from the earliest finds pointed expression in so many proverbs of the Arabic language during the early days of Islam. Some of them are reminiscent of the days of tribal warfare when a carefully educated son was a bulwark of strength for the tribe against a powerful enemy. "One who educates his son in childhood, cools his eye on looking upon him when he comes of age. "One who trains and educates his son humiliates his enemy thereby." In the works of the poets we come across that conception of mind which is akin to the description of tabla rasa in the history of psychology. They compare the young child to a sapling, applicable wood, a tender branch which rests so easy and graceful on its root but the grown up man is likened to a dried wood which cannot soften." "An individual may be likened to earth which receives impression only when it is moist." Some poets have expressed the spirit of the Prophet's Tradition in rhyme. A poet writes", "I have clean forgotten all that I had learnt in childhood. There is no knowledge except that which is acquired in the morning of life and no forbearance except that which is experienced in advanced age. If you open the heart of a scholar in his early years, you will discover there, knowledge inscribed as if on stone. What is learning after one has entered upon years when the heart, the sense of hearing and sight have deteriorated."

In the words of another poet, "Education in the morning of one's life is like the watering of the roots of a plant till it springs up green and refreshing after passing through a period of drought. As for an old man, he would never renounce his style of life until he is laid in his grave and when you leave him, he relapses once more into ignorance like one who has a relapse of a malady after he has recovered from it."

Before the Advent of Islam

It appears that the social usage of putting the children early to school was not altogether unknown during the days of Jahiliyyah while the Jews and Christians had educational institutions of their own where they imparted instruction in the sacred lore, although in the opinion of the Prophet it was all de-educating the child as they were indifferent to the importance of acting upon their knowledge. Once in the course of a conversation, he mentioned that such a thing would happen after the death of knowledge and when asked to explain it, he quoted the instance of the Jews and Christians who taught and learnt the Torah and the Bible but never acted upon them, which meant the death of knowledge.

Traditions supply the case of a child of ten who had learnt the Quran and could recite it according to a recognised form and style.

Modem age is a period of inter-continental missiles and artificial satellites; it is driven by an insane desire for speed and speedy results. Its impatient spirit brooks no delay. It is impatient alike to create and to destroy. Such a world can hardly have any patience with the slow and gradual processes of evolutionary growth.

On the other hand, it is controlled and directed by extreme individualism and even the most dogmatic socialist is a believer in individualism within areas of interests which are not controlled by his political ideology.

Both these characteristics of the modern age came into a direct conflict, with the development of the child. The process of his growth is determined by the natural laws of physical and psychological development and they can no more be quickened into peace than the growth of any other organism. But the modern techniques are trying to control and direct the rhythm of organic growth while believers in the processes of an industrial world are fright fully impatient with the slow paced movement of child education and training. They would like to quicken it into an unnatural peace.

But like other arts, education of a child demands great patience, persistence and disciplined control. It demands an intense, love and sympathy with the child and an innate or acquired understanding of the child mind. It is only these qualities of dead and heart which can produce lasting results in the domain of fine arts and child education.

Force of Love

According to a companion of the Prophet, he had never come across a person who was more affectionate towards children than the Prophet. Collections of Traditions contain chapters on his affection for children and they reveal his amazing sympathy with the child mind and a method for their informal training in daily life which persuaded the children to cooperate in a joyous enthusiasm for their training and education. Where disciplinary methods fail the dynamics of love and affection prevail and the great secret of preparing a young generation of brave souls like Imam Hussain lay in that stupendous faith that the elders reposed in the innate good that lay in children and the confidence that the younger generation entertained in the love and good intentions of the old.

A world which is being whipped into an insane drive on its mad course of speed and individualism could certainly learn a lesson or two from the technique that the Prophet developed for the training and education of young souls.

According to the Bible, "the Kingdom of Heaven belongs to children" but in the words of the Prophet "the Kingdom on earth also belongs to them".

He revelled in a sheer physical contact with children and would describe his sensuous experiences in poetic language. He would take them in his arms and clasp them to his bosom. Then he would inhale deeply the fragrance of their fresh bodies as if they were freshly blown flowers. He described them as blossoms of earth, and fragrant blossoms into the bargain.

Whenever he went to the house of Fatima, he would invariably send for his grandsons. He would enjoy the freshness and the fragrance of their blooming personalities and take them unto his bosom.

Just as a spark kindles up a blaze, his attitude found a response in the heart of his young friends. While he discovered hidden nosegays in children, they found in him the perfumer's casket.

Once he issued forth from the mosque after the Zuhr prayers. He was accompanied by Jabir bin Samurah. On the way, he met some children. The Prophet called them to him and started caressing their cheeks; he caressed the cheeks of Jabir also. According to Jabir, there was such a coolness and fragrance in his caress as emanates from the casket of a perfumer.

The reaction of his boy servant Anas was also more or less the same. According to him he had never felt anything, not even silk, so soft as the touch of the Prophet. He had never smelt anything more fragrant than the fragrance of the body of the Prophet; not even ambergris or must as compared with it.

He loved children with all the depth and richness of his great personality but his love was intensified through an allegorical interpretation of the paternal instinct in terms of Divine Beneficence for creation.

He was never moved so deeply by any spectacle as the expression of parental love for their progeny. More than once tears flowed from his eyes when he saw a parent tending a child. These occasions invariably reminded him of the immensity of that paternal affection which the Creator entertained for his creation. He had declared on more than one occasion that God's love for his creation is more abundant than that of the parent for his offspring.

He would frequently illustrate the positive and the negative aspect of this relationship by referring to the maternal instinct for the child. Once he pointed towards a woman who was suckling her babe in his presence and said, "Can that woman throw her precious darling into the blazing fire?" Even a mare keeps her hoof off the calf so that it may not harm it. So is the case of God with his creation, and according to the Quran, God has writ large Rahmat on his Divine Self.

Casual observers from the West have often remarked about the deep attachment which parents in Islamic society evince for their children and one who is not alive to the functional purpose of the love for children and respect for elders in Islamic society has no insight into its basic foundations.

According to the Prophet, one who has no affection for the young and no regard for the old is not one of us.

It implies that such a person has derived no inspiration from the social outlook of Islam and has no understanding of the social compactness which such an outlook emphasizes upon. The Tradition encompasses both the creative and the conservative aspects of educational development.

Education for Minorities

He opened out his great heart not only to the children of the Faithful but to the world of children as a whole.

He would visit Jewish children on their sick bed and had issued general instructions that children and women should in no case be put to sword during a campaign. Whenever Ibn Abbas was consulted on the subject, he decreed that the Prophet never put the children of the unbelievers to sword and they should also abstain from it.

According to a Tradition, the children of the unbelievers (Mushriks) were not denied the Grace of God.

Once the Prophet described a dream in which he saw the patriarch Ibrahim who was seated in paradise and was surrounded by a crowd of children. He remarked that they were those children who had died in the Natural Faith (Din-al-Fitrat) implying that they had died before they had reached the age of discretion, the time when they were expected to make a declaration of their faith. Then somebody asked him about the children of the unbelievers (Mushriks). He added, "And the children of the Mushriks, too!"

Elsewhere he has said, 'The Pen of the Lord has been lifted away from the children until they reach the age of discretion!

In fact in one of the rawayat, when Aishah heard of the death of the child of a companion, she said in the presence of the Prophet, 'O Messenger of God, may God bless him. He was a birdie out of the birds of Paradise. He committed no sin and he did not attain to the age of committing sin."

Children's Education

As the Head of the state he was keenly concerned about the rights of the weak and the unprotected. In case of children he had laid down clear injunctions against the separation of the child from the mother. In his infinite sense of pity for children, he realised that no nurse could replace the mother of the child. Hence he disallowed the separation of the child from his mother in case the mother was being sold out as a slave and changing masters.

"Don't distract the love of the mother from her child", he

commands and elsewhere "One who has separated the child from the mother, will be separated from his near and dear ones on the Day of Judgement." According to the Traditions, the child must be entrusted to the mother even if she is an Unbeliever because feeding the babe and nursing is permissible in the case of a woman who is an Unbeliever.

In the case of Rafi bin Sinan, when a dispute arose about the possession of his daughter who had been weaned or was about to be weaned, the Prophet decreed that the daughter should be handed over to Rafi's wife who had not embraced Islam as yet.

Once he asked the husband and wife to sit in two distant corners and then asked them to call their daughter to him. At first the child turned to her mother. Thereupon the Prophet prayed to God and said, "Oh God, show her the right path," Then she went over to her father who took her away.

Disputes over the guardianship of children were decided in favour of mothers by Umar and Ali bin Abu Talib also and when the uncle of an orphan claimed the child, Umar said to the child, "The affection of thy mother is better for you than the riches of thy uncle."

The opinion of Ishaq bin Rahwayh, an early professor of law is that the child should stay with the mother up to his seventh year and should have the option of selecting either of the parent.

In fact the spirit of the Traditions and the Islamic law is protecting and safeguarding the child's right to security, love and affection.

In the case of Bint Hamzah the claims of a person like Hadrat Ali were rejected in the interest of the child. Bint Hamzah was brought up at Mecca and when Ali and Jafar were leaving Mecca after Amrat al-Qaza, she followed them calling aloud, "Uncle! Uncle!" Thereupon Ali took her along with him. There were three claimants of the child but the Prophet finally decreed that she should go to Jafar because her mother's sister was married to Jafar and a maternal aunt could legitimately claim to take the place of the mother in love and affection. Here also the decisive factor was the protection of the interest of the child.

Children enjoyed certain priorities in his assembly. The first fruit of the season when brought to the Prophet was always given to the youngest in the assembly. This simple and naive usage of his can be appreciated only by those who have observed that first flush of pleasant surprise which comes to a child when he tastes a new fruit for the first time in his life. For him it is like a new planet which has arisen on the horizon of his sensuous experience and only a person with an intense sympathy with child mind can reach to such heights and go to such details in attending to the younger generation.

He would not forget his young friends when he received presents from distant lands. Once when he received embroidered sheets from Yemen, he sent for Um Khalid who was so young that she was actually taken to him in arms. He addressed her in loving terms and pointed out the flowered design with words of impassioned delight 'Sana', 'Sana' which means beautiful in the Abysinian language. In fact the little lady was born in Abyssinia and she could understand words of that language only.

Once he received a golden necklace as a present and he declared that he would present it as a gift to that member of his family whom he loved most. Then he called Amamah, the child of his daughter Zaynab who was a great favourite of his and put the necklace in her neck with his own hands.

Easy Regulations

He would even relax the rigour of religious injunctions for the sake of children. Women prayed along with men in the Prophet's Mosque and if he heard a baby crying while leading prayers, he would shorten the prayer so that the mother could attend to the child. The injunctions for purifying clothes soiled by the urination of a baby are less rigorous than otherwise. He would often pray with a child in his arms. Once he performed a prayer with Amamah, the daughter of Abul Ath bin Rabi in her arms. He would seat the baby on the ground when performing the prostration and take her up when he rose on his feet.

Once he got down the pulpit for receiving Hassan and Hussain who wore scarlet coloured clothes and were so young that they could hardly walk. They would stagger a few steps and then flop down. The Prophet got down from the pulpit, took them in his arms and then seated them in front of him. Then he turned to the assembly and made a frank confession of his human frailty in these words.

> "How true are the words of God that your property and your progeny are a means of test and trial. When I saw them staggering and again rising to their feet, I could not help interrupting my address and taking them in my arms."

He realised the great conflict which a person has to face between his duties and his family affiliations and had himself experienced the powerful instinct which created moral crises in the life of individuals. Once he issued forth from his house with a grandson of his in his arms and remarked while pointing to the child.

> "You turn us into niggardly misers, plunge us into ignorance and moral apathy and make cowards of us. But there is no doubt that you are a flower modelled by the hands of the Lord."

He used to have all sorts of playful games with children. He would give them a ride on his back or on his shoulders; he would give a child a joyride on his legs. Sometimes he would seat two of them. He would seat them on his thighs, take them in his arms, kiss and fondle them. Sometimes they rode on his shoulders and when any one accosted the Prophet with the words "what a nice ride!" He would remark with a smile, "and what a rider!'

Whenever he returned from a journey, children came out with their elders to welcome him to the town. On such occasions he would take up a child or two and seat them on the ride. In this way they shared the keen pleasure of a victorious entry with the Prophet.

The liberty which the children had with them reached his very person when some of them were attracted by the Sign of Prophethood, a protuberant mark on his back. He would permit them to touch it with their fingers and when an elder discouraged them from doing so he would ask them not to interfere with their innocent pastime and let them play on.

Children undergo a feeling of measureless isolation in huge gatherings of adults and they would choose some of the most solemn occasions to initiate themselves into his presence.

Hajj at ul-Wida was the climax of the Prophet's political triumph and in those days he gave more than one addresses to huge congregations. On the day of the Sacrifice, the Prophet addressed the people while he was seated on a white mule or a camel. The scene has been well described by Rafi bin Amr who was a child in those days and had attended the function with his father. In his own words:

> "When the day advanced, I gave a slip to my father, edged my way through the huge concourse of people who surrounded the Prophet, reached his ride and put my hand in between his shoe and his foot".
>
> "The Prophet gave me a smile of recognition and said, 'Oh, is it Rafi?"

Only one who has the heart of a child can realise the great surge of love and confidence which must have thrilled the small frame of the young child. During that instance, the child must have felt that out of this seething ocean of humanity, he had discovered at least one with whom he could claim unity of the soul.

Scheme for Younger Generation : Sometimes he would enter into the spirit of their boyish pranks and direct the superabundance of juvenile energy into educative channels.

On his way back from the Battle of Hunayn, the Muezzen called for prayers. Abu Mahzurah, a young fellow who had not accepted Islam as yet along with some of his friends raised their voices and repeated the words of the call to prayers. The boys were evidently enjoying the fun. The Prophet called them to him joined in the fun like a young boy and made them repeat the call one by one. Abu Mahzurah had a good voice. The Prophet liked him immensely, made him sit before him, passed his hand over his head and prayed for him. Then he asked him to give the call of prayers regularly in the Haram.

Anyone who has some knowledge of the social status of persons attached in any way to religious service in the Haram in the Jahiliyyah and the Islamic period can have an idea of the sense of gratification which must have come to the young boy through this simple act of confidence.

His contact with children began very early. Newly born babes were often brought to him. He would bless them, perform the custom of *Tahnik* (putting something in the mouth of the infant, a chewed date or any thing else) and he selected for them a good name. He performed the Tahnik of Abdullah bin Zubayr, the first child born in Islam after the migration to Medina and that of Abdullah ibn Abi Talha, the son of Um Sulaym, the mother of Anas. He would put the newly born affectionately on his thigh and select a good name for him.

Munzar bin Abi Usayd was taken to the Prophet on his birth. The Prophet took him in his arms and seated him on his thigh. Then some other business of urgent nature demanded his attention and he was so busy that he forgot about the infant. The baby was taken away but the Prophet suddenly recalled him and once more seated him on his thigh. Then he asked for its name and when he was told the name selected by the parents he said, "No, no, his name is Munzar" and the child was named accordingly.

When a child was born to Um Sulaym, the mother of Anas bin Malik, the boy servant of the Prophet, his mother asked Anas to take the child to the Prophet for Tahnik and the naming ceremony. The Prophet was at that time in a garden and was branding camels. He held in his hand an instrument for branding the animals. Anas says, "When I brought the child, he took him in his arms. Then he sent for the Ajwah dates, a variety of dates grown in Medina, softened it by chewing it under his teeth and put it in the mouth of the baby. The infant began to suck it. Thereupon the Prophet said, "Look how these Ansars love dates." Then he caressed his face and named him Abdullah.

His contact with children was not that of an elderly person who deigned to join their company in a half condescending, half patronising manner. He entered into the spirit of their simple joys and sorrows and like a genuine teacher gave them the feeling that he also belonged to the world of children and had the gift and vision to participate in their emotional experiences.

He had the great gift of opening magic casements into their hearts and enter the Forbidden Kingdom. This was made more realistic and easy through that fund of pleasant humour which sparkled with a subdued light in his contact with children.

According to Anas, his younger brother kept a sparrow and his grief was inconsolable when the birdie died. The Prophet knew the little boy as intimately as the bird and whenever he met him after this tragedy, he would say to him, "Well my dear, what about your little birdie?"

Commands of the Holy Prophet

His admonition of children was illumined with a sense of intense sympathy with the child mind and a sense of humour.

Once a boy who robbed his neighbour's garden was brought to him. He would constantly rain stones on the neighbour's date palms and take away the fruit. The Prophet asked him, "My dear, why do you throw stones on the trees?" The child replied innocently. "For the fruit." When assured of his intention, he told him that if he wanted to take the fruit, he should take only those which fell from the trees." Then he caressed the child and said, "May God bless you with a bellyful of dates."

According to the Islamic Law, no restriction can be imposed upon taking the fallen fruit but the simple naive humour of his prayer for the child needs hardly any comment as an instructive piece of informal education.

The children would often accost him on the way, accompanied him on his walks through the streets and sometimes has a chance of taking their meals with him. On all such occasions, they were being educated in an informal way either through direct instruction or through personal observation and imitation.

Once a child was taking his meals with the Prophet and they were both eating out of the same plate.

The Prophet saw that he was not taking his meals in the proper way. He instructed him politely to begin the meals in the name of the Lord to take them with the right hand and to take only from the portion in front of him.

He has left instructions on the minutest details of every day social etiquette and has gone to the extent of determining the form of thanksgiving prescribed for a Muslim when another presents him with a nosegay. All these instructions were meant both for the old and the young. What the elders did through direct instruction the children followed through imitation.

Children attended the Prophet's assembly and sometimes a sudden fear gripped their souls when they heard him describe the great catastrophe of moral crisis that man shall have to face in days to come or when he administered punishments for the criminals. In these moments he would comfort them with a word of love or clasp them to his bosom.

Al-Mughuab bin Shubah, when a young boy would go on asking the Prophet about the Anti-Christ (Dajjal). The Prophet obviously felt that the child had a morbid interest in the subject and had developed a fear complex. Then he said to him in loving tones, "My son, never mind the Anti Christ; he won't harm you". In this case also the Prophet had affirmed the great faith which he had in the innocence of youth.

A person belonging to the tribe of Banu Harith says, "I was on the scene with my father when Maaiz bin Malik was stoned to death for adultery. Maaiz had himself openly confessed his crime and had insisted upon the extreme penalty. When the stones rained on him, the witness who was a young boy was terrified whereupon the Prophet held him in his arms and comforted him."

We find in his domestic circle a number of children whom he loved with all the depth and dignity of his great personality and the colourful modes of expression which his emotions took had a richness and variety, all his own.

These beautiful vignettes of children on the family stage include that of Usamah, the son of his freed slave Zayd and Anas bin Malik, his domestic servant. He seemed to be particularly fond of Usamah whom he would give a joy ride on his thighs along with his grandson. Usamah must have been a child of good features. He would often fondle him and say, "If Usamah had been a girl I would have bedecked him with ornaments and would have acclaimed him as a beauty in the world."

He entertained an extremely delicate feeling for this son of his freed slave. According to Aishah, once Usamah the son of Zayd, slipped on the threshold and cut his forehead. The child began to bleed profusely and the Prophet asked his young wife to clean it. Aishah demurred but the Prophet put his lips to the wound and comforted the child. Then he said, "If Usamah had been a girl, I would have dressed him in nice clothes, set him off with jewellery and would have made him famous as a beauty".

Sometimes he would tidy up Usamah with his own hands. Once he asked Aishah to clean the nose of the child which she did not. So he wiped it with his own hands and made his well known remark so often quoted in the Manaqib of Usamah, "Love him because I love those who love him."

Some of his wives had children from their former husbands and they lived with him as members of his family. In his playful moods, he would be as frolicsome with them as a child.

Um Salma had daughters by her first husband. One of them Zaynab describes how the Prophet was once taking bath in the house of Um Salma when the girl approached him.

He squirted water on her playfully and according to her belief it added to the freshness of her appearance. She always felt an air of freshness about her throughout her life.

His grand-children were the object of his love and affection out of whom Hassan and Hussain were the greatest favourites.

Books on Traditions contain special chapters on the Manaqib (praise) of the two brothers. His expression of love for them was genuine and spontaneous.

With the unquestioned privilege of a child, they would interrupt his addresses and insist on staying in his arms when he prayed.

Anas bin Malik remained in the Prophet's household for a period of nine or ten years as a domestic and he was treated always by the Prophet with a pleasant familiarity as if he was an equal. He would often address him jokingly as Unays (the diminutive for his proper name 'Anas'). He would address him as "the little boy with two ears." Once he saw Anas picking the leaves of a vegetable and he named him after the vegetable. He would often call him "sonnie."

During this long period of ten years the Prophet never addressed him with even such a mild word of reproof as 'uf'.

During this period he never took him to task for anything which he had left undone or questioned him about anything which he had done. In his own words, "He found the Prophet the kindest of all creation".

Once the Prophet asked him to go on some business but like a spoiled child he refused to go. Anas says that he never meant to disobey the Prophet but he was just being playful with him. Then he came out of the house and joined a group of children who were playing on the street. The Prophet followed him quietly and touched the nape of his neck from behind and when he turned, Anas found him laughing.

Then he said, "Unays did you go where I had asked you to go?" Anas replied, 'O Prophet of God, I am just going".

Holy Influence : His great love for children had an extremely contagious influence on his Companions. Hard hearted Beduins who never knew how to kiss their children and wondered when they saw the Prophet caressing a child, would melt and grow gentle hearted under his genial influence. Some of the Companions grew so interested in children that they would sometimes try to while away the hours of approaching death by playing with them.

There is the case of Khubayb. He had killed Harith bin Amir in the battle of Badr. Later on he was bought by the family of Harith, for satiating the demands of vendetta and was condemned to death. Khubayb prepared himself for the end and asked for a razor for removing hair. The razor was given to him inadvertantly when he was playing with a young child of the tribe who was having a joy ride on his thigh. The child's mother was alarmed about the safety of her son. Khubayb discovered her fears, went on fondling the child and said to the mother, "Do you fear that I will kill the child? I will never do so."

Then he performed two rakaat of prayers and recited those

beautifully touching verses that have comforted the heart of many a man under similar conditions. These couplets were often recited by men who fought with Shah Ismail Shahid and Sayyad Ahmad Barelwi. They ran as follows:

> "And I never care on whatever side I collapse as dead so long as I die a Muslim and lie unto the Lord. If he desires he can bless every limb of my dismembered body".

The hearts of the Companions went out move abundantly towards those street urchins who were deprived of the simple and innocent pleasures of life. According to Abu Aqba, once Abdullah bin Umar was passing through a street when he came across two Abysinian children who were most probably slave boys. Thereupon he stopped gave them two Dirhams.

His great love for children had a mellowing influence on those hard-headed Beduins who considered it unmanly to caress children or give them a kiss.

Once a Beduin came to visit the Prophet and was surprised to see him kissing a child. In his opinion, it was a human frailty unpardonable in a leader of the people. He told the Prophet that he had never given a caress to a child in his life. Thereupon the Prophet said, "It seems that God has deprived you of the milk of human kindness".

On another occasion when he was kissing Hassan, a bystander confessed that he had ten sons but he had never kissed anyone of them. The Prophet remarked, "One who does not treat others with affection, receives no affection in return."

The spark of enthusiasm that the Prophet had ignited into the hearts of his younger followers blazed more gloriously than in the case of their elders.

Once their sincerity and enthusiasm were instrumental in averting an extremely dangerous rift among the Muslims of Medina.

Abdullah bin Ubi, the chief of the dissenters (Munafiq) took advantage of a difference between an Ansar and a Muhajir during the Ghazwah of Banu al-Mustaliq, and declared that on his return, he and his party who were men of noble lineage would expel the low bred Muhajirs. On this occasion, elderly persons kept counsel for reasons which were more politic than moral.

It was a boy hero Zayd bin Arqam who defied Abdullah bin Ubi and told him that it was he who was low bred and was considered to be such by his own people. There was every danger that Abdullah would try to create mischief on his return. But when Abdullah bin Ubi returned to Medina, it was once again a boy follower of the Prophet who came out of the town and challenged Abdullah. He was Abdullah, the son of Abdullah bin Ubi himself. The boy stood nonchalantly in his way and refused his father an entry into the town until he declared openly that it was he himself who was a low bred churl while the Prophet was high and noble.

The situation created by Abdullah bin Ubi was in fact one of the most serious dangers to the internal solidarity of Islamic society at that stage and it was the implicit faith and trust which the younger generation of the Ansar reposed in the Prophet which stimulated them to stand heroically against such disruptive tendencies.

Acts of Bravery : Offering for active service was one of the usual channels through which the idealism of the younger generation often found its expression.

Asad al-Ghaba gives a long list of young people who offered themselves for active service on the eve of the battle of Badr and Uhud but were rejected by the Prophet.

Abdullah bin Umar and Bara bin Azib were both refused permission to join the ranks in Badr and they were so young that when they applied one year later to join on the eve of the battle of Uhud, their requests had to be turned down once again.

Quite a large number of young persons were rejected on the eve of Uhud. The list included the names of Abdullah bin Umar, Zayd bin Thabit, Usamah bin Zayd, Zayd bin Arqam, Bara bin Azib, Amr bin Hazm, Abu Said Khuzri, Samurah bin Jundab, Rafi bin Khudayj and several others. They belonged to the age group of 13-14.

Rafi's father pressed the request of his son on the plea that he was a good marksman with the bow and Rafi himself tried to add a few inches to his stature by raising himself on his toes when he was presented to the Prophet. He was permitted to fight.

But when Abu Said Khudri was recommended by his father because he had a well built constitution and had a strong and stout frame, he was not approved by the Prophet. According to Abu Said, the Prophet looked up on him and then lowered his eyes. He was finally rejected.

Samurah bin Jundab challenged Rafi bin Khudayj after his approval to a personal bout in which he floored him in no time. Samurah was also permitted to join.

Some of these boy soldiers performed wonders on the scene of battle.

Abu Jahl who had been described as the Pharaoh of the Age by the Prophet was killed in the battle of Badr by two young men.

According to Abdur Rahman bin Awf, "As I stood in the fighting rank on the battlefield of Badr, I looked to my left and to my right in order to find out who stood by me and I discovered myself between two young boys from Ansars who looked so tender in age. I wished that I were between more tried soldiers. Then one of them signed to me and whispered, "O uncle, do you know Abu Jahl." I said, 'And what is your business with him?' He replied, 'I have been told that he reviles the Prophet and by God who has my life in His Hand, if I encounter him to day, I will stick to him until one of us gets killed.'

> "1 wondered at these words of his. Then the other boy also said something similar to me".
>
> "Soon after I saw Abu Jahl moving about and I said, 'Don't you see, here is your man, about whom you were asking.' Upon this they advanced towards him with their swords until they killed him. Then they returned and reported themselves to the Prophet".
>
> "When he asked who had killed him, both of them claimed the credit. Then the Prophet examined their swords and said, 'Both of you have killed him".

"But he allowed the Salb or the booty of Abu Jahl to Muadh. These two young men were Muadh bin Amr bin Jumuh and Maadh bin Ufra."

Roots of Knowledge

The supreme confidence which the Prophet had in the naive faith of children has been expressed in a number of Traditions. In one of the Traditions, he has described the True Path as the Luminous one which can be traversed easily even by the ignorant Arab of the desert and the children at school.

He has described how the innate understanding which grew out of a child's innocence would sometimes light upon truth while their elders were lost in the wilderness of their prejudices and passions. In the literature of Traditions we come across three occasions on which an infant declared the truth and averted a great moral calamity. One of them was Jesus Christ. The story has been told with magnificent restraint in the Sura Maryam.

The second was the infant born of an evil woman who charged Jurayj the pious man among the Israelites with fornication. When Jurayj prayed to God and patted the belly of the babe, he told them the name of his real father.

The third was the sucking babe who absolved a slave girl from the serious charge of adultery and theft.

It is the touching story of a mother who was sucking her baby when there passed by her side a man who rode a splendid steed and was clad in magnificent garments. The mother said, "O God make my child like him" and the child left instantaneously the sucking, began to look up and when his eyes met the man, he said, "O God, don't make me like him', and once again began to suck".

Abu Hurayrah who has narrated the Tradition describes how completely the Prophet was carried away by the touching scene he was painting in words. In the ccurse of this description, the Prophet appeared to have identified himself with the infant hero of the story. He actually put his forefinger into his mouth and began sucking it like a babe.

According to the story after that there passed a slave girl and the people were beating her black and blue. They had charged her with adultery and theft but the poor wretch protested "God is sufficient for me as an evidence and a supporter!" Upon this the mother prayed, "O God, don't make my son like that slave girl." But the baby left once more his suckling, looked at the slave girl and said, "O God, make me like her", and there ensued a discussion between the mother and the son in the course of which it became known that the infant was right in both the cases.

The babes in all these fables represent honest, straightforward, sincere humanity which speaks the truth with all the frank boldness and courage of a young child.

The fable of the boy Prophet throws light on the story of Ashab al-Khudud (the People of the Pits) as given in the Quran and describes in a moving manner the great faith with which the word of God inspires young hearts.

A tyrant who did not believe in God apprenticed a young boy to a sorcerer who had served his master, the king well and was nearing his end. The boy learnt the art of sorcery but on his way to his master, he came across a Christian monk and was initiated into the true faith. The story runs how the king came to know about the monk and got his body sawn in two. The boy was a witness to the scene and the king asked him to recant from his new faith.

The boy peremptorily refused and the king condemned him to a cruel death. He was thrown down a precipice but he escaped miraculously and when the king failed twice in his attempt, the boy suggested a way out of the difficulty. He asked him to gather the people in the market-place and impale him on the trunk of a tree or a pillar. The procedure was carefully detailed by the boy. The king must take an arrow out of the quiver of the boy and let it fly by announcing the formula, "In the name of the Lord of this boy."

The king did the same and sent the arrow flying which struck the boy on the temple. The boy died on the spot. But the moving spectacle ignited a spark of faith among the people and it was fanned into flame by the great tragedy. They rose to one man and cried out "We believe in the Lord of the boy. We believe in the Lord of the boy." And then the king ordered large pits to be dug on the mouths of the streets which were filled with glowing ambers. These pits were filled with men who did not recant from their faith.

The fable which describes the heroic career of the boy Prophet is rounded up by the determined resolution of another boy. When a woman came up to the Pit, she hung back for a moment but a boy who was with her said, "Mother, be steadfast because it is all for the sake of the Lord."

It would be interesting to study how his words of lòve and sympathy made an undying mark on young hearts and how they were cherished as loving mementoes throughout their lives.

Anas bin Malik, his boy servant is one of the most prolific narrator of Traditions and his narrations are often richly coloured with flashes of human touches.

Usamah bin Zayd who had been described by him as only second to his father Zayd in regard and affection, has a number of Traditions to his credit.

Imam Hassan who was only seven years and some months when the Prophet died used to recall vividly his sayings. He has thirteen Traditions to his credit. He describes graphically how the Prophet asked him to spit out a date sent as a charity that he had put into his mouth by chance.

His brother Imam Hussain, who was six years and odd months when the Prophet passed away had narrated eight Traditions.

Even young children of five recalled his words and remembered even more vividly how spontaneously he joined them in their playful activities.

According to Muawwid bin-al-Rabi, the Prophet visited their house when he was a tiny toddler of five. He remembered vividly how the Prophet took water from a well situated in the house and spurted it on his face playfully with his mouth.

16

Education for Women

The oral expression of the Prophet had a ring of sincerity about it and the rhythmic harmony of his words haunted the memory long after they had been heard. The Traditions are inspired with a feeling of deep humanity, genuine simplicity and felicity of diction peculiarly their own. They are a natural outcome of the great rhythm of life that moved his entire frame.

It is interesting to discover that some of the women who came to see him took unconsciously after him and express themselves in a beautifully expressive language.

When a woman was divorced by her husband and she came to him for the protection of her right as the guardian of her son she said, "He is my child, my womb has been his receptacle, my breasts his water-skin and my arms his cradle."

And when he had asked Hind, the wife of Abu Jahl on the fall of Mecca to give a pledge against infanticide, she said, "We suckled them as young and you killed them when they grew old. So you and they are the better judges thereof."

Aishah who had been brought up in a family with literary traditions would often narrate a tradition in a language illumined with expressive similes and figures of speech.

While commenting on the Prophet's interpretation of dreams she said, "Every dream that he saw came true as the dawn of the day." The Prophet experienced a great psychological strain during the moments of revelation and would often perspire heavily on such occasions and she described his worked up countenance by saying, "Drops of perspiration rolled down his brow like pearls." And when she passed sleepless nights during the days of Ifk, she says, "I rarely applied the collirium of sleep to my eyes."

But when her emotions were thoroughly aroused, she presented an impressive example of an ancient woman oracle and spoke with a fiery eloquence and her bon-mots and witticisms are like unto sparks when compared to that glorious blaze of scorching eloquence with which she addressed the army in the Battle of the Camel.

The opening lines in which she recounts her claims on the regard and affection of the people seem to grip the attention and have an air of remarkable pointedness about them.

> "O Men, be quiet, be quiet. I have the privilege of a mother on you and I exercise the authority of giving advice. The Prophet died with his head in my arms. I was the most cherished of his wives. God saved me from others (she had no previous husband) and through me were distinguished the believer from the Doubter (the accident of Ifk). It was for my sake that God revealed the injunction on Tayammum."

After summing up in one glorious repertory her claims to be listened, she speaks about her father.

"When the string of religion was set a tremble after the Prophet, it was my father who held its ends in both his hands. He controlled the reins of dissension, he dried up the sources of renegacy. He extinguished the fiery plans of the Jews. He took those who had been watered to their resting place, and brought those who were thirsty to the water side and watered again those who had slaked their thirst before.

And when he had nipped the dissension in the bud and had blazed the mighty conflagration of battle for the unbelievers and had secured the bundle of provisions with a string he was called away by God."

With such remarkable gifts of eloquence women could very well help the Prophet in his great work.

Women Teachers

Some of the women companions rendered services as teachers of the new cause and they did so at a great personal risk to themselves.

Um Shank Dawsiyyiah started her secret propaganda among the women of Mecca during those days when the Muslims were still a persecuted minority and she was ejected from the town by the Quraish. At Medina her residence was the rendezvous of the visitors from outside who came to learn about the new religion. And there was such a crowd of them always coming in and going out of her place that the Prophet did not permit Fatima bint Qays to prolong her stay when he had quartered her with Um Sharik after her divorce.

Another woman Ghuziyyah who worked among the women of Quraish was evicted from Mecca under appalling circumstances. She was secured tightly with cords on the naked back of a camel and was kept without food and drink for three days during the journey. It is said that the Quranic verse: In Wahabat Nafsaha linabi — if she has offered herself for the Prophet — had been revealed to commemorate her great sacrifices in the cause of truth.

Women in the days of the Prophet served on the battlefield and were responsible for a variety of duties. They would prepare meals on the way and in the camps on field service they supplied drinking water, attended to the wounded and looked after the injured and the sick. In some cases they were entrusted with the responsibility of carrying the dead to Medina.

Some of the more outstanding among those who accompanied the Prophet on his military operations were Um Sulaym, the mother of Anas bin Malik, and Um Atiyyah. Um Sulaym was an extremely courageous woman and was never daunted by the most grievous reverses. She had served with Aishah bint Abu Bakr on the battlefront of Uhud.

According to an eye-witness, they had tightened up their garments a little so that their anklets were visible. They would carry skinbags full of water on their back poured water into the mouths of the people and again hurried back to fill them up again.

Services like these were highly prized and Umar gave precendence to Umm-e-Kulthum bint Ali because she had taken part in the supply of water on the day of Uhud.

Umm-e-Sulaym kept always a cool mind under extremely trying conditions. When Muslims received a setback in the first encounter on the day of Hunayn, she was seen going about with a dagger and when the Prophet asked her what purpose it could serve, she replied that she would tear open the belly of the first unbeliever who would approach her with evil intentions. Um Atiyya another lady companion took part in seven campaigns with the Prophet and proved extremely useful on such occasions.

Um Umariyyah, a woman belonging to the Ansar was an early convert to Islam. She had embraced the new faith with the third group of Medinites who had embraced Islam at Aqabah. She served in the fighting ranks in the battles of Uhud, Hudaybiyyah, Khyber, Hunayn and Yamamah.

A description of the part played by her in the Battle of Uhud reveals the great spirit of service and sacrifice which the Prophet had awakened among his women followers. She was performing at the same time the duties of First Aid to the injured and acted as a personal bodyguard of the Prophet.

She had a water skin and took drinking water to the wounded. She had rolls of bandages kept in a piece of cloth that was secured to her waist.

She experienced a narrow scrape when she attempted to ward off the enemy who were heading towards the Prophet. She formed one of the trusted band of followers with Musab bin Umayr and others who defended the Prophet at a great personal risk when he was beset by tried and determined warriors like Ibn Qamiyyah and others. She received twelve or thirteen wounds in the affray. One of them which she had received on her shoulder took more than one year to heal. She gives herself an interesting description of her fighting technique. According to her, "We were fighting at a great disadvantage. The enemy fought on their rides and we were mostly on foot. Whenever a soldier attacked me, I would check the onslaught with my shield and when he retreated

I would give a sword thrust on the legs of the horse and make it rear and fall. Then the Prophet who was close by called out my son to help and we finished him between ourselves."

Um Umariyyah had joined the battle with her whole family, her husband and two sons serving in the ranks. She followed her military career with equal zeal after the death of the Prophet.

And when Muslims fought the great battle of Yamamah against the renegades she took an active part in actual fighting. She received eleven wounds and one other arms was severed on the occasion.

This was not an isolated example of women joining a battle, with her whole family.

Khansa, the great elegist fought in the battle of Qadisiyyah in 1 A.H. along with four sons all of whom met their end in the sanguinary fight. The brave mother offered thanksgivings when she heard of their martyrdom?

Examples of personal bravery on the part of women were not uncommon in the Prophet's family. There is the case of Safiyyah, an aunt of the Prophet on the paternal side who killed a Jew with a tent peg during the Battle of the Ditch when she could not find a more handy weapon. Hassan bin Thabit, the poet who was staying behind with the ladies in those perilous days when the Muslims were seriously threatened by the Jews of Medina could not gather up his courage to meet the man who was approaching the fortified retreat with evil intentions. When she had killed the man, she asked him to go and despoil him. But he refused to go and bring the armour of the victim which was a legitimate right of the victor. Thereupon Saffiyah issued forth once again, severed the head and threw it amidst the Jewish melee who had gathered below.

In addition to these brave women who were more known, there were several unnamed heroines who served with equal zeal and self-sacrifice. An unnamed woman took part in six battles out of twelve acting with her husband and performed duties of nursing and first aid.

Although there had been no sea campaign during the lifetime of the Prophet there is one distinguished instance of a lady companion who participated in naval engagement. She was Um Haram, the wife of 'Ubadah bin Thamar, the companion who was described as 'Kamil' or the perfect man in the language of the Jahiliyyah, one of the qualifications for earning the title being skill in the art of swimming. She was a sister of the redoubtable Um Sulaym. It is interesting to know that Ubadah was the first companion of the Prophet who had joined maritime warfare and was accompanied by Um Haram.

One of the chief traditions, in fact the main tradition on the blessings of sea warfare, is related on her authority. She gives a graphic picture of the whole scene. 'The Prophet visited my house and took his meals. Then I began to massage his head and he dozed off. He woke up all of a sudden and laughed out. I said 'What makes you laugh, O Prophet of Allah', and he said 'A group among my people were presented to me (in the dream). They were fighting on the path of the Lord and they had mounted the waves of the sea as kings mount their thrones.' Thereupon Um Haram said, 'Pray for me O Prophet of Allah, that I may be one of them'. So he prayed for her.

Um Haram had accompanied her husband in the sea campaign against Cyprus during the reign of Muawiyyah. As she was disembarking from a boat she slipped down from her mount and was drowned in the sea.

Women's Role

The position of women in some of the Muslim countries today raises the important question how far the state of affairs is directly inspired by the Traditions of the Prophet.

A careful study of this literature brings us evidence of an overwhelming nature which proves that the deterioration in the status of women set up with the capitalistic society of a later age which believed in the proprietorship of woman as a commodity rather than treating her as a conscious being.

According to the Traditions, woman has an extremely important role to play in society. Although her primary duties lay in the creation of a rich and fuller life in the family, she was in no way barred from participating in the life outside home whenever there was a demand for such help on social or personal grounds.

Woman's place in the Muslim society of subsequent periods in no way reflects the spirit of those traditions which determined her role in society. They provide rich and abundant opportunities for the development of her personality within the framing arch and outside it. They provide means for the growth of healthy moral attitude and variegated modes of expression for her social, economic and even physical aspirations. And the annals of Islamic history reveal a rich variety of social, educational and spiritual occupations through which womanhood of Islam expressed itself under changing times and climes.

The perennial source of information for this freedom of expression can be traced out to the original teachings of the religion.

In this context, it would be interesting to make a critical study of two problems of an extremely controversial nature and see how far his teachings accorded with the eternal verities of human nature and moral and social good and how his injunctions provided ample facilities for a colourful variety in their modes of expression so long as they preserved the basic principles on which these injunctions had been framed. They are purdah and birth control.

The problem of purdah or the segregation of the sexes has been made a highly controversial issue for more than one reason. It is difficult to discover the origin of the so called harem life in the injunctions or the practice of the Prophet. It was the growth of a later stage that was far removed from the genuine democracy of early Islam. It developed during a period of kingship supported by a landed and commercial aristocracy that seriously jeopardised the freedom of the common man and woman. Started as a symbol of social prestige by the higher classes, it percolated down to the lower strata and recognised as a social institution was given the sanction of a religious institution by the clergy who tried to discover religious injunctions for it.

In its essence it was the product of a society that was essentially oligarchical and which tried to justify its undemocratic institutions by invoking the support of religion.

The Quran and the Traditions are fairly clear on the subject. They provide injunctions for regulating the life of men and women in a democratic society and establishing their relationship on an equable basis.

In fact the issue has been complicated by the two sets of injunctions, those for the wives of the Prophet and for the rest of women.

In fact social conditions of the town and the unfriendly intentions of the dissenters demanded special precautions for the preservation of the dignity of the Prophet's household.

Hence certain restrictions had been imposed on the Mothers of the Faithful and the Sura of Hijab had been primarily revealed with specific reference to the Prophet's wives.

The Sura was revealed on the occasion of the marriage of Zaiynab bint Jahsh with the Prophet. According to Anas after this event the wives of the Prophet began to observe Hijab. The injunction forbids the believers from entering the Prophet's residence without permission.

It appears that before this event visitors entered the Prophet's house without permission and would sometimes prolong their stay indefinitely. Henceforth they were to seek permission for admission. This specific injunction was further implemented by the Prophet's wives by taking the Hijab. But the practice cannot be interpreted as a general commandment for the entire womanhood. This is not an isolated example when the Prophet had imposed restrictions exclusively on himself and his family. He had denied to his family any right of inheritance to his worldly possessions. The restriction had no force for others.

The women of Medina continued with their routine share in the normal life of the community, and did so without purdah, at least purdah as understood today.

There is abundant evidence to prove that women addressed the Prophet with uncovered faces.

Once in the course of his address to women on the Eid day the Prophet declared that most of them were faggots for hell. This was a device to set their moral frames atremble. On this occasion it was a woman belonging to the masses described as Saflat Annisa, Safal Khadayn (lowly woman with black spots on her cheeks) who stood up and cross questioned him on the subject. According to the traditions, she was marked with dark spots on her cheek. Obviously the woman could not be described by an eyewitness in these words if she was veiled.

On another occasion, in the words of the tradition (a woman had raised herself on her knees so that the Prophet might see her.)

The books on Tafsir mention the episode of a fair complexioned woman who used to join the prayers in the Prophet's mosque and how there was a larger rush in the back rows than the front rows.

Instances where women attended mixed gatherings without a veil during the lifetime of the Prophet can be multiplied indefinitely. The very nature of the work performed by women on the battlefield, in the gardens and the field, the pastures and the grazing grounds of Medina precluded the possibility of the use of a veil.

A fairly large number of women worked in the fields and engaged themselves in agricultural operations. These included both women belonging to the Ansar and the Muhajarin. In the early days the Prophet had granted tracts of lands to the poorer section among the Muhajarin. These grants had been made out of the landed property of Banu Nadhir. These persons were helped by their women folk. Women living in the desert must have led even a more free life. They looked after the flocks and attended to guests in the absence of menfolk. During the Prophet's time one comes across women who looked after goats transacted petty business like selling of milk to the travellers. The Prophet and his fellow traveller had been entertained by such a woman on their way from Mecca to Medina.

It would be interesting to make a study of the Traditional evidence on the subject in greater details.

Attending Holy Prophet's Assembly : Women attended his assembly along with men and he would discuss very intimate topics like that of sex in such mixed gatherings.

Once he addressed the people about a person who let out his bed chamber secrets to others. There were present on that occasion both men and women and they were seated in separate groups.

He asked them frankly whether there was any one who behaved like that. All kept quiet. Then one of the women raised herself on the knees so that the Prophet might be able to see her and listen to her. She said, "There are persons like that both among-men and women." This incident throws light on the frankness with which women used to discuss things and how they addressed the Prophet and the people with uncovered faces.

Women would come to him for clarification of legal points concerning all sorts of matters including their conjugal relations and some of them would express their views in a language which might be considered too frank. Questions like these don't indicate any morbid curiosity about sex affairs. For the Arabs, these matters had no air of morbidity about them. They were as normal as other features of their every day life. What stimulated them to ask such questions was the great desire to learn the Prophet's injunctions on all matters and to preserve them for future generations.

There is the case of a woman who demanded separation before she had performed coitus with her husband. And when she preferred her case, she raised the edge of a piece of cloth and told the Prophet that her husband's limb was as supine as the cloth. On another occasion a woman had actually put him a question on bed pollution in case of women and when Um Salma, the Prophet's wife expressed displeasure on the question he told that there was no harm about the query.

Attending Prayers : During the life time of the Prophet, women enjoyed considerable freedom in their movements and they attended the Prophet's mosque regularly for morning and for other prayers. According to Aishah women used to join the morning prayers that were led by the Prophet. They used to have their sheets on them. The Prophet was extremely considerate for children and he would often cut short his prayers if he heard a child crying for its mother who had obviously joined prayers led by the Prophet.

The chapters on Salat as given in the authentic collection of Traditions contain instructions as regards the participation of women in prayers with men. According to Ibn Umar no woman should be disallowed from visiting a mosque and elsewhere he has said that she should be permitted to visit the mosque even at night and when a son of his refused to accept the statement he grew so violent that he abused him. According to another source, he struck his fist against his chest and said, "I am telling you a command of the Prophet and you have the facetiousness to say that I won't accept it." According to Ibn Umar, a wife of Umar bin Khatib attended the mosque regularly for morning and night prayers. Umar was rather over strict as regards movement of women as evidenced from the episode of Sawdah, the wife the Prophet. He did not like it personally that his wife should join the night prayers in the mosque but he did not prevent her from attending the mosque out of his great regard for the Prophet's injunctions on the subject. Atikah, a wife of Zubayr had married him on the express condition that he won't check her from attending night prayers in the mosque.

Certain other injunctions are concerned with the actual act of praying.

According to a Tradition in Bukhari, women are not permitted to rise from prostration until men had seated themselves. A number of chapters in books on Salat deal with injunctions concerned with women praying along with men.

Women used to join Eid prayers and other prayers like those offered during a solar eclipse. According to Um Atiyyah, the Prophet ordered us to take unmarried women or married and even those in menses to the Eid prayers.

They were not silent spectators on such occasions but would call out the Takbir also.

Maymunah used to call out Takbir on the prayers for the Eid of Sacrifice and women would recite Takbir when they joined prayers with men under the leadership of Aban bin Uthman and Umar bin Abd-al-Aziz during the nights of Tashriq.

The Prophet insisted that women both married and unmarried and even those in their menses should go forth out of their houses on the Eid day and join the prayers. He enjoined on them to lend scarfs to one another for dressing properly for the occasion.

Women attended the addresses of the Prophet on Fridays and the Eid days and on other occasions along with men. But as they sat at a distance, apart from men he had sometimes the feeling that he was not easily audible to them.

For a number of years he used to address men and women together and afterwards he would come down from the pulpit and address the women separately. It was also necessitated by the appeal for the poor relief which the Prophet would make to them on the spot. A ready collection was always possible in case of women because they would donate their ornaments on such occasions, a form of contribution not possible in case of men. On such occasions Bilal or some other person was always at hand to collect the donations in a piece of cloth.

Sometimes he would appoint a particular day for addressing women alone. Once a representation was made that men had an easier access to him than women so he named a special day for them on which he gave them spiritual counsel and told them about the commandments of God. He gave a special address to women on Eid days also.

Social Responsibility

The Prophet visited some women at their homes too. They were either women like Um Sulaym the mother of Anas bin Malik who used to accompany him on his military campaigns and Um Haram her sister, a brave woman who met her end in a naval campaign during the period of Muawiyyah. She belonged to the family that had fostered the Prophet in his early years, and was a sister of his foster mother. She lived at Kaaba, quite a distance from the Prophet's mosque and whenever he visited Kaaba he would make a point to visit her and take his noon day siesta there. Um Haram would scurry his hair and he would go to sleep. It was in her house that he saw in a dream how some of his followers rode the waves of the ocean as kings mount their throne. This had occasioned the well known tradition on the excellence of naval warfare.

He would often take his siesta in the house of Um Sulaym also who would collect his perspiration as a sacred memento in a phial.

The Prophet used to pass his noon day hours some times at the residence of Shifa bint Abdullah, a learned lady of those times who had taught writing to Hafsah, the wife of the Prophet.

Women would often visit him at his residence and discuss

things, obviously without any purdah restrictions as interpreted today and even the presence of the Prophet did not deter them from raising their voices to the loudest pitch. It is interesting to note that women exercised such a freedom only in the presence of the Prophet. They would take every precaution for more decorum if Umar bin Khattab appeared on the scene.

Once Umar sought permission to see the Prophet who had with him at that time some women from Quraish who were talking with him and they would often shout at the highest pitch of their voice. When Umar bin Khattab sought admission (from outside) they hastened to cover themselves (Yabdarun al Hijab). When Umar entered the house he found the Prophet laughing.

Thereupon Umar said, "May God keep you laughing", and the Prophet explained, "I was tickled by these women who were with me. When they heard your voice, they hastened to cover themselves."

Upon this Umar said, "O Prophet of God, you have a better right to be feared by them than myself and then he turned to the women and said, "O enemies of your souls, do you fear me and do not fear the Prophet". They replied, "Yes, because you are more strict and harsh."

The phrase 'Yabdarun al Hijab implies that the women were sitting without any Hijab.

Female Workers : In the case of a town like Medina which was the settlement of an agricultural community it was natural that some women should have engaged themselves in agricultural operations. They were not essentially Ansars, some of the Meccan emigrants had also taken to this profession when they were allotted pieces of land out of the property of Banu Nadhir after their exile. One such piece was allotted to Zubayr, the father of Abdullah that brave and redoubtable claimant for the Caliphate under the Umayyids. His wife Asma bint Abu Bakr describes how she used to go often to the land and bring fodder for the horse carrying it all the way on her head. She would often mend the leather bucket for drawing water for her husband. This piece of land was situated three quarter of a Farsakh (league) from her house.

It is interesting to learn that Asma belonged to the highest of the high. She was the daughter of Abu Bakr and one of the most courageous and renowned women of early Islam. She had revealed an amazing sense of loyalty to Islam even during the Meccan period as a young girl and she must have enjoyed all the social prestige and precedence she deserved. But all these things did not prevent her from following an occupation which belonged essentially to out of door life.

A large number of unnamed women occupied themselves with agricultural operations. Sahl describes how a woman used to sow beet root along the channels of her field and would give them a treat by making a preparation of the beet root mixed with flour every Friday.

Women used to look after herds of animals, specially goat and sheep both at Mecca and Medina. Um Ayman, the freed slave girl of the Prophet's family used to look after goats.

Once the master of a slave girl who used to tend his flock of goats gave her a beating because she had lost a goat. The Prophet had asked the man to set her at liberty as a compensation for his harsh treatment.

Some of the women at Medina followed professions involving operations which could in no way be performed with a covered face.

Rufaydah was a surgeon and she used to perform minor operations in a tent like structure adjacent to the mosque.

Shifa bint Abdullah was a scholarly woman of the age who knew reading and writing, she dabbled in medicine and was often put in charge of supervision work in the market place by Umar.

The Prophet's injunctions on birth control revealed an extremely objective outlook on an issue which can hardly be 'discussed in this scientific age of ours without arousing considerable feelings. For him it does not seem to have any moral significance, good or bad, it is 'a moral' to all intents and purposes.

Birth control was practised in the days of the Prophet for more than one reason, its chief reason in the earlier years being scarcity. It was practised under war conditions too. Sometimes it was practised in case of a woman during the suckling period.

One of the chief traditions on the subject has been narrated on the authority of Jabir bin Abdullah who had married after the death of his father in Uhud. His father had left a rather heavy debt which the Prophet helped to pay off. But he had left a more burdensome legacy of seven or nine daughters and it was not easy for Jabir to feed so many mouths. Jabir took a widow for a wife and the news reached the Prophet after the marriage had been celebrated. When Jabir saw him next, the Prophet said, "You should have married a virgin. She would have proved more playful with you," Thereupon Jabir told him that he had married a widow so that she might look after his sisters.

Now according to Jabir, birth control or Azl was commonly practised in those days. In his own words "We used to practise Azl during the days that the Quran was being revealed. It may be any time before A.H., the year of Hajj al Wida. It was represented to the Prophet that some of companions practised birth control but the Jews objected to the practice and described it something in the nature of burying a child alive. The Prophet said, "They lie. When God intends to create, nothing can stand in His way."

According to a tradition by Abi Said, "When birth control was mentioned in his presence, the Prophet said, 'Why does anyone practise birth control.' He did not make any further comments and he did not prohibit it."

According to Muslim, the Permission for the practice is negative in nature. According to Abu Said al Khudzari when they practised Azl during the battle of Bani Mustalaq and the opinion of the Prophet was sought on the matter he said, "There is no harm if you don't do it because a soul that God has ordained to be created any time till Doomsday will be created."

According to Iman Malik, it is essential to obtain consent for its practice in case of a free woman.

Education for Girls

The Prophet had a soft corner of his heart for the girls who had suffered most from that callous indifference to human life and dignity which was the darkest spot in the social life of the Pre-Islamic Arabia. An inordinate feeling of tribal pride led to the cruel custom of infanticide. The Prophet once wept like a child when one of his companions related to him the pathetic description of an infanticide he had committed before he had accepted Islam; the memory of the innocent voice crying out from the bottom of the pit where he had heartlessly buried her calling upon the departing parent to reclaim her from a living grave, set his moral fibre atremble.

Any expression of motherly feeling had always a profound influence on him and when a widow visited Aishah with two other daughters and on receiving a single date from the Mother of the Faithful, divided it equally between them, the Prophet was evidently overwhelmed with emotion and called out his blessing on all who tended their daughters because verily they were a covering of protection from the consuming fire of Hell." There is a tradition on the authority of Shaabi that "one who has imparted good education to his daughter, trained her on sound lines and provided for her a matrimonial alliance, verily for him there lay a reward in God." Again according to Abi Said al Khudri, one who has brought up three daughters, educated them, married them and acted otherwise handsomely towards them has won his title to heaven.

We have made a passing reference already to the fact how the Prophet had relaxed the formal discipline of the prayers when a child chanced to approach him on such occasions with the privilege that its naive and unconventional nature gave him. According to Abu Qatadah, he prayed while Amamah, the daughter of Abi-al-Ath bin Rabi rode on his shoulders; the Prophet would place her gently on the ground when performing the prostration and lifted her up after completing it. Innocent hands played with his mighty frame. They rollicked and frolicked about him boldly and freely and he always beamed into smiles. Once the tiny daughter of Khalid bin Said played with the Mark of Apostolate a scar-like formation on his back and he permitted her benevolently to continue with her innocent mischief uninterrupted. He won't forget his little friends amidst more respectable company and even when engaged in important affairs of state.

Once he was presented with a black 'cheddar' and he sent for Um Khalid who was sc small that she was actually carried to him. When the child arrived he pointed out to her lovingly the flowered embroidery of the piece and called out, 'Sana, Sana, ('Beautiful' in the Abysinian language) and he spoke the word because the little lady was born in Abyssinia and it was the only language which she understood. She began to play with the Seal of Prophethood, a purple coloured protuberance on his back. Thereupon her father tried to check her rudely, but the Prophet requested him not to prevent her from doing so.

It appears that the shades of gloom had lifted from the girlhood of Arabia on the advent of Islam and we have evidence that they sang, played on musical instruments, revelled in joy rides on the swings and shared with the girlhood of all ages the pastime of doll playing and had toys as fantastic and grotesque as found in any other country of the world. Women enjoyed more freedom and liberty to move out in the days of the Prophet than the orthodox Muslim women of today and naturally women who accompanied warriors on the battlefields and rendered First Aid service must have had ample opportunities for playing and physical exercise in order to train them for such an arduous duty. There is the instance of Aishah running a race with the Prophet in the earlier years of their married life and winning it. She lost the second race which she arranged with him in later years.

Aishah's house appears to be an educative and a playing centre for girls in the earlier years and the rendezvous of scholars and intellectuals during the later period. The pleasure of her company and the attractive display other playthings of the days of childhood must have brought to her the girls of the neighbourhood in numbers who had a chance to benefit by her talk and experience. A breath of joyous life appeared to have passed over the house when they joined company with Aishah and they were not daunted by the presence of the Prophet in their merrymakings.

We have it on the authority of Aishah that once two girls were singing war songs of the battle of Badr in her house and the Prophet came and lay on bed for some time. At this stage, Abu Bakr arrived on the scene and reprimanded the girls. Thereupon the Prophet asked him to let the girls alone and they continued with their songs for some time.

A group of Abyssinians had arranged a display of war games and probably war dances on an Eid day, and Aishah stood behind the Prophet with her chin resting on his shoulder while the Prophet urged them on with encouraging words. Such displays and public performances must have been a good training ground for instilling in women a spirit of discipline and physical agility.

Women were taught reading and writing and we have it on the authority of Shifa bin Abdullah, a scholarly woman of the period, whom the Prophet visited frequently and often had his siesta at her house. Once the Prophet visited her and she was with Hafsa; thereupon he said, "Why did not you teach Hafsa the incantation for Namlah (minor swellings on the sides) as you had taught her writing."

It is remarkable that more specific injunctions and promises of higher rewards were held out specially in case of girls education. The Education of the boys was most probably a normal feature of the social life and the Prophet was more solicitous about women's Education because it was one of the most neglected spheres of social and cultural activity during that period.

The Companions of the Prophet were equally solicitous for the education of girls and Jabir stated in the presence of the Prophet that Abdulla his father, died leaving behind daughters of tender age and that he had married a widow for their instruction and training.

That the objective of women's education was not merely the raising of the sociai prestige of womanhood but it derived its sanction on account of an intense faith in human worth in general, is revealed by the traditions containing instructions on the education of the slave girls.

The chapter on Slaves of the same book contains instructions to one who owns a slave girl and how she should be educated and trained into an exemplary behaviour.

17

Co-education

It is not difficult to understand the attitude of Islam with regard to co-education, if one realises that its conception of sex equality is founded on a differentiation of functions as between men and women. Islam insists on married life both for men and women. It regards the home and domestic life as the natural and most important sphere of a woman's activity. It dislikes the free intermingling of men and women except under the strain of a serious emergency. It is, therefore, obvious that co-education is opposed to the whole tenor of Islamic teachings, because the system rests on presuppositions and postulates which are quite different.

Co-education is based on the assumption that there are no psychological and temperamental differences of any great consequence between man and woman, that after completing their education they have to pursue like careers and enter identical spheres of activity and that no sexual aberrations are likely to occur from the herding together of boys and girls in the same institution, or if they do occur, their consequences for, the stability of the family, the happiness of married life and the general character-formation of men and women are not serious enough to warrant social condemnation. All these assumptions are very questionable and since the modern education of girls has been mostly based on them, the results have been none too happy, as the following paragraphs will show.

Education for Upliftment

In the earlier phase of the movement for women's emancipation in England, the British feminists did not allow their aspirations to run amuck. They had a practicable and sane ideal of women's freedom which did not run counter to the fundamental traits of feminine nature. As early as 1864, Miss Emil Davies wrote in the *Year Book of Education:* 'We are not encumbered by theories about equality and inequality of mental powers in the sexes. All we claim is that the intelligence of women, be it great or small shall have full and free development. . . the object being the awakening and strengthening and adorning of the human spirit.' Totally different have been the ideas of later feminists whose educational and other ideals have fallen in the same line with men. Under the assumption that the female brain was capable of intellectual pursuits equal to the male, the modern educational system for girls is a copy of the educational system for boys. The results of this policy have been commented upon in the report of the committee appointed in England in 1923 to consider the differentiation of curricula between the sexes in secondary schools. The authors of the report remark: 'Basing their policy on the belief that girls could equal boys at least in intellectual matters if favourable conditions were afforded, the leaders of the (women's) movement implicitly assumed that what had been done for and by boys was in general suitable for both sexes.' A complete lack of feminine ideals and a thorough imitation of masculine ideals have been the most outstanding features of the educational system for girls.

To a considerable extent this defect in the education of girls is the outcome of co-education. When boys and girls are made to learn and receive their education under the same teachers and in the same schools, it is naturally difficult to give sufficient consideration to their psychological, emotional and temperamental differences and yet these differences are deep, abiding and all-pervading. Let us examine them one by one.

In his book entitled *The Psychology of Education*, Professor Wilton points out that while man lives by reason, woman's outlook is moulded and determined by feeling. 'She approximates the emotional temperament even when she does not show it in all its fulness. Intuition is a special quality of woman; and therefore she does not care for abstract thought. It is not that she does not generalise, but that she generalises without preparatory analysis.' He cites the example of sc eminent a woman as Hume de Sevique who acknowledged that 'abstract reasoning was repugnant to her.' Man, therefore, he points out, analyses and applies principles deductively, but a woman takes the special case and its value for feeling. The differences in the mental outlook of the sexes become, according to the observations of this author, clear from early life. A little girl of four is essentially a little girl; and a little boy, a little boy. The girl, says he, is precocious in speech, is less often troubled with stammering. Her play has not the force and expansion of movement which characterises the boy's: it is comparatively quieter and assumes a definite meaning.

Wilton sees intellectual distinctions also. Intellectual distinctions colour the learning of the two sexes as soon as the studies provide an opportunity for their respective intellectual qualities. Thus, girls do well in all that demands neither originality of thought nor abstraction. They, therefore, keep pace with the boys, or even surpass them, in the earliest school studies most of which are concerned with concrete wholes. They learn by heart with ease, take delight in neatness and in the embellishment of their written exercises, they work out with accuracy all detailed processes with the general form of which they are familiar or which they can imitate from example. They appreciate beauty of feeling and of form; and that is why study of literature has a special appeal to them, and they can show here more progress at an earlier age than what boys could do.

These mental and intellectual differences, says Wilton, are sadly ignored by the advocates and promoters of equal education to the sexes. He is, therefore, opposed to co-education. Boys and girls, he says, may be taught together in the same subjects only in the earliest age, say, up to ten years of age, because in these years 'the matter put before them gives little scope for their characteristically different modes of apprehension'. But the intellectual differences come into prominence with advance in age. Soon boys and girls begin to retard each other's progress, the girls being held back for slower boys in some subjects and, in their turn, impeding the advance of the boys in other subjects, So, different schools for the sexes with different curricula would seem to give the best intellectual results. And this, he says, is very marked out by my own somewhat extended observations.

One point, however, Wilton makes clear. It states that it must never be supposed that woman is an imperfectly developed man. That woman differs from man in intellect does not mean that she is in any way intellectually inferior to him. To deduce intellectual inferiority from woman's ineptitude for abstract thought is to apply a false standard to reach a wrong conclusion. 'Neither is inferior to the other. Each is essential to life; and in this difference of attitude, as in all that follows from it, man and woman are complementary. There is no question of superiority or inferiority: and any course of action based on the assumption that woman should try to become intellectually like man rests on a very insecure psychological foundation.'

Practical Aspects

Another ground on which Wilton proposes a different type of education for women is their functional difference from men. The functions of men and women, he says, are essentially distinct. Evolution does not mean the identification of sex qualities, but their more perfect mutual adaptation. 'Equality in value of complementary functions, not the obscuring of differences already established, is what the whole course of man's evolution leads us to expect.' In his book, *What Do We Mean by Education*, he sadly deprecates the tendency of the course of women's education which seeks to prepare them for various forms of professional and commercial life which, he points out, involves strenuous intellectual application during the years of adolescence and thus becomes trying on their nerves. In his opinion the present education on the same lines as that of males disturbs the nervous equilibrium of girls and thus injures their health. This breakdown of health may become serious in the rough and tumble of competitive examinations, and still more so when the competition is with boys.

In his book, *The Mixed School*, Howard comments on the psychology of women. Howard does not admit much intellectual difference between the sexes, but he lays special emphasis on temperamental difference. He says that boys are less emotional and more practical. The girls are more subjective in their outlook while the boys are more objective. Similarly, the girls are distinguished by greater passivity so that they are inclined to rely more on authority than on reason and argument. The girls have also a certain power of rapid intuition. They jump to conclusions all too easily and reason back from them to test their accuracy. Howard, therefore, advocates a different system of education for girls and boys. He bases his conclusion on the fact that girls are liable to fatigue more readily after puberty when the amount of haemoglobin in the blood becomes lessened. This fact, he says, is of far more importance than is generally believed. For this, he cites Dr. Adams who has summarised his observations as follows. Girls in general are (1) not so strong physically as boys; (2) highly strung and liable to nervous strain which possibly is associated with the fact that physiologically they are liable to heavier drains upon the circulating calcium of the blood, and (3) with their thinner blood with lowered haemoglobin content after puberty, they are nearer to the threshold of anaemia.

This consideration of her physiological aptitude, in the opinion of Howard, must weigh when laying down a particular system of education for girls. 'The sex-changes during adolescence are followed in the girl by recurring periods of strain when general efficiency may temporarily be impaired.' He, therefore, fears a risk of overstraining the girls through unsympathetic treatment at this period. Moreover, there is a definite risk which, in his opinion, may fail to do her abilities full justice at a moment when she specially needs it.

Howard, therefore, suggests that, as far as games and physical exercises are concerned, the sexes should be entirely separated as soon as their physical differences become significant. As regards intellectual education, first boys and girls may be separated for those subjects which are usually only studied by one sex; secondly, wider choice of optional subjects may be given in girls' schools; and, thirdly, overstrain on the part of the girl may be minimised by an easier optional subject.

Mrs. Dora Russell says in her book, *Hypatia*, 'Is there something wrong with the education of women and, if so, what? I think we must judge that there is. The reason lies in, the sense of inferiority bred in women by so much operation, and the natural result that their chief aim, as they struggled upwards, was to prove that they could jolly well do without men. This effort is mistaken. Each sex has that to give to the common stock which alone it can give, and robs itself and community by inferior imitation.... Feminist ideals of education, then, had the defect that they did in a certain measure deny sex or ignore it.'

That there is such a thing as a female mind is proved beyond doubt by psychologists. And this female mind requires a suitable education for its own culture and development, irrespective of what the corresponding standard is for men. As Dr. Rabindranath Tagore pertinently remarks in an article published in *The Nineteenth Century and After* (August 1927): 'If woman's nature were really the same as that of man, it would be a superfluity, a mere tautology.... If women acquire the view that sex' difference is only physical, and that mentally and spiritually they are of the same nature as men, and if they act on this assumption- (thus giving life a one-sidedly masculine form), then our civilisation would sink into utter confusion and chaos.'

Pros and Cons of Co-education : The most vital defect of co-education, from the point of view of female nature and woman's special functions in society, is that it prevents the training of woman for motherhood. How can a common educational institution run alike for boys and girls make adequate provision for training women in those arts and branches of knowledge which are necessary for her future life as a mother? Education for motherhood is the crying need of the world today. Because the vast majority of girls become mothers in after-life, every girl should be required to specialise for a definite time "in those subjects which will make her a good mother. When the whole curriculum of girls is hopelessly congested with subjects on the line of boys which cost them their mental equilibrium and physical health, their essential function in life is allowed to pass off in ignorance. Girls expected to manage somehow, without any adequate training, their function of motherhood on which in a great degree depends their own happiness and the preservation and welfare of the race. As a woman herself writes: 'The human mother gives poisonous mixture to her infant in place of Nature's food. She feeds its lungs with poisoned air in overheated, stuffy rooms, whilst its nervous and physical vitality is undermined by the noises and distractions of over-civilized life. Teach, train and direct instinct in women if you will, but supplement it with knowledge that is essential for child bearing in our social organization.'

Not only is there a thorough lack of training in maternity, but, on the contrary, that female education today incapacitates women for motherhood and marriage. It is because the strain of higher education is so enervating and exhausting that they cannot bear the strain of childbirth. Dr. Cyrn. Esdon has remarked on this point: 'Many educated women are so exhausted before marriage that after bearing one or two children they become wrecks.' Dr. Taylor writes very much in the same strain in his book, *The Nature of Women*. He says: 'This much we do know that probably at no other time in history has childbirth been so difficult, so unhealthily difficult, as now, and that this has manifested itself chiefly in the last fifty years, a period of increasing educational strain for girls.'

Similarly, Dr. Knealy writes in *Feminine and Sex Education:* 'When adolescent girls are strained by athletics, by over culture or industrial exhaustion, the vital resources are so diverted from the evolution of function as to cause incapacitation in them, partial or complete, for wifehood and for bearing of fine offspring.' Finally, the author of *Whither Woman*, Y.M. Rege, says:

> No feminist of however extreme views-can deny motherhood to be the flower of all woman's individuality, physical and psychical. If higher education on male lines has done anything wrong to women, it is this: it has by arresting the full development of her physique, by enervating her nerves, made her incapable of attaining the full growth of womanhood of which motherhood is the final symbol. There is no surprise that the graduates of English and American universities, with their physical energies sapped for any healthy reproduction, should come out in the world with a-maternal feelings and should try to cover this up with false pretentions that their unmarried state is due to their desire to devote their lives to some social service. It is really a pity that many a fine girlhood which, if

> spared of this overstraining education, would blossom into fine womanhood and would give real service to society by giving it healthy and vigorous children, is victimized under an entirely false and misguided idealism.

All these defects in the modern system of female education can be remedied if co-education is entirely given up, separate institutions for boys and girls are set up and, consistent with the special needs of each sex, two parallel systems of education and curricula of studies are evolved, so that the large mass of girls who are to be the future mothers of the race may receive preparatory training for their special calling. A limited number of women there will always be whose special gifts may entitle them to a different kind of education, but the interests of the many should not be sacrificed for the chosen few. And even these women of special gifts and endowments should not refuse the call of motherhood because they can reproduce and enlarge their gifts by becoming mothers. In a country which is backward like our own, there may be difficulties in obtaining the requisite number of female teachers for higher arts and branches of knowledge, but this difficulty does not tilt the scale in favour of co-education. Islam allows men and women of advanced age who have lost sexual attraction to mix with members of the other sex, under the stress of social or religious necessity. To prepare and train women teachers in the higher branches of knowledge, male teachers and professors of advanced age can be employed in sufficient numbers. When an adequate number of women have been trained, the need for even this amount of co-education will disappear.

18

Common System

Lighting arrangements were not necessary in the case of colleges because lectures at night were more an exception rather than the rule. But for the composite structure comprising a mosque and a college they were an important accessory of the equipment. They had a glamorous place in the celebration of certain festivals like the Lail-ul-Wuqud or the Night of Illuminations.

Lamp of enamelled glass were frequently used during the fourteenth century and came into vogue later on. These were either in the form of a truncated pyramid with a hook for hanging while the other was the lantern or the candelabra. These lamps were ornamented with inscriptions from the verses of the Quran and the names of the owner or his armorial bearings.

The chandeliers for lighting purposes were very often marvellous combination of aesthetic taste and utility and the more important institutions were provided with a generous supply of them. They were mostly used on festive occasions and specially during the fasting month with its night vigils and religious activities. About 400 A.H., large candelabras were made in Egypt which were called Tanvees or stove on account of their shape which resembled an oven.

Some of these *tanvees* were constructed on a magnificent scale and one which was ordered by Al-Hakim for the mosque of 'Amr' cost 100,000 dirhams of silver and was so huge that the doors of the mosque had to be widened in order to admit it. Al-Hakim, that large hearted Macaena of his age had presented three silver tanavees and thirty nine chandeliers made of silver to the foundations constructed by him out of which two tanvees and twenty seven chandeliers were specifically meant for Al-Azhar and one tanvees and twelve chandeliers for the Friday mosque of Rashidah, with the condition that they were to be used during the month of Ramadan only and returned to the store after the fasting period was over. The candlesticks used in Al-Azhar and other places were made of silver and sometimes of gold.

The festivals and ceremonial occasions were celebrated with illuminations on a magnificent scale. On the Night of Illumination, 18000 candles were made for the mosque of Amr and eleven and half a kintar of good oil was used.

Ibn Zubayr describes how the Khatm (Completion of Quran reading) ceremony of a boy belonging to a well-to-do family was observed in the holy Sanctuary of Mecca. The whole Sanctuary appeared to be a blaze of light. The chief feature of the decoration were four trees made in wax while candles were arranged in a circle on the rim of a spacious basin.

While beauty and magnificence was the prominent feature of lightening arrangement in the college mosque those used in the individual cells of the hostel were examples of severe simplicity and the student working late in the night had to plod through his books in the flickering light of the humble earthen lamp which was in most cases without a glass globe. Sheikh Abdul Haq, of Delhi narrates how sometimes he lost himself so completely in his books that his lock of hair which hung over the flame of the lamp caught fire and he won't realise it until it singed his skin. In the earliest period the pupils found considerable difficulties in providing for themselves adequate lighting arrangements.

There were students who would study in the light of the mosque's lamp in a standing position for hours at a stretch, others would try to study in the flickering light of the lantern carried by the night watch in the streets. With the establishment of the colleges the pupils were ensured these facilities and in some institutions they received their ration for oil regularly. In some cases endowments were made in favour of particular individuals for lighting facilities.

The Infrastructure

Kursi was a composite structure made of a desk and a seat on which the reader could sit cross legged. They were specially meant for the Readers of the Quran. Ibn Zubayr remarks how he visited a mosque where the preacher spoke from the *mimbar* (pulpit) and the readers of Quran who always preceded the preacher in the programme were seated on teak wood *Kursis* for recitation.

Some of these old world *Kursis* were marvellous pieces of workmanship and taste. Briggs gives a reproduction of some of the inlaid and carved *Kursis* with the name of the owner inscribed on the top.

Instead of seats and desks the audience used to take their places on the floor which was covered which mattress. There were more than one variety of these and a warm covering was used for the winter season.

Ibn Tulun, for instance had floored his mosque with Abbadanian and Samanian mats. In some cases there was a rich padding of mats one above the other the mosque of Amr at Cairo containing ten layers of carpets, one above the other.

The mattresses were changed at least every year. In the mosque of Mecca they were renewed every Ramadan while in the Mosque of Jerusalem, 800,000 cubits of carpets were used every year. The annual budget of Al-Azhar contained a regular item for the annual replacement of the mattresses. The budget of Al-Hakim's Academy at Cairo provided ten dinars for abbadanian mattress, five for felt carpets for winter and four for the covering in summer.

In some cases the founder gave the institution a magnificent carpet as a free gift for the celebration of the inaugural ceremony and other functions. The Taybariyyah College which was close to Al-Azhar and whose generous hearted founder had washed all the account books containing the expenditure incurred on the college in water so that none might knew what he had spent in the name of the Lord, had a carpet with patterns of arches worked into it. The carpet was used only on Fridays.

Sometimes, these carpets were presented by persons other than the founder. When the building of the Iqbaghaviyyah college was completed the Muhtasib of Cairo who aspired to be the Head of the Institution made the costly-gift of a carpet priced at 8000 dinars to the Collage. Chests were used also for storing of lamps, for the Bait-ul-Mal or the property and for keeping rose-wreaths; they were in charge of a special attendant.

The craftsmen of the Islamic world gave evidence of wonderful skill and artistic talent in making these chests.

One of these chests specially prepared for the Caliph Abdul Momin of West Africa was manipulated mechanically and was worked with the help of a key. As soon as the key was turned its sides opened out and a case emerged from inside which contained a *Kursi* and a *Rihl* as a rest for the Quran. The rest would open out automatically and the sides closed by themselves. When the key was turned in the opposite direction, the sides opened out once again and the *Kursi* (seat) and the book rest were drawn inside while the sides closed over them.

Water Supply : The water supply was mainly needed for two purposes, the ablutions and drinking. As mosques and colleges were buildings of public utility, they formed sometimes a nucleus of more than one charitable foundation and some of them had facilities of drinking water for beasts and also cisterns for washing purposes.

The supply of drinking water was provided either by a cistern in the middle of the courtyard often covered with a marble pavilion resting on graceful columns which had a permanent supply from a reservoir and the water was led through lead pipes as observed by Ibn Zubayr at Damascus or it was stored in pitchers made of iron or other material which was iced in certain cases.

The ablutions were made either at the central cistern in case it was not reserved for drinking purposes or at the ablution place.

The mosque-colleges had a Midaa, a place of ablution which had a regular supply of water in most cases. Sometimes the ablutions were made at the central cistern, a common usage in the East at present, but in other countries a special place was set aside for this purpose. Ibn Jamaah gives specific instructions to the pupils for the use of the ablution place and bath rooms which were generally adjacent to them.

The Al-azhar had more than one such places. There was a variety of means and methods for ensuring an adequate supply of water in the college building. Where ever water was easily available the supply to the public institutions was generous and abundant.

According to Yaqut, he did not come across and mosque college or monastery in the town of Damascus which did not have water flowing into a birka or cistern in the courtyard.

Ibn Zubayr has given a delightful description of the water supply in the college of Nuruddin Zangi at Damascus. The college was located in a well planned and graceful edifice which contained also the tomb of the founder. The building was as magnificent as a royal place. It contained a fountain and the water of the fountain collected in a reservoir from where it flowed into a channel which passed right through the building. The entire layout was amazingly beautiful.

The college contained a number of dormitories for the mystics. They were styled as Khanqah. These were very graceful and each of them had a supply of running water. The mystics lived with princely ease in these quarters.

But even in countries where water supply was not so abundant, the founders tried to ensure an adequate provision of water supply which had not only a hygienic, but also a religious importance.

Ibn Tulun whose splendid mosque at Cairo once comprised a college on its precincts had constructed an aqueduct which was supplied from a deep well on the slopes of the Muqattam Hills and the water was raised by means of a Saqiyah.

Al-Nasir, a Turkish Mameluke Sultan of Egypt who built colleges at Cairo and in Palestine constructed an arched aqueduct leading from the Nile to the citadel in Cairo in 1311.

Amir Tankaz who constructed a splendid college adjacent to the Western Rawaq of the mosque of Al-Aqsa, laid out an aqueduct for the city of Jerusalem. It led up to the middle of the mosque of Aqsa and a tank was constructed for storing purposes between the Dome of the Rock and Al-Aqsa.

Water supply provided several opportunities for reconciling art and utility. Fountains at work were often the most relieving feature of the courtyard which provided an elegant break in its spacious emptiness. Ibn Zubayr mentions a number of mosques which contained such fountains. The mosque of Umayyids at Damascus contained three Cupolas, the central one resting on marble columns, below it was a basin with a spring of drinking water surrounded by an iron grille which was called a water cage.

Many colleges in Egypt had Sabil Kuttab attached to them. It was a composite building comprising an elementary school which formed in many cases an inalienable adjunct of the college and a drinking fountain. The Sabil Kuttab attached to the Qait Bey College and the mosque of Al-Ghoury at Cairo are fine specimen of this kind of structure according to Saladin.

The Sabil contains a small fountain on the ground floor in a richly decorated room. The school which is constructed on the first floor is sheltered in a pent house with joinery work which projects out and is highly graceful and delicate. The composite building comprising the fountain and the small school is named "Sabil-Kuttab ". A number of colleges at Cairo including those built by women founders had such fountain-schools attached to them. A reproduction of the fountain at the college of Umus Sultan at Cairo is given by Saladin.

The water supply arrangements had a prominent place in the celebration of college functions. The central birka or basin was filled with sugar lemonade or other sweet drink on the inaugural day for public use. Maqrizi mentions a number of such occasions when common people celebrated the occasion by drinking to the welfare and prosperity of the college.

Turkish Baths : Like the Romans, baths in the Islamic world were not meant primarily for physical cleanliness, they functioned as places of social gathering. Mulla Sadruddin Shirazi made his first acquaintance with a great teacher when he was visiting a bath at Asfahan. They were means of good income for the owner and a savant under the Osmanides had a bath which yielded, him a rich profit.

A number colleges in Egypt and Syria were endowed with baths attached to them. They were a source of income like the booth shops, and the market places which very often formed a part of the endowed property. But the baths must have been of a more direct and immediate use for the students than these.

The Zahiriyya College built by Salahuddin at Damascus had the Zahiriyya bath attached to it. A number of colleges in Egypt and Syria contained baths and one of them, the Badhaiyyah College had two, one to the East and another to the West of the College building. Other institutions which contained baths were the Qaimariyya College, and the Azrawiyyah College with the well known bath called the Dar-al-Saadat. One of the ancient Baths adjacent to the Zahiriyya College at Damascus is extant still.

Collection of Books

The Islamic world had some of the most magnificent libraries the world has ever seen, both public and private, which were not only renowned for their rich collections but also for their organisation and general management.

The free and easy accessibility of the books in a public library is as much important as the intrinsic worth of its collections and there was a generous provision of such facilities in at least the more outstanding libraries of the Islamic world and it was through these means that they became dynamic institutions of informal education for the public and rich and inspiring treasures for the learned.

There were no restrictions on the study or the copying of manuscripts while in some cases paper and other stationary requirements were supplied gratis to the reader. Very often the libraries transformed themselves into learned academies and workshops for authors. When Hakim bi Amrillah established his House of Learning in Egypt, he appointed a number of juriconsults, physicians, logicians and mathematicians, who were to pursue their special branch of study on the premises and create an atmosphere of love for knowledge and learning.

The founder took a keen interest in the establishment and paid frequent visits to the library. The Egyptian Caliph often invited scholars to his library for a debate held in his presence while Nizam-ul Mulk also paid visits to the library of his college when free of official duties. But this chapter will be confined to a study of those libraries and collections, which were either attached to the college or located in their precincts and accessible to the teachers and their pupils.

The library or the Treasury of books as it was styled, was located in one of the wings of the Nizamiyya College and Nizam-ul Mulk endowed the library with a rich collection of manuscripts. As the great vazier was well known for his love of learning, he often received books which came to him as gifts or dedicated volumes and he invariably presented them to the Nizamiyya Library.

The Library of the Mustansiriyya was richly endowed by the founder and one hundred and sixty camel loads of books were transferred from the palace Library to the College for this purpose.

Very often, the donors took special care in appointing distinguished scholars as librarians or Khazins. These institutions functioned as learned academies and meeting ground of savants for discussions and debates and served very often as retiring places for the cultured donor when he could gleen some hours from his busy life. The donor took care to provide the librarians a handsome remuneration for their services.

Nizam-ul-Mulk appointed the famous scholar Abu Zakaria Razi as the Librarian of Nizamiyya, who was rather fond of good living and when the Khawajah came to know of his high standard of life, he doubled his remuneration. Razi was succeeded by another distinguished scholar Yaqub bin Sulaiman Isfraini as the Librarian of the college. Every great college had a library attached to it and sometimes more than one library were built up and endowed by latter benefactors on the premises of an old institution. A new Library was erected by the Caliph Nasir bi Dinillah in the Nizamiyya, which was endowed with a rich collection of books from the palace Library.

We meet also traces of the seminar system but the books were not distributed among the various departments or sections of the college, but were placed in the various rawaqs or nations in which the hostels were organised. The library system of Al-Azhar was organised on this system from old days and it was as recent as 1314 A.H. when the authorities recalled the books for the purpose of establishing a central library and even then all the books were not returned and some of the Rawaqs or Hostels insisted upon retaining a separate seminar for themselves.

It appears that in the beginning the kings and the aristocracy were chiefly interested in establishing public libraries, but with the opening of the colleges, their enthusiasm was diverted to these seats of learning and they took more interest in the college libraries. In the earlier days scholars met together in the public libraries which served the purpose of a literary club for the Elect. Abu Zaid the hero of Hariri's Muqamat comes across a group of dilettante in the public library of Halwan which was the council hall of scholars and the meeting place of residents and strangers.

Although private collections were extremely popular and found abundantly all over the Islamic world, the public libraries with the exception of those attached to certain mosques were few and far between. But the advent of the colleges and specifically the foundation of the Nizamiyya group of colleges helped considerably in propagating the library idea and in no time the Islamic world or to be more exact, its Eastern parts were covered with a network of libraries. Nizam-ul Mulk had issued a general decree that wherever there was a distinguished savant in the Islamic countries, his scholarship should be recognised by the foundation of a college and a library.

By the time of Yaqut Hamawi, the college libraries appear to be a more universal feature of the intellectual life than the public library. The colleges had turned into resting houses for the wandering scholar, who was sure of a hospitable welcome and good company on the precincts of a college. We know how abundantly Yaqut made use of the splendid collections in the college libraries at Marw. These libraries helped him in completing the major portion of his geographical compendium.

The endowments were mostly made by great vaziers, the collection of books in the Nizamiyya college library at Marw being the gift of the illustrious founder. At least one of these libraries had been founded by a woman. They were rich treasures and one of them contained two hundred volumes costing two hundred Dinars apiece.

19

Boarding Facility

The organisation of hostel life in the palmy days of Islam has a special significance for those interested in the development of University education in the West. The influence crossed over to the Continent from Sicily where a high intellectual life had been cultivated by the Arab teachers. The findings of Aman and other orientalists reveal the deep influence which the Islamic institutions had on the evolution of higher learning in Europe. Words like Baccalaureate, Alma Mater and others tell the tale of this age-long influence.

The hostel life of medieval Universities like those of Bologna and Paris was organised on lines radically different from the monastic and cloistered life of the medieval monks. The origin of this great change is traceable to the influence from the Orient. The experiment in cooperative living which began in the Islamic Institutions of higher learning was not organised as a convenience, it functioned as a vital educative force in the building up of the students personality and social attitudes.

The rules and regulations of the hostel life do not insist so much upon the rights and privileges of the individual as on his duties and obligations to the social group. They were inspired with a democratic regard for the rights of others, a deep reverence for scholarship and a profound respect for the terms of the Waqf Deed. A section of those regulations, which aims at a better integration of hostel and college life was a logical sequence of the close proximity of the hostels to the college building, very often one and the same building serving the purpose of the hostel and the college.

Hostel Rules

The hostels formed a part of a composite plan which often included a mosque, a mausoleum and a college. The sanctity attached to these buildings naturally had a restrictive influence on the freedom of the students.' The social code expected exemplary standards of moral and cultural life from the member of the learned profession. As a large number of the members of the staff and chance visitors lived in the hostel, the pupils had to be all the more careful in their movements and general behaviour. In spite of the squalor and dirt outside, the standard of cleanliness in the mosque was always and everywhere above reproach and it had a healthy influence on the general standards maintained in hostel life.

The hostels were often two storeyed buildings. The rooms on the first floor were much sought after by the diligent pupil for secluded application to his studies. According to Khatib, the garret was the choicest place for memory work.

The ground floor was reserved for the weak and the old. One of the duties often performed by the teachers was the issue of the Fatwa or religious decrees, on debatable points. In some cases there was a special functionary in the staff for this purpose and the work was entrusted usually to the professor of Fiqh (Law) in the institution. Such persons were expected to reside on the ground floor as they were constantly in demand and had a large number of visitors.

The hostels with two storeys had more than one stair case, one leading from the main gateway or the passage to the second storey and the other opening out into the courtyard of the college. The second staircase was reserved for the use of the teachers who could have an easy access to their rooms and could proceed directly from their lecturing chambers to their residential quarter. The supervision of the hostel must have been the duty of those teachers who resided there and the various regulations concerning the relationship of the elderly residents and the pupils reveal that some members of the staff lived in the hostel: some of them stayed with their families.

The hostels like the colleges were cosmopolitan and often attracted pupils from different parts of the Islamic world. The main function of the hostel life was to stimulate in this incongruous mass a group consciousness and cultivate social and moral values demanded by religion and society. Books on Education prescribe instructions on hostel life and specially the maintenance of good relations with other residents of the hostel. According to Ibn Jamaah "It is incumbent upon him to greet fellow residents, express his love and respect for them. He should safeguard the right of neighbourliness, companionship and religious and professional brotherhood."

> "He should overlook their mistakes of omission and commission and guard their secrets. He should render them thanks for the good and forgive them the evil that they do."

The educational institutions were mostly located in crowded thoroughfares and the compactness of structure and lack of space often demanded a strict regulation of hostel life in certain aspects. Its nature is revealed in those minute and detailed instructions which Ibn Jamaah gives on various aspects of the day to day life in the hostel. There were rules for the use of residential rooms on the first floor, the use of staircase, the college gate the courtyard and the place of ablution. Another set of instructions deals with peeping through the doors, pointing towards windows and unclothing.

The pupil was expected not to eat anything while walking, not to move with a swagger or raise the chest like a bravado, indulge in outbursts of laughter and climb on the roof which commands a view of the neighbourhood without purpose.

The pupil had to observe certain rules as regards his movements outside the college hostel.

He was strictly prohibited from frequenting places of suspected reputation and resorts of irreligious nature. He was not permitted to lodge in his room a person who disliked the residents and carried their tales outside, indulged in calumnies or one who interfered with their education and enticed them away into other pursuits. A handsome student or a child was not allowed to stay in the hostel without a proper guardian.

It seems that the hostels had women residents also in some cases. According to Jamaah, women could not reside in those rooms whose door opened on to a passage frequented by men or had a window which commanded a view of the college courtyard.

The pupils also were not permitted to seat themselves in the passage frequented by women who were in any way connected with the college.

There was obviously no provision for recreational activities in the hostel and the pupils had to seek their pastimes and pleasures outside the precincts of the college. Popular resorts were the gardens outlying the town, the banks of a neighbouring stream, the ante-chambers of a hath.

Within the college campus, the courtyard of the mosque could be used in the afternoon for recitation of poetry and discussion on stray topics while gateways which usually opened out into a busy market place supplied a colourful panorama of the town-life.

The students would often seat themselves on the gateway in order to relax themselves after their studies. In the case of some colleges the gateways were magnificent structures with provision for seating accommodation. Ibn Batuta would often seat himself on the gateway of the Nizamiyyah, Baghdad and meet chance visitors.

The students were discouraged from seating themselves on the gate or in the passage except when needed. Writers on education recognise the need for relaxation and permit the use of the gateway for seating purposes in case one is feeling out of spirits and is disconsolate.

Whenever young spirits congregate, strong likes and dislikes were bound to arise. Sheikh Saadi, who was a stipendiary at the Nizamiyya College once complained to his teacher Ibn Jauzi of the jealousy of his companions. His teacher curtly told him how keenly he had observed the mote in others eyes but could not discover the beam in his own. While he complained of the jealous temperament of others, he did not realise what a terrible back-biter he was.

The pupils were enjoined to make due allowance for the failings of others and in case of differences, they were instructed to retire and contemplate over the matter in calmer moments. But on no account were they advised to transfer themselves to another college because frequent change of institutions was not advisable in the case of beginners.

The proximity of the hostel with the college building could prove a serious source of distraction for the students and the pupils were exhorted to be singleminded in their study while in *Majlis* or the *Halqa.* There were set of regulations for checking the tendency of frequently leaving the class group and going into the rooms. The pupils were instructed to keep to their room during college hours when not attending lectures and not to make frequent excursions to their room during a discourse in case they were attending lectures. They were positively discouraged from inviting outsiders during college hours. They were enjoined not to stroll in front of a class group and also not to take their constitutional in the courtyard of the college.

The Setup

The organisation of hostel life and administration in Al-Azhar provides an example *par excellence* of the residential arrangement in case of colleges planned on an ambitious scale. The present day university building and the campus of Al-Azhar is the outcome of an organic growth and continuous development.

As planned originally by Jawhar the Fatimide general, it was a congregational mosque without any residential facilities. It was the Caliph Al-Aziz Billah, who raised a hostel adjacent to the mosque for residential purposes which must have provided ample accommodation for the thirty-five persons attached to the mosque in the beginning. He also granted stipends payable in cash.

But gradually as need arose, further accessions were made to the original plan and more hostels were constructed along with accessories like baths, ablution places and kitchens. All these structures were closely connected with the central mosque and all the buildings form such a self contained unit that the pupil has on no account any necessity of going outside the portals of the University and can spend the whole of his academic life within its precincts.

The internal organisation of the hostel was planned on the basis of "nations" or separate hostels for various nationals from the earliest days. According to Miqrizi this system was introduced from the earliest days, as early as the year 818 A.H. the necessitous pupils who numbered 750 were divided into four groups, the people of Ajam, Zialah, Riff in Misr and North Africa and each group had its own Rawaq which was named after them.

The organisation appears to be similar with that obtaining in the Universities stadium of Bologna or other medieval universities. At Bologna, the students were divided into the cis-alpine and the Trans-alpine block while there was a Spanish college for students hailing from the Iberian Peninsula. The University of Paris which was essentially a Teachers' guild as opposed to the student's guild contained 'nations' for students belonging to various nationalities.

The history of medieval universities is tense with a struggle for power between the teachers' and pupils' organisations. In fact, as most of the universities had to start from the scratch without any encouragement from the state or support from the public, universities had to levy fees on the pupils in order to provide subsistence for the teachers and there was a widespread feeling amongst the students that one who paid the piper should call the tune. Moreover they demanded special rights and privileges similar to those conceded in the case of the clergy.

But the tendencies which gave rise to a tussle between the teachers and their pupils in the West did not exist in the institutions of the Islamic world. They were richly, endowed institutions in the majority of cases and the endowments were amply sufficient to provide the salaries of the teachers and the full maintenance charges of the necessitous pupils. The question of fees, never arose. The clergy did not exist as a class in Islam, hence one and all enjoyed equal rights of citizenship and were responsible for the performance of the obligations imposed upon them as a citizen of an Islamic State.

Even today the hostels of Al-Azhar were classified into "Rawaqs" or "Nations" which signify a furnished hostel with residential quarters and accessory buildings. The residential rooms in these institutions were generally cubicles reserved for single students but in case there was a rush for admissions, two or more pupils were assigned to a single cubicle. Rooms in the Al-Azhar hostels contain wardrobes for clothes and books. They were floored with mattress which was changed every six months.

The administration of the Rawaqs was organised on democratic principles and the residents of the Rawaq elect their own Sheikh, who looks after their extra-curricular interests, settles their disputes, safeguards their rights and privileges and functions as their representative with the Head of Al-Azhar. Normally the pupils live in the Rawaqs, but in case there was a rush of pupils, they were allowed to stay outside the university, but they receive their daily rations and stipends from the Rawaq to which they are attached.

The Rawaqs serve, more or less the purpose of a residential Hall in a modern university combined with college Bursary. Attached to these Rawaqs were Haras which may be likened to reading rooms because they do not contain any suite of retiring rooms.

The teachers and the pupils of the university were divided into two classes for purposes of financial assistance.

The first group comprises the teaching staff and those pupils who receive stipends in the form of cash payments. The second group includes the teachers and those pupils who receive meals and a suit of clothes in certain seasons of the year.

As regards, residence, the hostels were classified in two main groups, those meant for the Egyptians and others which were reserved for the non-Egyptians. Out of the Egyptian Rawaqs, two were specifically reserved for the Hanbalites and the Hanafites while one of them was serving as a hostel for the blind. The more important of the non-Rawaqs are for the students belonging to Hijaz, Syria, Iraq, North Africa, Sudan, Turkey, Yemen, Kurdistan, Indo-Pak region, Afghanistan and Indonesia.

Various Facilities

The period may be divided roughly into the early, the middle, and the later stage as regards the provision of boarding facilities.

In the earliest period there was no organised system for providing board and lodging and the pupils had to meet considerable difficulties in making these arrangements. But the tempo of student life and the pupils' attitude towards this aspect of their educational life was determined by the sayings of the Prophet, and the precepts and the life of the teachers. They enjoin a discipline of the most rigorous nature in the pursuit of learning.

The second stage was introduced with the first beginnings of an organised system of colleges and the provision of simple and adequate facilities for board. The third period was that of plenty and pelf when wealthy philanthropists and large hearted rulers vied with one another in founding colleges and making princely arrangements for that purpose.

Authorities on education rule out sumptuous meals for students on account of their adverse influence on the intellectual growth of the pupil. A certain class of victuals was condemned because it had a baneful effect on memory and intellect. They advocated also moral and religious reasons for abstemiousness and moderation in meals.

The economic factors also influenced the provision of such facilities to a considerable extent. In the early period industrial and economic life was yet to be developed and organised.

With the expansion of the dominions, and the growth of peace and prosperity, ampler economic means became available for establishing the educational system on a sound economic basis.

The Islamic educational system primarily aimed at the development of the religious and cultural aspects of personality and although the physical aspect was not ignored yet sumptuous food was not approved in the case of the pupils for more than one reason.

In the early period, plain living and high thinking was the guiding principle of student life. The pupil was enjoined upon to take precaution from gorging himself with food and books on education supply a rich variety of sayings and instructions on the subject. According to Jesus Christ, 'make your lives devoid of food and your bodies of clothes so that your hearts may look upon the Heavenly Vision'. According to the Prophet, man never Stuffed up a worse receptacle than his stomach.' 'Man thinks that eating would straighten up his back. But if he can manage, he should fill up one third of his stomach with food, the second with drink and should keep the last free from respiration.'

Injunctions like these were taken in right earnest and most of the students accepted the rigorous discipline as an essential part of their educational life. They were not daunted in their pursuit of learning by the danger of dire privations and starvation. There were pupils who eke out existence on one loaf daily. Hajjaj of Baghdad, the famous traditionist set forth on his educational travel with hundred loaves prepared by his mother and used to take one loaf daily. The hard crust offered stubborn resistance and he had to soften it by moistening it with the water of Tigris. The great Imam Bukhari had to subsist on the roots found in the forest for three days at a stretch when he was stranded in his travels. Another savant lived on the leaves of beetroot as a student.

Cheap rates and simpler standards of living among the masses helped the poor scholar to pay his way easily during his educational career. Imam Barqani left his home with three dinars and a dirham; the gold dinars parted company during the journey and he was left with a single dirham which he deposited with the baker who continued to supply him with two loaves daily for a month.

In the absence of a well organised system of colleges with boarding facilities, the students in the early period met considerable difficulties in arranging for their meals but it could not damp their enthusiasm for learning. Memories of these trials were cherished as the privileges and triumphs of student life.

According to Ibn Ali Hatim (d. 327 A. H.) he and his companion stayed for seven months in Egypt but had not a single opportunity to prepare curry for want of time. They attended lectures of various teachers in the day and copied manuscripts and collated them at night. He relates how once they had a vacant period as one of the teachers had fallen ill; he and his fellow students made haste to purchase a fish from the bazar, but as soon as they returned with the purchase to their house, it was high time for attending the lecture of other teachers. So they went out again and they had hardly any time to eat it for three days when it went bad. So they ate it up raw because they could get no time to fry the fish.

But this does not imply that pupils and teachers subsisted on coarse and scanty meals as a penance.

Good food was always welcomed and was a regular feature of the special feasts held on festival days or on ceremonial occasions. The savants justify the luxury of a sumptuous feast by quoting those verses of the Quran which enjoin on the faithful to avail fully of all the blessings which God had bestowed on man. And the later period gave them plenty of opportunities for the purpose.

In case of the more outstanding institutions, the menu of the dining table could be described as sumptuous. In the Mustansariyya College of Baghdad, the pupils were provided with a sweet drink and fruit besides daily rations.

Ibn Batuta who had frequently enjoyed the hospitality of these colleges during his travels relates how in a college at Tastar four courses were laid in addition to sweet dish which was served at the end.

Firoz Tughlaq the Sultan of Delhi in the thirteenth century had founded a college at the Metropolis and a teacher of the college had celebrated the sumptuousness of the feasts given in the college in verse.

He describes the variety of fowl, fish and mutton provided in the college with dessert of dry fruit like almond and pomegranate. The dinner was dressed up with perfumes of sandal wood, saffron and musk. There were two varieties of almond cakes, dry and wet while there was a special variety of baked bread. The feasts of the period had a course of Sherbet and two varieties of cook drinks were provided in the college. When the dinner was over the guests were served with betel leaves in plates of gold and silver.

And in a college at Bijapur, meat pulao was a daily feature of the menu, a dish which is served not more than once at the dining tables of college hostels at present.

The pupils were advised not to partake of the meals in the bazar or frequent hotels and eat in the presence of others. The practice of bringing meals from the bazar and partaking it at the residence was also disapproved as they were prepared under insanitary conditions.

The father of Imam Muhammad bin Fazl used to visit him every Friday and brought provisions which lasted for a week. Once he found a piece of baker's bread in his room and was so much annoyed that he did not exchange a single word with him on that day. When Imam Muhammad came to know of the cause of his irritation he preferred profuse excuses and told him that it had been brought to his room by a friend of his.

Medical Aid Facilities

The period of great colleges synchronises with the advent of Maristans (public Hospitals) in the Islamic world and there appears to have been adequate arrangements for medical advice and treatment for the pupils and teachers in the colleges or outside them. The Mustansiriyya college had a hospital attached to it and the building was situated on the campus of the institution.

The college needed a hospital in close vicinity more specifically than other institutions because it was in most cases endowed with a chair of Medicine and a hospital was a necessary corollary for purposes of practical demonstration.

In fact these chairs of Medicine along with a staff of assistant teachers must have provided ample facilities for medical advice in the case of the pupils because in most cases the department formed an organic part of the whole college and the pupils following purely academic studies had a claim for consultation and attention upon the members of the sister department. According to Ibn Zubayr, there was a hospital in Alexandria, which was specifically meant for students and aliens, who were staying in the colleges or inns. The hospital contained, a number of physicians and there was a large staff of medical attendants for nursing and feeding the patients.

A special class of attendants was appointed to visit those patients, who were too ill to attend the hospital in person at their residence and prescribe for them in consultation with the physicians.

The physician class as a whole seemed to entertain a kindly regard for the student body. It is related that Aminud Daula, the chief of the physicians in Baghdad under the Caliph Mustadhi, who resided next to the Nizamiyyah would take the ailing students of the college to his own house, a house which often served as a nursing home for ruling princes, tended them with the greatest care and after they had regained their health, sent them back with a gift of two dinars each, obviously for the celebration of their recovery.

The members of the medical profession in general and its outstanding personalities in particular had a keen interest in education and those engaged in the pursuit of learning. Muhiyy-ud-din, the chief of Physicians in Egypt had established more than one college with chairs of medicine and it can be safely assumed that when the top ranking men in the profession were keenly interested in education, the pupils were not denied the best medical advice available in those days.

Each collection of the Prophet's traditions contains a chapter on medicine and the students were expected to know the treatment of common ailments as professed by the Prophet. They were advised to keep with them a book named Tib-un Nabi edited specially for this purpose by Imam Mustaghfari.

Special Arrangements

The college hostels often functioned as a guest house for distinguished scholars and students who chanced to visit the town on their grand tours. It was a part of educational etiquette for the wandering scholar to pay a courtesy call on the distinguished savants of the towns. They received free board and lodging in the hostels or monastery schools. Ibn Batuta had several opportunities to avail of the generous hospitality of these institutions during his travels.

According to him at every stage of the high roads in Asia Minor there was a monastery or a college where every traveller received food for himself and fodder for his ride. In the country of Tastar the expenses were defrayed from the income of the royal endowments, one third of the revenue having been earmarked for educational purposes.

Similar facilities were afforded in the centres of those socio-political organisations called the Akhi (Les freres).

The usage of staying in college hostels is hallowed by great names. The father of Maulana Jalaluddin Rumi stayed in the boarding house of the Halawiyyah college at Allepo and when the Maulana proceeded to Damascus he took his abode in one of the colleges in the town.

In fact scholars maintained a life long association with academic life even after they had discarded the profession for the career of a diplomat or a minister.

When Ibn Khaldun went on a peace mission to Timurlane who was besieging in those days the town of Damascus, he stayed at the Adibiyyah College in the town along with other Faqihs and Ulama.

Ibn Qadi Baalbak, who was appointed as chief of the physicians and surgeons and oculists in Damascus in 637 A.H. used to live in the residential rooms in the Qalijiyyah college and studied during his stay books on Fiqh, literature, Exegesis and Quran readings.

20

Teaching Devices

Text book had an important place in the educational system because the educational career was initiated by the study of Al-kitab (The Book) or the Quran and was followed by a study of the Traditions. In both the subjects the text formed a significant feature of the learning process. The copying of manuscripts, collation and correction of punctuation formed itself a part of the pupil's education.

Textbooks

The preparation of text books was a normal feature of the teachers, programme, some of whom would set apart one third of the night to the task of authorship. Again the very method of teaching, the Imla or the Dictation method provided opportunities for the preparation of a text book because in this case authorship was transformed into a cooperative effort between the teacher and the taught and the text was constantly revised or amplified in the light of the pupils' needs and remarks during the period of its composition.

The teachers were expected to prepare text books only when they had attained intellectual maturity and when they had the scholarship and professional eminence needed for the responsible task of authorship. One advantage in writing books was that it led him to research and investigate, enquire into and check references. According to Khatib Baghdadi it makes the capacity of memory more lasting, purges the mind, sharpens intellect and adorns the power of expression.

According to the writers on education, the subject for the composition of books was of universal interest and such as was commonly needed by the pupil. He should make the best of efforts in order to write in a clear and lucid style and he should abstain from a style involving sickening prolixity or exasperating brevity.

The book in no case was released for publication before correction, re-edition and revision.

Preparation of Text books : In the majority of cases, the teachers were stimulated to compose a text book in order to meet the requirements of their pupils, the inner urge of presenting their own view point or the desire of gaining a name in the academic world. The original was meant to be an authoritative volume on the topic while he would prepare sometimes an abbreviated text for the use of the pupils. In this case the lecture work and explanation by the teacher made amends for its brevity desirable in the case of a text book on account of the labour involved in copying. The commentaries were generally prepared by the pupils.

Sometimes the book was prepared at the request of a pupil and there were instances when a teacher made such a request to a pupil. Sometimes a ruling prince was instrumental in preparing a text book for general use or for the immediate use of a younger member of the royal family.

A scholar often draws the attention of the prince to the need of a better text book in a particular subject. Averroes was requested to prepare a book on the works of Aristotle when Ibn Tufail suggested to the king the need of presenting Aristotle's writings in an easy and more comprehensible manner.

In the absence of any publishing agencies, the authors had to devise means for the circulation of their works. In spite of the limited means of communications it can be affirmed that the exchange of books and ideas in the Islamic world, was quicker and more easy in those days.

The Dictation method and the usage of Ijazah was the most educational and popular method for publishing a text book. The copies of the work as dictated by the author to his pupils were countersigned by the author and the pupil was given an Ijazah (authority) to teach the work.

Teachers in affluent circumstances used to order copies of their works and send them abroad as presents. They were mostly sent to important centres of intellectual and religious life in the Islamic world.

Rich authors gave endowments to ensure publication facilities for their works on a permanent basis. Rashiduddin Fazlullah (d. 718 A. H.) the minister of the Tatar Ilkhanis had founded a waqf in his university town of Raba Rashidi which he had founded near Tabriz. The proceeds of its income, were to be utilised for the preparation of two copies of his monumental work, Jami-al-Tawarikh, one in Persian and another in Arabic which were to be sent to different parts of the Islamic world.

There were scholars who rendered a more useful service in this connection. Ali Muttaqi, the Indian savant who had taken a permanent abode at Mecca used to acquire useful and rare manuscripts from distant quarters of Arabia, ordered their copies to be prepared and despatched them to those countries where they had not been published as yet. He would acquire important text books whose text had been debased on account of limited circulation and prepared a correct version by collating a number of manuscripts.

There were teachers who had adopted copying as a subsidiary profession which brought a much needed addition to their meagre income. Manuscripts copied by good scholars fetched higher price than those prepared by the professional copyist.

The work of publishing was sometimes made easy by the dedication of the work to a prince and in this respect some of the princes showed the keenest interest in a wider circulation of the book because the publicity of the book-meant a wider fame for the prince as a patron of learning.

When Qadi Adhd wrote his great classic, the Muwaffiq, Muhammad Tughlaq, the sultan of Delhi in fourteenth century despatched a special messenger to Shiraz for inviting the author to India and acquiring the dedication of the book for himself. But the Sultan of Shiraz returned the reply that barring the Queen, he was prepared to sacrifice all his worldly belongings, even his kingdom to retain the scholar in Shiraz and obtain the dedication of the work.

The supply of text books was a formidable question in the days when there were no printing facilities and paper was not so easily available as it is today. The pupils often resorted to the college library for copying a book or preparing a summary and there were no restrictions for the use of library books for the purpose, but the well-to-do pupil was positively discouraged from borrowing books from others or copying them. The spirit of the regulation was to help the indigent pupil or the copyist, who could earn something by copying for others and save the pupil in easy circumstances the drudgery of copying.

The pupil was advised to buy the text-book, or if not possible, to acquire it on hire or loan but he should not direct his entire energy to the acquisition of books and their safe custody. Maqrizi relates how a person needed a copy of the Hamasa for his son and he consulted a savant on the subject whose attendant displayed thirty five different manuscripts of the famous classics. Thereupon the savant advised him not to bother the child with different editions of the same work and buy him a decent single copy for one Dinar.

The teachers were keenly alive to the tremendous wastage of time and energy in copying out manuscripts and recommended that the pupil should not insist upon a flawless hand in calligraphy but he should devote more attention to correct transcription and improvement of mistakes occurring in the original manuscript. The transcription was to be made in a bold hand. In the words of Abu Hanifa, 'if one writes an illegible hand, he would be ashamed of himself during his lifetime, and cured after he has passed away"; according to another savant, whenever "we wrote in a small hand, we were thoroughly ashamed of ourselves, when we summarised a text (instead of copying out at length) we felt very much worried and whenever we did not collate the copy with the original we were invariably miserable." Another has put it in a more epigrammatical form. "Write in a way that may stand you in good stead in the hour of thy need and refrain from writing in a way which may bring no benefit at the time of your need."

The above sayings refer obviously to the old age when the failing eyesight would have to struggle hard with the close type. In fact, the educative process was conceived as a life-long mission by the Muslims and for them these companions of their youth were to remain bosom friends for the whole of their life, hence all the more insistence in transcribing them correctly in a bold hand.

The pupil is positively discouraged to acquire books on loan and in case he is compelled to obtain one, he should take scrupulous care not to spoil it by corrections and annotations.

According to a common usage of the time the authors and other benefactors often gave books as endowments to the libraries. In this case it was permissible for a competent person to make corrections preferably with the permission of the keeper of the collection. In any case special care is enjoined in handling the book with care while copying. The paper or the inkpot should not be placed on the body of the book when copying and the pen should not be traced bluntly over the written words.

Other Devices

Educational apparatus and appliances in certain subjects formed an important part of class room equipment. The teacher of Euclid carried with him a board and pencil for drawing diagrams. The teacher of calligraphy had his stylus ; the oculist and the surgeon had his set of instruments. But quite a formidable assortment of apparatus was required in the teaching of astronomy and normally every institution had an astrolobe, an astronomical globe and other accessories. The more enthusiastic teachers would prepare a model of the heavens and a Spanish scientist planned one showing stars, clouds, lightning and thunder.

The art of constructing astronomical instruments had developed into a regular branch of the science, the work not only requiring technical skill, but also an exact knowledge of astronomy. The knowledge and skill of instrument making seems to be fairly widespread from the earliest times. Ibn Nadim gives a formidable list of the practisers of the art. The scientists in charge of the college clock tower had an opportunity to make a practical use of their knowledge and some of them employed their skill in making astronomical apparatus. Al-Mizi, the time keeper of the Friday mosque at Damascus (died beginning of 750 A. H.) had a great skill in making astrolabes and quadrants. His astrolabes were priced at one hundred dirhams apiece while the quadrants were sold for fifty dirhams.

Al-Badi, an astrolobe maker of Baghdad had a remarkable inventive genius and had introduced significant improvement in astronomical apparatus and appliances.

Sometimes, the teacher availed of the good offices of their pupils in preparing such apparatus. Abu Bakr Yahya-al-Biyasi, the pupil of Ibn-al-Naqqash who knew cabinet making used to design geometrical instruments for his teacher and had prepared quite a large number of them. The art of instrument making had attracted the attention of the greatest among the scientists who published works on their various methods of construction, uses and corrections. Some of them had specialised in their construction. Others in lyrics over such an unpoetic topic as an astrolobe and celebrate its excellencies in verse.

Royal interest in the science sometimes inspired the astrolobe makers to more ingenious efforts The instrument commonly used in the indigeneous colleges in India was called astarlab-i-Humayuni because it had been prepared by Sheikh Allah Dad, an expert under the direction of Humayun the Mughal ruler who was keenly interested in the science and used to impart instruction in the subject.

Indian astronomers used as a rule the instruments similar to those installed by Ulugh Beg at the Samarkand observatory but Raja Jai Singh of Amber who raised the splendid observatory of Jantar Mantar at Delhi had invented some instruments for himself.

The libraries contained not only books, but apparatus of educative value. Once Ibn-al-Sanbadi, an astrolobe maker of Egypt had an opportunity of visiting the royal library which was being recatalogued by a minister of state. He had the opportunity to see there an astronomical globe prepared by Ptolemy which was one in the possession of Khalid bin Yazid bin Muawiyyah. According to his computation it was 1250 years old. There was another globe which was made for Malik Abdud-Dawlah which weighed 3000 dirhams and was priced at 300 dinars.

The student of surgery the oculist and optician had their set of apparatus. Geography did not form a regular subject in the curriculum, but the books contained fairly accurate maps showing details of human and physical interest.

21

Classroom Administration

The management of the classroom or the assembly chambers was mainly determined by the traditions of the Prophet concerning general behaviour in those gatherings which attended the addresses or informal talks by the Prophet. The early teachers strictly adhered to these injunctions.

But as the simple and unsophisticated Caliphate developed into the Empire of the Umayyids, other influences might have crept in to change the ideals of class management. They began to reflect also the social ideals of the day. Human contacts played a very important role in life and there were minute details of social behaviour and etiquette which had been worked out by tradition and experience. Educational ideals might have been unconsciously influenced in some cases by the regulations of court life and monasteries, both of which had a definite set of rules. Again the teachers realised the significance of rites and rituals for the purpose of creating a proper atmosphere and imparting that momentum to the educational machine which could only be provided by the fly wheel of regular routine.

The Soul

There were teachers who believed that the inner spirit of the educative process needs strengthening by the outer form and some of the lecture assemblies looked quite impressive affairs with costly carpets, glamorous chandeliers and richly ornamented censors.

The social and cultural life of certain periods demanded that the teacher should give special attention to such externalities as appearance, dress and organisation of the assembly. Preparation in the physical senses helped him in developing a mental orientation towards his professional work.

Teaching was essentially a social process and the savant was to begin his daily intention by beginning his profession daily with a prayer that his teaching might be useful for others. There were a number of other sacred formulae to be recited on various occasions during his round of daily routine, one of them being a prayer for the founder of the college to which the teacher was attached.

The teachers would make special sartorical preparations for their lectures. Imam Malik would make ablutions, put on his best clothes, dress his hair and use his favourite perfume. Then he would seat himself in the middle of the mattress and spreading out his beard assumed a grave and dignified deportment.

According to Ibn Jamaah, the teacher should seat himself cross legged on reaching the college, the easiest and most comfortable posture for an oriental and face the Holy Mecca.

Some teachers would recline against a pillar and it is said about a teacher that as he rested in this posture, great scholars like Imam Ahmad bin Hanbal stood on their feet before him and asked questions.

The use of a dikka or a dais was also permissible; in case of recitations he could use a kursi (chair).

The teachers kept to their seat and left it only under abnormal circumstances. Not only it resulted in an interruption of the educative process but it meant considerable inconvenience to the assembly who had to rise en masse, when the teacher stood on his feet to receive a visitor. It is said that Yahya, the distinguished pupil of Imam Malik never rose to welcome any person during his life time except once when Abdullah Ibn Mubarak came to visit him. Imam Malik once evidenced remarkable capacity of endurance in continuing his work. A scorpion had crept into his sook and stung him several times in the course of a lecture. Every time the scorpion stung him, he would change colour but continued courageously with his work. At the end of his lecture he told that he did not do so in order to display his power of endurance. He did so in order to express his deep reverence for the traditions of the Prophet which he was dictating.

The teacher was expected to maintain a judicious moderation in the pitch of his voice which should be neither high nor low. His voice should not transcend the' confines of the audience and neither should it be so low as to be inaudible by his listeners. He could raise the pitch of the voice in case some members of the audience were hard of hearing.

The teacher should not speak fast, rather he should adopt a deliberate easy style of speech and should give an opportunity for thought and contemplation to himself and to his audience.

The savants followed in this respect the instructions of the Prophet who spoke deliberately and often repeated each sentence thrice.

The teacher should stop for a while when he has done with a particular topic or section. So that one who felt like putting a question might have an opportunity to do so.

The lectures of distinguished teachers were attended by all sections of the population ranging from kings and nobility to the commoner specially when the subjects of address had a universal appeal. Such representative gatherings would include princes and nobles, scholars and judges.

Role of Scholars

Scholars and savants who had completed their education and had been vested with the academic gown and some times even Imams or scholars who were held to be an authority in their particular branch of knowledge would attend the lectures of another teacher for enriching their store of knowledge or to study a different subject. Books on education lay down special instructions on the seating arrangement in case of such persons. The teacher was expected to be specially considerate to them even if they arrived in the course of the lecture. Precedence in seating arrangements was accorded on the basis of character and scholarship.

The members of the audience received equal treatment in the class. At least the great masters of the profession adhered to this principle in a rigorous manner and the rulers and the nobility submitted themselves to the discipline with willing resignation.

When Amir Mansur, the Caliph of Spain attended the lectures of the famous thinker Ibn Rushd (Averroes), he would address him with the following words 'Listen, O my brother.

There are instances when the members of royal lineage were reprimanded publicly by the teachers for a transgression of assembly regulations. Imam Silfi once chastised the ruler of Egypt who started talking with his brother in the class of the savant.

In spite of all these stringent regulations as regards etiquette of the assembly chamber, members of the ruling class often relished these intellectual treats immensely. Once when Sultan Muhammad, the conqueror of Constantinople attended a lecture by Maula Ali, he was so ravished by his exposition that he would rise on his feet and seat himself again and again during the lecture.

On the close of his address, he presented the teacher with a robe of honour and ten thousands dirhams while all the pupils received five hundred dirhams each.

Reading aloud was controlled and directed by specific signs on the part of the teacher. He would indicate the mistake by raising a finger or thumping with his hand the mattress on which he was seated. With more sensitive pupils a mere raising of the eyes would serve the purpose.

The pupils freely exercised their right of questioning and books on education enjoin upon the teacher to encourage the pupils, specially the more diffident type. 'He should help him in expressing his views in clear a and confident manner and in case he is unable to do so, the teacher should give a bucid exposition of his objection himself and give a rejoinder.'

If a person puts him a question or joins issue with him on a debatable point, he should particularise him out of the audience, and show special attention towards him, face him squarely, whether he is young in age or low in station.

Sometimes, instead of putting test questions for estimating the scope and nature of pupil's knowledge, the teacher interrogated a distinguished member of the audience who happened to attend his lecture, thereby seeking advice on an abstruse point.

Once Abdullah Ibn Mubarak attended the assembly of Imam Malik and in the course of teaching, Malik continued asking him about certain traditions and religious injunctions. Ibn Mubarak replied in a quiet and unobstrusive manner.

It required a good deal of courage to criticise a savant in his assembly, but there were persons who would attempt to beard the lion in his den and in most cases such criticism was received in a calm and objective manner. They would often maintain a composed demeanour under extremely exasperating circumstances. When a person condemned Maulana Rum in his assembly because he had declared that he was in agreement with all the seventy two sects, and used strong language against him, the latter replied with a disarming smile that he was in agreement with all that he was saying against him too. There were teachers who would take criticism as a worthy challenge and were stimulated to further intellectual effort on that score. There were others who would beat an ignominous retreat, never to return to their work.

But with their own pupils, questioning and answering was a happy, joyous, cooperative venture in search of truth and it had its humorous aspects also.

Once Ibn Durayd was giving Abu Nasr who was inclined to frivolity and raillery, a lesson in poetry. Ibn Durayd was explaining the word Rabaith which means spears with broad heads. Abu Nasr interrupted him and said he was mistaken. The other pupils were amazed at his contradicting an authority like Ibn Durayd. The teacher who was so gentle in disposition asked what the word meant. Abn Nasr gave ostensibly a nonsensical reply and continued the lesson with more vigour. All the class laughed at him.

Some teachers would arrive at the college on a ride which was usually a mule in the case of savants. And they would sally forth out of their house amidst a crowd of pupils who surrounded him. Ibn Jamaah deprecates this practice and gives instructions concerning the deportment of the teacher after the dismissal of the class.

The educational system was essentially teacher centered and a considerable number of pupils received instruction at the teachers' residence. This was specially the case with the more advanced or the backward students. Some teachers continued their professional work at their residence at an advanced age of their life when physical disability prevented them from attending the college in person. Ibn Khallikan remarks about a very old teacher of his who would sit muffled up in warm clothes with a brazier constantly in front of him.

There were teachers who would hold classes both at their residence and in the college.

The pupils of Maula Khusrau used to visit him at sunrise and spend their mornings with him. Then he mounted his mule and rode in state to the college with his pupils in front of him. He pupils accompanied him on return journey also. The teachers took particular care about keeping their study chambers at their residential quarters neat and clean. Maula Khusrau would sweep the room himself and personally attended to the heating and lighting arrangements.

The Attendance : There were no hard and fast rules for attendance and the teachers did not maintain a register in the modern sense of the term, but the surest guarantee against slackness was the singleness of purpose and enthusiasm with which both the teachers and pupils pursued their work. Ancient traditions of regular and punctual work helped a great deal in maintaining the general tone of discipline as regards attendance. In some cases even the death of a kinsman could not prevent a savant or a pupil from attending classes.

As a rule the teacher was expected to know the names of his students, their families, their place of origin and specially their kuniat or the title with which they liked to be addressed.

The teacher was expected to enquire about such absentees who attended his lectures regularly either in the capacity of students or private visitors. In case the period of absence was unusually prolonged, he must make enquiries about the pupil's circumstances from his friends and in case no such person was available, he should send some one to his residence; but the more meritorious act would be to visit him in person.

He should attend upon him if he is sick; console him if he is in sorrow and if he has departed on journey, he shculd take care of his family and his dependants. He should try to see that they were not left in want. If the student himself was in difficulties, he should try to help him, or otherwise he should cheer him up and pray for him.

There were teachers who maintained a register also. It is related of Umar-al-Ruwasi that when he started lecturing on traditions in Sarkhas, he took down carefully the names of the company in his own hand when he began for the first time. By the next turn he had learnt the names of all the persons, who were seventy in number approximately by heart and never felt the necessity of asking their names again.

22

Examination System

The state conducted examinations in medicine, opthalmic surgery, pharmacy and other branches of medical profession. These examinations were carried out normally by the Muhtasib.

Maalim-al-Qurba, a book on the duties and functions of the Muhtasib reveals the nature and scope of such examinations. They included both oral and practical tests. The oral examination was based on a classical text book and the practical work included physiology, skill in the manipulation of instruments and drug making.

The muhtasib must exact the oath of Hippocrates from all physicians, causing them to swear that they will never administer to any one nor prescribe poisons as medicine to the public nor mention to any woman a medicament for procuring abortion of the embryo nor to any man one which will prevent procreation.

'Oculists must be examined by the muhtasib on the 'Book' of Hunayn bin Ishaq, namely the 'Ten discourses on the Eye.' Those whom he finds competent in the subjects of the examination,— Those, namely, who know the structure of the layers of the eye and their number (seven) and of the number of the humours (three) and of the diseases of the eye (three) and the ramifications of these diseases ; who know, further, how to compound the salves (Kuhls) and to mix the various drugs—these shall be licensed by the muhtasib to undertake the treatment of eyes. The practitioner must not be negligent with respect to the instruments of his craft such as hooks for removal of sabat and pterygium, lancets for bleeding, the case of kuhl-pencils, etc.'

'Setters of (broken) bones shall not be permitted to practise until they have acquired knowledge of the sixth chapter of Thesaurus of Paul, on 'Bone-setting,' and know the number of the human bones—According to human science there are only 206 bones in a human body—and the appearance, shade and size of each one, so that if it is broken or dislocated it can be restored to its original state. The muhtasib must examine them on these subjects.'

'Surgeons must have knowledge of the book of Galen known as Kata Genos (on wounds and dressings) of the members of the human, body and what muscles, veins, arteries and nerves they contain, so that these may be avoided when abscesses are being opened or haemorrhoids excised. The surgeon should have with him a set of lancets, some with round heads, some with square and some cross-cut ; also knives, a frontal hatchet, an amputating saw, an earpiercer, a set of leeches, a case of dressings and the remedy which stops the flow of blood."

Besides the usual examinations conducted by the Muhtasib special examinations were held sometimes under express order of the ruling prince and they were conducted by the chief of the physicians, an important official who examined the applicants and granted them licence for practice. These examinations were occasioned sometimes by an instance of gross professional misconduct on the part of a practitioner. Sometimes they were held in the interest of a more efficient medical service for the army.

Amin-ud-Dawla Talmiz, the chief of Physicians at Baghdad and a distinguished Christian doctor of the Metropolis examined the practitioners in the days of Mustadhi bi-Amrillah and according to Qifti under Muqtafi and certified those applicants who stood the test.

Eye trouble has been the common scourge of Egypt. Muhazabbuddin Dakhwar (d. 628) a teacher of the author of Tabaqat who was the chief physician for Egypt and Syria was appointed examiner of oculists and issued licenses to those who passed the examination. In this case the licences indicated the extent of the possessor's knowledge in the science.

These examinations were held orally and the repertory of questions and answers by the examiner and the candidates form interesting reading.

A more practical method was used for the examination of apothecaries in certain cases. Once the Abbaside Caliph Mamun asked a chemist to examine the apothecaries of the Metropolis. He fabricated the name of a drug and sent persons to various apothecaries with the prescription. All the apothecaries supplied a different description of the drug and sent back the messengers with something or the other ranging from the splinter wood to a stone or a seed.

When Afshin the Turkish general of Mutasim was sent against Babak the army included a number of apothecaries. One day he asked for a list of the traders in the camp. The clerk read out the list and when he came to the list of apothecaries he turned towards Zakaria-al-Taifuri and asked him to prepare a selective list after a thorough examination. Zakariya selected twenty names out of a book on pharmacopea and sent persons to procure them from the apothecaries in the camp. Some of them claimed to know the drugs and supplied them after receiving the price ; others refused point blank and acknowledged their ignorance of the medicine. Afshin ordered all the quacks who pretended to know the drugs to be ejected from the camp and requested the Caliph to replace them with others.

The rest who had given evidence of their integrity of character were allowed to continue with the business. It appears that such examinations were fairly common in the Islamic world and books were composed on the subject by medical authors. A book on the Examination for physicians was composed by Ibn-al-Khammar under the instructions of Amir Khwarizm Shah who desired perhaps to prescribe it for state examinations.

Another author Abu Said Yamami had written a book on the

subject wherein he had fixed grades of physicians according to their knowledge and experience and had laid down methods and rules for such examinations.

The late Dr. E. G. Browne has inferred from a word Mutakharrij occurring in the preface to Firdaus-al-Hikma by Ali Ibn Rabban that it means graduate in the modern sense of the term. He justifies his conclusion by referring to the state examinations in medicine.

It is difficult to say whether the State diploma alone could authorise the possessor to practise in the absence of an Ijazah and even in the case of state tests the examiner would enquire from the candidate about his teacher and his medical education.

The aim of these examination was akin in nature to the registration work of a medical council. The word Mutakharrij is still used for students who have completed their course of education and have been awarded a diploma by an educational institution. In those days the Ijazah was the only diploma issued to the pupil. The state examinations might have secured for the pupil a recognition by the state, but for the people in general the medical practitioner had to depend entirely on the Ijazah issued by a distinguished teacher.

Internal Assessment

The day to day tests conducted under class room conditions were meant to assess the achievement of the pupil and his capacity for comprehension. They could prove extremely valuable for the class teacher in estimating how far his lectures had imparted to the pupil that intellectual discipline which would help him in further deductions.

According to Ibn Jamaah, "The teacher should often make an attempt to examine the pupils in the portions covered previously specially those which deal with important principles and their exceptions. He should invite them to explain to him the inferences deduced from the principles established by him in his lectures, or those based on arguments discussed in the class."

Old Pattern

The scholars took special care in preserving the text and the chain of narrators (Asnad) associated with it. According to Masaar while teaching traditions he had a feeling as if he was supporting over his head a basketful of glass-ware. He wished to god that this precious load might fall to earth and broken to pieces rather than he should take on himself the responsibility of narrating them. The traditionist had to maintain a high standard and had to fulfil the rigorous conditions laid down by the authorities in this subject.

Mistakes occurred generally in the names of the narrators and their chronological order. The examinations were both public and private.

Great traditionists had to face the ordeal in public. Incorrect names were introduced in the chain of narrators on purpose and sometimes such changes were made in their sequence also and the examinee was expected to correct them.

When Imam Bukhari visited Baghdad for the first time, he had to undergo such a test. The traditionists selected one hundred traditions and introduced in the text of each the spurious name of a narrator and gave them by tens to ten different persons. Bukhari corrected all the wrong Asnad. The assembly acknowledged his authority in the subject and he was styled the butting ram (whom no one could withstand).

Public examinations were rather uncommon but examinations conducted in the classroom or the assembly were more commonly used for their educative value both by the teachers and the pupils. Sometimes a pupil would give such a test to his teacher in order to discover the soundness of his knowledge.

A group of pupils visited Al-Hassan bin Sufian (died. 303 A. H.) and one of them declared that he had noted down a number of traditions related by him. The teacher invited him to read them out and as he read the chain of narrators he forged into the chain a number of fictitious persons whereupon the teacher corrected his mistake. He repeated the trick again and once more the teacher showed remarkable patience in correcting the pupil. When he attempted the forgery for the third time the teacher told him that he should not be so calumnious with his teachers. Thereupon another pupil explained that he just wanted to test the exactness and accuracy of his knowledge.

The test was used for other parsons besides the pupils also. Once a scholar changed the words of a tradition and recited it in the presence of Abdur Rahman Ibn Mahdi who pointed out the mistake at once.

Good authorities on the subject had a wonderful grasp of such details and had acquired a remarkable capacity for spotting out weak points.

Ibn Mahdi used to say that he could discriminate the correct version of a tradition from the incorrect just as a physician knows the sane from the insane or a money changer discriminates a good coin from the counterfeit.

Riddles : It was a formidable challenge for the pupil's intellect and it formed as much a feature of educational method as the examination system. In some cases it had an essentially prognostic value.

Some text book writers used the riddle and the style as a selective test of prognostic value for higher stages of education. These authors felt the need of devising ways and means for eliminating the indifferent type of student and they composed text books for higher stages in such a difficult style as would tax the comprehension capacity of the pupil to its breaking point.

Riddles were universally popular as educational tests in the later period and batteries of riddles were prepared by teachers in their particular branches of learning. Interesting stories are told how pupils burnt night oil over their solutions.

Najmuddin-al-Qamrawi and Sharfuddin-al-Matani, two scholars once visited Sheikh Kamaluddin bin Yunus at Mausal when the savant was engaged in lecturing. They took part in the discussion and evidenced superiority above other members of the audience. The lecturer offered them a seat near his person. At noon they requested the teacher whether they could have his book on philosophy which contained a famous riddle of his. The teacher refused and told them that he had never come across a single person who could solve the riddle and it won't serve any useful purpose.

They supplicated him once again and preferred the plea that they had come from a foreign country in order to benefit by his learning and study his works. They promised to stay in the premises of the college at night, go through the book and return it to the teacher in the morning. The savant agreed and both of them fell furiously to copying the book, one dictating and the other transcribing until they had finished and compared the copy with the original. It was followed by an attempt to solve the riddle. They continued in their efforts and daybreak saw them still engaged in the process. At last a trace was discovered to its solution and step by step they worked it out successfully.

They carried the book to the savant who was lecturing at that time and declared that his book and the riddle contained in it was too easy for them. In fact they had come in quest of his Greater work which contained riddle of an advanced nature. The savant was surprised and asked them to give the solution which they did in an eloquent and effective manner.

These riddles were composed in various subjects and they formed a common feature of the text books written in the latter period. Their value as a part of educational method was certainly doubtful and they were introduced as such during a period when the teachers had begun to emphasize the form at the expense of this spirit. As achievement tests, they were more challenging and full of interest.

Type of Tests

The educational system provided examinations in professional subjects like medicine, law and teaching.

According to Al-Maqarri no person was appointed a Mufti nor was his evidence accepted unless he had attained standard of knowledge. Such persons were given a test in an assembly of discussion.

Language and literature formed an important part of the curriculum and variety of tests were used in this case. Besides the old tests like recitation of the text and questions as regards its comprehension, bilingual students were expected to translate Arabic poetry into the mother tongue in verse and vice versa. They were also asked to cap a hemistich or to add verses in the same rhyme scheme.

Grammar Test : Examinations in grammar were quite formidable affairs and they took frequently the form of a public debate. Grammar like law had different schools and every scholar was expected to support the viewpoint of his own school with a battery of arguments in a public assembly.

Muimmah (enigma) was an interesting device, more in the nature of educational playwork for assessing the linguistic ability of the student; it was popular in bilingual areas. It assessed the capacity of discovering synonyms in two languages and an accurate knowledge of their spelling. It was related to the ability which spots out harmony of meaning or form in words. The device was worked out into a regular subject of study in central Asia. Mir Hussain (d. 912 *A.* H.) had composed a small Risala on the art and kings, ministers and the nobility would send their sons to him for the study of the book.

Education had not been institutionalised as yet and the system had its weaknesses and strong features. They were reflected in the system of examinations which lacked in uniformity of standards but had a validity of its own.

They had net become as yet a universal scourge for the educational system in form or spirit.

There were no examining universities or state departments for awarding diplomas. The educative process was an intimately personal affair between the teacher and the taught and the most common form of examination was the individual test applied by the teacher himself. Individual colleges did not conduct their own examinations. The duty of examining students rested with the teacher individually.

Under these conditions the form of examinations was individual rather than that of group examination, oral rather than written. They had prognostic or achievement value and were both private and public. In the oral examination the pupil repeated in the presence of the teacher memorized verses of the Quran, text and chain of narrators (Asnad) in case of traditions and pieces of literary, historical and biographical knowledge. The teacher might ask the student to read aloud from a book and discuss with him different readings, inquired about the authorities for those readings and arguments supporting different view points. Sometimes he would mark the important passages and confined his questioning to these portions.

In the class rooms he would give them tests to estimate their capacity for apprehension and intellectual training in deduction work in logic or law. He would put them sometimes a 'lughs' or a riddle. In some cases the pupils had to undergo a public test in the form of a debate. A victory at this performance signalized the attainment of the highest qualifications in the subject during a period when public debates had caught the imagination of the people.

Qualification Certificate

The Ijazah : The Ijazah could be classified into two kinds, specific and general. This distinction was made with reference to the nature and scope of the permission granted to the pupil. By a specific licence he was allowed to teach only those books, their parts and chapters as were specifically indicated in the Ijazah. The general certificate permitted the pupil to teach all that he had learnt from the teacher without any specifications of scope or other limitations.

Another classification of the Ijazah was based on the instructional method employed in the course of teaching. The teacher would issue a variety of Ijazah on this basis. They included certificates for (1) the knowledge received through oral instruction from his teachers, (2) knowledge imparted through teacher's reading aloud from a book (3) reading aloud by a pupil in the class, (4) knowledge received by the teacher from his professors as indicated in his special or general licence. (5) or by Izn or permission by word of mouth (6) or through Wasiyyat (will) (7) or Manawilah (authoritative interpretation). Other categories refer to the form and contents of teaching material whether oral or written, prose or poetry, traditional knowledge or creative ; knowledge imparted through personal discussion or exchange of opinion through correspondence. Ijazah included those books and those aspects of knowledge which were studied in the course of the impact of one mind on another when the pupil showered a volley of questions and the teacher gave a reply to his objections. It covered also notes of lectures taken by the pupil during lecture hours.

The Ijazah contained also a brief history of the educational career of the teacher with date of birth and other important data like the names of his teachers and the dates of receiving a licence from them, a list of his works and compositions. In case of a specific certificate the teacher would indicate books or their parts which the pupil had studied with him.

Sometimes a teacher would include one or more traditions of the Prophet with Asnad or chain of narrators reaching from the Prophet to himself. These traditions dealt either with knowledge in general or with that particular subject for which the licence was being issued. Very often the tradition expressed a cherished ideal of the teacher.

The Ijazah was wound up with a fervent prayer for the pupil in prose or verse.

There were no hard and fast rules for the classification of licences in rank or merit, only the teachers used the most appropriate terms out of their repository of qualifying remarks. These qualifying words were not of a vague or an indeterminate nature. They had a specific meaning and connotation for the subject for which they were used.

The teacher used to issue a special kind of certificate called the Wasiyyat (will) in case of those pupils who had earned their high regard and affection. It was in the fitness of things that the teacher who was loco-parentis for the pupil should bequeath to him the legacy of intellectual and moral wealth as preserved in a book of instructions which was passed on from generation to generation, providing guidance and solace for generations of teachers and pupils. The small Risala, named 'O thou my son' by Ghazzali and the Wasiyyat of Abu Hanifa are documents of this nature. They differ essentially from the Ijazah in their being general rather than particular in nature. They are a book of guidance for the pupil to follow in his after school career. They had a profound influence in moulding the general outlook of the pupil and the words of the teachers would often bring a ray of hope and comfort in the darkest moments of their lives.

As a rule the Ijazah was issued only when the pupil had completed the book with the teacher. But if the teacher realised that the pupil had acquired the intellectual discipline needed for the proper comprehension of the text book without the aid of the teacher, he would issue him a licence without finishing the book.

According to Haneburg licences could be obtained from the descendants of a teacher and a scholar obtained such a licence for Sahih Bukhari from the descendants of Imam Bukhari three hundred years after that great work had been compiled. But such an authority as exercised by the family of a great teacher could at best amount to a certification of the correctness of the text acquired from the family and could confer in no way the licence of teaching the book unless a member of the family actually taught the work and issued licences to that purpose.

The Ijazah was sometimes inscribed by the teachers on the book which the students had studied with him. Ibn Khallikan came across many of these licences in the handwriting of Al-Hanafi a teacher of philosophy testifying that the possessors had read the book with him. In this he followed the general usage of the teachers.

In other cases they were attached to the albums of the text.

Sometimes the Ijazah formed a small book by itself. According to Ibn Shaddad he possessed in the handwriting of his teacher nearly forty pages in which was indicated all that he had read under him and matters which he himself taught orally and which he might teach on his authority.

Sometimes teachers with a knack of versification would write the Ijazah in verse. Once a teacher wrote by way of Ijazah.

I have permitted them to relate on my authority all that they have received from me faithfully and correctly. I abjure all additions or omissions on their part.

Licences were not only issued by teachers of religion and literature. They were equally common in science and philosophy. In the case of the mystics the award of the licence was accompanied by an investiture ceremony of the Khirqa, the cloak of a mystic. Ibn Usaibiah gives the text of one of these licences issued to his uncle Rashid-ud-din by his mystic preceptor with all the formalities of signature and date.

Women scholars also exercised the authority for issuing a licence and many distinguished scholars count women among their teachers. Ibn Batuta received such a licence from a woman savant who was called Rahilat-al-alam and was visited by students from the four quarters of the globe.

Transfer Certificate : Under a teacher centered system of education, the pupil had to make frequent changes of teachers and hence arose the need of a transfer certificate which took usually the form of a letter of recommendation to a comrade in profession. Such letters provided a general idea of the scope of studies already covered by the pupil and his keenness for prosecuting them in the same or a different direction. It contained teacher's opinion about the character and personality of the pupil, his power of memory and other intellectual qualities.

The text of a letter written by Al-Barqani, the teacher of Khatib Baghdadi to Al-Hafiz Abi Naim, the traditionist of Isphahan gives an idea of this kind of certificate, 'Our brother Abu Bakr Ahmad bin Ali is proceeding to you with a determined will and may god help him to avail of your learning and store of Traditions. He is one of those who has acquired marked precedence over others in the pursuit and he possesses resolution of spirit and keenness of intelligence. He is setting out in search of learning and has acquired more learning than the majority of other pupils. All this you will discover in him when he meets you but along with it he has other virtues which will endear him to you and exalt him in your estimate. He is endowed with virtue, a powerful capacity for memory and exactitude in learning knowledge.'

I hope that when you have testified these qualities in him you would favour him with nearness to your person and bestow upon him abundantly your rich store of knowledge. You will bear patiently the trials which he would cause you by his enthusiasm for cross questioning for such has been the usage of teachers hallowed by time ; the older generation has always borne patiently with the new and has benefitted generously the deserving pupil. They have singled him out for mark of special favour and precedence, socially and intellectually, something which was not the good fortune of the rest.

The Award : There were no strict regulations controlling the award of an Ijazah. They varied considerably with individual teachers. There were teachers who were extremely generous in this respect. It is related about one of them that he had covered the earth with his certificates and testimonials.

In the case of a pupil with whom the teacher had not the opportunity of coming into a long and intimate contact, he would specify clearly the scope of studies with the names and chapters of the book he has studied with him. With others who had sit at his feet for years he would issue a *general certificate* signifying a permission to teach all his works and repeat all his lectures which he had noted down in his assembly. Personal considerations counted a great deal and young teachers who were often on friendly terms with their pupils would be most generous in their compliments to the pupil when issuing a certificate.

There are cases when teachers relaxed their standards for considerations other than strictly educational, but they appear to be the exceptions rather than the rule.

Ibn Jazri relates how a teacher issued a certificate with the 'excellent' mark to a pupil of Qirat who did not perform well in the class. When another student objected to the remark, the teacher replied that he had excelled through gold.

Some teachers were highly exacting in their standards and the indifferent type of student had to make many an attempt before he could obtain the Ijazah. Ibn Khallikan mentions the case of a scholar of Cairo who was unsuccessful in getting a certificate.

According to Ibn Jazri, Ibn Bazhan, a teacher of Qirat did not allow the pupil to slur over even a Ghunna, Tashdid or other matters of minutest details in recitation without pointing out the mistake and correcting it. When the pupil committed a mistake he would strike the mattress on which he was seated with his hand. If the pupil corrected himself he would allow him to proceed otherwise he would try to reduce the correct reading from him and if unsuccessful gave it himself. He would note down all the places where the reader had stumbled.

When the pupil applied for a certificate he would examine him again about the incorrect readings If he was satisfied he would issue him the certificate otherwise he asked him to complete once more the reading of the Quran with him. He did not issue more than two certificates during his lifetime.

23

Sports and Games

It is very difficult to say how far physical education formed a regular feature of the school programme under the Islamic system but there were manly exercises and pastimes which were popular with the savants; here, as elsewhere, it is always the example of the Prophet who left behind something edifying in all activities of life and the scholars and their pupils collected and studied the Traditions on the subject with enthusiasm and made their best efforts to follow them.

Out of leisure time activities, the Prophet had expressed special approval of four. According to Jabir, "Everything else beside praying to God is frivolous except four. These are archery, horsemanship swimming and amusing oneself in the company of one's wife."

The Archery : There is a chapter in Bukhari on popularising archery and it contains a description of its exercises and how the Prophet divided his Companions into two groups and encouraged them in the exercise of healthy rivalry in marksmanship. He took part himself in the pastime and would join a side but his attitude was always of a sportsman who belonged to no party and who joined the sport for sport's sake. When the members of a group objected to his joining the opposite party, he would reply with a disarming smile that he belonged to all of them.

The pastime was taken up zealously by some of the teachers and there is the case of Imam Shafii, who attained considerable skill in this art and once when he saw a person exhibiting marvellous skill in archery, he pulled out his money-case and presented him with all the money he had, for his fine display.

There is a brochure on archery in Manuscript in the Rampur Collection of the Aligarh Muslim University Library which opens with relevant Traditions on the subject. A study of these Traditions reveals the importance which the Prophet attached to this manly exercise. Archery was practised not only as a training for war but it was a healthy kind of pastime, which provided opportunities for a wholesome emulation and exhibition of skill. Once the Prophet recited a verse of the Holy Quran from the pulpit, "Wage war against them with all the strength at your disposal," and he emphasized three times that the term 'strength' used here implies archery. On the evidence of these Traditions some legists have decreed the learning of archery, a religious obligation. It is interesting to note that he blessed a renowned archer in words which he had never used for any other person, a mark of honour for which he singled out Saad bin Abi Waqqas for whom he emptied his quiver at the battlefield of Uhud and encouraged him to shoot at the enemy saying, "May my parents be thy sacrifice, O Saad."

Another Tradition states that one who shot an arrow on the path of the Lord earned merit equal to the manumission of a slave.

The Empires which lay on the borders of the Arabian desert and their hostile attitude towards Islam forced the Muslims to keep a vigilant eye on the war programme and the supply of war material became a thorny problem in a country with poor economic resources and few handicraftsmen. In the economy of the desert life which forced every individual to be self-dependent there was no possibility of the growth of a class of skilled workers. Hence a Tradition blesses in one breath three persons — the arrow-maker, the purchaser and the thrower. Most probably the high cost of the arrows in those days gave rise to another Tradition, "One who brings back the arrow from its target would receive merit equal to the manumission of a slave for every step he takes in that direction."

The Prophet condemned strongly all those who left the practice after learning archery, "One who discards archery after once learning it discards my Sunnah."

Islamic literature contains interesting works on archery, falconery horsemanship, chess playing and other games, and such books always open with a chapter containing Traditions relevant to the subject; the books on Fiqh and Hadith contain chapters on games and sports, all laying down legal regulations in case of lawful games. The latter class of books created an interest in games and sports, among the learned class which percolated to the masses while the former class of books occupied a prominent place in the libraries of the aristocracy who had more leisure and means for such pursuits. The books on Traditions contain invariably a chapter on the excellence of keeping horses and the great interest which the Prophet evinced in this hobby.

Horse Riding : Horsemanship was a national trait of the Arabs and horse races with stakes was a popular and common pastime. Once they arranged links, five to six miles in length and race horses were specially trained for the occasion. Abdullah bin Umar outstripped others in the race but could not control the horse on the finishing spot and the animal stumbled into the mosque.

It would be interesting to study the conditions under which races were organised during the lifetime of the Prophet.

There is a Tradition which insists on the addition of a third party in a race when two parties run a race for stakes. As a rule stakes (Qamar) were not permitted.

He is called a Muhallil or the Legaliser because his participation make stakes legal and in fact the spirit of the injunction which insists on the addition of a Muhallil was to transform playing at stakes into a genuine form of sport.

In case of two parties only, the race is run in a competitive spirit and the dominant factor appears to be speculation rather than genuine sport.

But all earnings which do not give a return in terms of labour have been discouraged by Islam and there is no distinction in stakes of speculation or any other form of transactions in this respect.

While the two parties were certain about the success of the horses they backed, the Muhallil should be a person who was not sure whether his horse would win or lose. He had no stakes, but in case he won he would get the money. The device was introduced to counteract the spirit of economic competition or betting or a means of acquiring wealth without any return in terms of work and labour. The collections of Traditions contain chapters on 'Jalab and Janab'. Jalab was a device for keeping an extra horse behind the competing animal in order to keep it going faster.

According to Jamah, the extra horse was kept beside the horse competing for the race for a change in case the competing horse was tired.

Animal Race : Standard collections on Traditions contain chapters on the good and bad points of horses. Like a true Arab the Prophet loved the animal for its use in war and its graceful beauty. He liked to preserve its attractive features and condemned the practice of cutting the forelock because according to him Khayr (Good) is tied up in its forelock.

The first horse race in Islam was organised in A.H. and it was won by the horse of Abu Bakr.

There were separate race courses for the Mudhmar (horses specially trained for races) and the untrained. According to Ibn Umar the Prophet ordered a race course between Hafiya and Thaniyyat-al-Wida, a distance of six miles for the trained horses and another course between Thaniyyat-al-Wida and the mosque of Bani Zuriq, a distance of one mile. Ibn Umar himself backed a horse and the animal cleared off a wall in its impetuous course.

Camel Riding : Although the Prophet knew a good horse from a bad one and loved the animal, he usually preferred to ride a camel. Camel race was as popular as a horse race. Ghasbah, his favourite dromedary took part in a camel race which the Prophet had arranged in 6 A.H. The race was won by the camel of a Beduin.

Ghasbah which was a highly trained and swift-footed animal was once stolen away in the course of a battle and miraculously saved a woman captive from the Ansar who had fallen into the hands of the enemy. In the dark of the night, the woman crept out softly and tried to catch hold of a camel but every animal which she approached would stamp its feet or kick.

By chance she lighted upon Ghasbah which was a quiet and docile animal and managed to escape with its help.

Racing Competition : Once when the Prophet was returning from a campaign he was accompanied by one of the Ansar who was unrivalled in foot race. He began to challenge others and invited them to join in a race with him up to Medina.

He went on calling aloud, "Come along if there is anyone to compete."

Then Salma asked the permission of the Prophet to run a race with the man and on receiving his approval he cried, "Look up, I come."

Salma ran with the economy of a trained runner, carefully spacing his race with breathing intervals until he overtook the man. He punched him with his first between his shoulders and said. "Verily have beaten you." Salma reached the town before the challenger.

The Prophet ran a race with his wife Aishah more than once. He was defeated on the first occasion and retrieved his position on the second.

Holy Prophet's Examples : The Prophet had challenged Rakkana, a renowned athlete of the times, to a fighting bout and made him measure his length on the ground on three different occasions. Such an inexpensive exercise of manly vigour and ingenuity should have appealed to countless generations of scholars and savants and although we don't have much historical evidence to support the contention, they must have joined sometimes in such contests of physical strength. Fighting bouts were held between young boys and the Prophet was himself the witness of such a challenge on the eve of the battle of Badr.

The Prophet and his Companions presented a fine example of fully developed personalities, physically and morally. Some of them were styled as ' Kamil', a title used in the days of Jahiliyyah for a person who was a poet, a warrior, a scribe, a swimmer, an archer at the same time. Sawid bin Samar was named Kamil for this very reason. The children of Medina had plenty of leisure to indulge in frolic and play and we come across frequently among the Traditions accounts of chance encounters of the Prophet with groups of playing children. They never scurried away at his approach in alarm; as they did sometimes in case of Umar. They would continue with their pastime and the Prophet would always greet them with a kind word when he approached them.

He had the broad sympathy to enter the heart of the child and share his joys and sorrows, his interests and activities. He was very indulgent to young persons whom he sent on business but who were attracted by the children playing on the way and joined the riotous fun. A young friend, the young often tender his condolence on the loss and sympathise with him on his sad bereavement. According to Ibrahim, the Companions allowed the children to play with all kinds of games and pets with the exception of dogs.

Glorious Playing : Once the Prophet intended to present the children of Medina with a glorious plaything in the form of the Evil one, tied to a pillar in the Prophet's mosque. The episode reveals his implicit faith in childhood and the high trust which he reposed in the strength which lay in the inborn innocence of human nature as it comes from the Creator. We can trust the child to meddle, nay to frolic with Evil and he is bound to come out unscathed from such a dangerous pastime! So secure is he in the stronghold of his nature and innocence.

Horse with Wings : Young girls in their, days had toys as fantastic and interesting as girls of any other age. Aishah kept a store of all her playthings and after her marriage, now that she had grown into a woman, she kept these dear little things carefully hidden behind a curtain. Once the Prophet discovered her cherished treasure by chance and found a winged horse among the toys. "A winged horse! Has a horse wings? asked he. "Yes", said Aishah, "I have heard that Solomon's steed was winged." Thereupon the Prophet burst into laughing. The Tradition throws some light on the place of educative material in the system of Islamic education.

Health Care

Health according to a Tradition of the Prophet is a Khaslah or an inborn natural tendency of the physical system and he described its neglect as a case of swindling or 'Ghabn against the system. "There are two 'Khaslat in which many a people commit misappropriation. They are *sihat* (health) and *Faraghat* (freedom from want).

One who begins his day with sanity of his health and the security of his flock, and has enough to feed himself is like one who has the entire world at his command.

Health is the first blessing from above about which man will be questioned in the next world implying thereby, that the first charge he shall have to account for will be his contravention of the rules of health.

According to this Tradition, the following query will be posited to Man:

> Didn't I set right your physical frame and refreshen it by means of cool water.

Most of the Muslim prayers include an invocation on the Almighty to bless man with good in this world and the next. The good in this world is generally interpreted as good health.

The Prophet had said, Ask from God Faith and Afiyah (health), because Faith is a guarantee against punishment in the next world and health provides security from the ailments in the present.

Elsewhere he has said, Ask for *Ufw* (reprieve), *Affiyah* (security in the present) and *Maafat* (security in the future) thereby seeking good for the past, the present and the future.

Afiyyah and Maafat have been interpreted by Ibn Qayyim as referring to good health in the present and the future.

Prevention is always better than cure and in one of the Traditions, the Prophet has issued an injunction which tantamounts to security measures against the propagation of disease, through 'germ carriers. Although he has insisted upon visitations of the sick by those sound in health, he has disallowed the sick to visit those who are sound in health (Abu Hurayrah).

The world of early Islam knew something about epidemics and how their contagion was carried from one place to another. A Tradition narrated on the authority of Usamah bin Zayd, who was brought up from his early childhood in the family of the Prophet, says, "Plague is one of the inflictions which came down upon the Jews and on the people who lived previous to them.

Whenever you come to know of an outbreak of plague in a particular area, you should not enter it. And in case it breaks out in the area where you happen to be, you should not leave the area in panic."

He had issued special instructions as regards lepers and had advised that while talking with a leper you should stay off at a distance of one spear-length or two.

First Aid : As regards actual treatment of disease, collection of Traditions always comprise a chapter on the treatment of disease. They prescribe very simple and naive treatment of a few common ailments.

Countless generations of commoners, scholars are students have followed these instructions. They develop in the average individual a consciousness of his health problems and a mental awareness to study the functions of the organism in an intelligent manner. The main outcome was to emancipate the individual to some extent of that blind faith in the medical man, a subject which has provided material for scathing criticism for Bernard Shaw in his Doctor's Dilemma.

Treatment of Diseases : The treatment prescribed by the Prophet consisted of two kinds, physical and spiritual, and one of his sayings on this subject provides a perennial source of hope and comfort for the sick, "For all ailments, there is a treatment" (Muslim).

On another occasion he was consulted by some Arabs of the desert on the treatment of disease and he said, "O Believers in God, treat your maladies because there is no ailment for which God has not created a treatment with the exception of old age. One who makes an effort to know, learns it up and one who does not, continues to be in a state of ignorance."

This Tradition urges upon men to make a quest for medical knowledge because it is possible for them to make progress and reach perfection in the art of healing.

According to Hadrat Ibrahim, medical practitioner is one who has been elected by God to bring solace to the heart of the afflicted, a proud privilege which would inspire the heart of any member of the medical profession.

Once Hadrat Ibrahim asked the Lord, "Whence is the malady, God replied "From me". Thereupon Ibrahim said "And what for is the physician." The reply came "He is the person through whom I send the remedy."

Holy Prophet's Medicines : The chief works on Traditions always include a chapter on medicine and according to Zarnuji, every scholar should have some knowledge of medicine for keeping his physical frame in good order and he recommends a treatise on medicine called 'Tib-an-Nabi' (Pharmacopeia of the Prophet) written by Sheikh-al-Anam Abul Abbas-al-Mustaghfari.

According to one of the Traditions, there are only two kinds of knowledge, the knowledge of *Adyan* (Religious) and the knowledge of *Abdan* (Bodies); a proper knowledge of the treatment of disease for those who professed it appears to be a religious obligation from a tradition wherein the Prophet had decreed *Dit* (monetary compensation) in case of the demise of a person treated by a quack. "A person who treats others without a proper knowledge of medicine shall be held responsible for the death of a person who died in his hands and he must pay the monetary compensation."

The Prophet treated sometimes simple ailments and his treatment was often coloured with a pleasant sense of humour. Once an individual suffered from stomach-ache and his brother came to consult the Prophet who prescribed honey. The man returned thrice and reported no improvement in the condition of the patient. On his fourth visit, the Prophet told him that God is True while his brother's stomach was false. He advised him to give him a dose of honey once again. This time there was a marked improvement.

Ibn Khaldun views the whole subject in a genuinely scientific perspective, worthy of the great thinker. In his opinion, the treatments prescribed by the Prophet cannot have the force of religious injunctions because his mission was not to propagate the art of medicine. But these treatments can be used for the purpose of faith healing, not because they are strictly in accordance with the principles of medical science but because faith and belief play a great part in medicine. Ibn Khaldun supplies thereby the psycho-therapic basis of such a treatment.

Psychological Treatment : And in fact his approach towards disease and ailments had a deep psychological and moral significance. He took the period of ailment as an extremely pliable period in the moral sense. It seems that the lowering of the physical level of activities raised other levels and in some cases a person is more prepared for an inner revolution during an illness than at any other period of his life.

According to a Tradition, "Allah causes the sins of the sick to drop away just as the tree drops its leaves (in autumn.)"

He emphasized the edifying influence of disease on another occasion when he visited an ailing woman who was cursing fever in her delirium. The Prophet said :

> "Don't you curse the fever because it cleans men of impurities as a furnace purifies iron, and even a person who is pricked by a thorn or with something slightly more painful will receive the reprieve of one sin from Allah."

All the Traditions concerning the sick have been listed by the collectors of Traditions under the heading "Religious reward for the Muslim who is afflicted by an ailment or other troubles."

These Traditions have a high psychological value for the patient. They release within the inner being of the patient, tremendous reserves of physical and moral energy. The lowered level of physical energy is supported and strengthened by the moral and vice–versa.

In that extremely sensitive and emotionally exercised frame of mind, the patient realises that he is losing in physical vigour and as a technique of psychological compensation, he makes an effort to balance it by gaining in moral stamina. In this pliable mood he regains faith and confidence in his moral and thereby in his physical self. He resolves to do more good and the resolve has a healthy reaction on his physical frame. The physical basis when renewed reacts once again on the moral and in this way the process of his physical and moral renewal continues. It is specially helped by the psycho pathological conditions of the patient.

Traditions like those given above stimulate in the patient the first beginnings of an inner revolution which is sustained in spite of failing energy and is brought to a certain culmination either in convalescence or even in his final collapse.

24

Fiscal Aspects

One of the chief sources of income for the maintenance of these institutions was the monetary assistance by the state, which was offered without any restriction of code rules or grant-in-aid regulations ; this help was rendered in a rich variety of forms.

There were rulers, who had allocated a certain percentage of their annual revenue for educational purposes. For instance Nur-ud-Din Zangi used to spend the entire revenue of the town of Damascus on its colleges and mosques, half of the proceeds went for the maintenance of the Friday mosque while he divided the other half into eleven parts, two of which were allocated to the Shafiyya and Hanafiyya colleges. Ibn Batuta mentions the ease of a Sultan in Asia Minor, who devoted one-third of his revenues to the maintenance of colleges and monasteries in the realm.

There were others, who made grants in a lump sum for education and works of public welfare. The grand Vazir Nizam-ul-Mulk had earmarked 700,000 Dinars annually from the public exchequer for his college in addition to an equal amount of grant which came from his privy purse. He had settled one-tenth of his private income on educational institutions.

It is related that once Malik Shah, his master criticised the lavish expenditure which he had made on the college. In his opinion, he could raise such an army with the help of that money, which would have razed Constantinople, the stronghold of the

Byzantine Empire to the ground. The great Vazir was deeply moved by his remarks and told the king that the blade of his soldier's sabre did not exceed two yards in its swoop while their arrows could not reach beyond three hundred footsteps, but he was rearing up an army the shafts of whose prayers will scale the very heavens.

ibn Zubayr visited Egypt during the reign of Salah-ud-Din and has supplied instructive details of the patronage of learning by the king. According to him, the Sultan defrayed the entire expenses of the colleges of Misr and Cairo from the public treasury and the total budget came up to 2,000 Egyptian Dinars or 4,000 Momina per mensem. In addition to this, the expenses of the wandering scholars and the aliens who visited Egypt in pursuit of learning were met from the state coffers. Every person, who came to Alexandria in search of knowledge was supplied well furnished residential quarters and was provided with a generous allowance. He had the facilities of Turkish bath and medical attendance at home or in the hospital, free of charge.

Budget for Education

According to a royal decree, any person founding a college in the town of Damascus was to be paid the bill for its total expenditure from the royal treasury. The salaries of the teachers, who taught in the institutions within his kingdom amounted to 300,000 dinars annually and the amount was paid from the public exchequer.

Nur-ud-Din Zangi, his able successor, who was renowned for his love of learning went one better. In addition to earmarking a portion of the revenue for educational purposes he made rich endowments from his privy purse. He spent eighteen thousand Suria Dinars per mensem on the college teachers of Damascus and Allepo and twenty two-thousand Dinars on the mosques and colleges of Himat and Hims. These endowments were maintained long after he had passed away. In certain cases, the ruling princes allocated salaries to the teachers and in others assigned to them the proceeds of the property given in endowment. Sultan Salah-ud-Din had sanctioned a monthly salary of eleven Dinars for the principal of Sayufiyya College. The Qamhiyya College or "the College of the Wheat" received its name from the proceeds in kind which came from the property endowed by Sultan Salah-ud-Din for the purpose of teachers' remuneration.

While the average philanthropist, so common in the Middle ages founded a college or two, there were large hearted benefactors like Nizam-ul-Mulk, who laid the foundation of a whole network of such institutions and there is at least one instance where another Maecena of the age planned a whole town for the advancement of learning.

Rashid-ud-Din Fadhlullah, the Prime Minister of the Mongol ruler Ghazan Khan founded at Tabriz a city named Rab-i-Rashidi and his bounty attracted the greatest scholars and most eminent professional practitioners. There were 200 Quran readers with fixed salaries for reciting the Holy book and they had forty selected acolytes for training. The scholar's street provided accommodation for four hundred savants with suitable salaries and allowances, who directed and supervised the studies of one thousand students, who had flocked from distant lands for education and instruction. There were fifty skilful physicians, renowned practitioners in various systems of medicine, who resided in the street of the Healers and had ten students assigned to each with definite duties in the hospital.

The endowments made by the rulers from the public exchequer or their privy purse took various forms, according to the popular usage in the country or the conditions under which the endowment was made. A common practice was to assign the proceeds of income from arable lands or other property to a particular foundation and when Caliph Mustansir Billah opened his college, he endowed it with a number of villages and other property; whose annual income exceeded 70,000 Mithqals in gold. A list of the names of these hamlets is available in Zahabi.

Government's Role

Sometimes the ruling class made endowments for the benefit of some renowned college outside the kingdom and Al-Azhar has been the beneficiary of such an endowment by a Tunisian ruler.

There were also other heads of public revenue which were earmarked for educational purposes. Jahangir, the Mughal ruler of India decreed that all the property left by a trader, who had died in the kingdom of the Great Mughal and which lapsed to the Public Treasury in absence of any legal claimant was henceforth to be utilised for the foundation, maintenance and rehabilitation of educational institutions and other works of public welfare. In the words of the author of Naasir-i-Jahangiri, the Farman had a profound influence in tenanting once again those colleges and schools which had turned into a wilderness in the past.

But even more important than the endowments and benefactions of the ruling class and the aristocracy was the active support and help of the people and the spirit of reverence and love for learning which inspired them ; therein lay the chief strength of the Islamic educational system.

One of the earliest colleges was established through private donations when the people of Nishapur invited the great divine Abu Bakr Foruk to their town and subscribed generously for the building of a college for the savant. The accounts of important towns of the Islamic world glow with a rich and varied description of the colleges raised through the benefactions of private individuals.

It appears that in certain cases, trade guilds and other social groups were responsible for establishing educational institutions of the higher grade. A number of colleges were associated with the names of trade guilds and although in the case of the college of Warraqin in Misr we know definitely that it received its name because it was located in the street of Warraqin, the same may not apply to the case of the two colleges founded in the town of Allepo, a great industrial centre where such guilds must have been rich and influential. These two institutions were called the college of the glass makers and the college of the ironsmiths respectively.

According to Ibn Khaldun, the usage of making endowments for educational purposes was popular in Egypt among the aristocracy. The chief motive in his opinion was the preservation of the property in the interest of the eldest son who was to manage the trust on behalf of the institution for which it had been made. But he adds that all were not actuated by this motive and the tradition of making charitable donations for education was getting strong in the country. These benefactions took various forms and included arable land, gardens, inns, street shops, Turkish baths and even flour mills. Sometimes savants and scholars of means made a personal adventure in this field and laid foundation of the colleges which were erected and maintained by themselves. Ibn Batuta mentions a family of learned scholars who maintained a College in their home town and the family members formed the teaching staff of the institution.

As a general rule there were no restrictions on the persons who could avail of the financial assistance given out of the income of an endowment, but in case the benefactors had stated clearly the conditions which were to be fulfilled before an allowance was granted, they were adhered to by the Nazir (Manager) of the Waqf. For instance certain donors made endowments in favour of a particular sect while in one case at least the benefactors had clearly stated that it was exclusively meant for the Arabs. But such individual distinctions were not a common feature of the endowment system. Sometimes the donor indicated in the deed a clear preference for people coming from a particular area and it was not necessary that they should be his compatriots. Sultan Nuruddin Zangi for instance made an endowment in Damascus for the people of Maghrib.

The management of these trusts and endowments rested entirely in the hands of the teachers of the college and in the accounts of these colleges one invariably comes across the phrase, "endowed in favour of the savants of the Hanafite, Shafiite or Malikite faith." The endowment was managed by the teachers in most cases through a Nazir. According to Ibn Zubayr there were thirty colleges in Baghdad whose endowments were managed by the teachers themselves. In the case of the Nizamiyya, the first manager of the trust was the son of the founder, Khawaja Abu Nasr bin Nizam-ul Mulk, who managed the property with the help of the teachers.

Even in the presence of a department of public endowments in the country, some part of its management remained in the hands of the teachers. For instance in the Al-Azhar, the heads of the various Rawaqs or hostels have been performing the function of the manager for the trusts partially while the major portion of the trust was under the supervision of the State department. But this department is a recent addition to the system of administration and in all probability, the teachers held undivided responsibility for the management of the endowments in the past.

Sometimes the State held judicial enquiries into the terms of the Waqf deed in order to see that the income is being utilised for the specific purposes indicated by the benefactor. There is the case of Nuruddin Zangi how he made a public enquiry into the Waqf deed of the great Mosque of Damascus in the presence of all the savants and chief personages of the town and how the finest and most subtle distinctions of law were thrashed in the presence of the august assembly.

Role in Education

As a general rule the Waqf deeds were honoured by the kings and the courts and they were respected by the public opinion. But there were exceptions and endowments were sometime misappropriated by unscrupulous persons although the irresistible pressure of public opinion got the wrong redressed in most cases. The history of the college of Amir Jamaluddin Astadar in Cairo indicates the vicissitudes through which a Waqf deed might pass.

The founder of this college had established six chairs for various branches of learning and had endowed them in a magnificent manner. Every pupil pursuing a course of study in the college was to receive three Ratl of bread daily and thirty dirhams per mensem as stipend while the teachers received a salary of three hundred dirhams a month and the surplus of the proceeds of the trust was to go to his progeny. The founder did not own the site personally but obtained it in exchange for a tract owned by the State.

Upon his death doubts were raised about the legitimacy of the exchange and the conditions of the Waqf deed and when the judges decreed the deed null and void, the king Malik Nasir purchased the site for 12000 dinars from the descendents of the founder and ordered the cancellation of the waqf deed. A new Waqf deed was drawn up whereby the clause which made the descendants of the founder, the beneficiaries of the surplus was abrogated. A portion of the property left by the founder which could suffice for meeting the conditions of the trust was retained for the college while the rest was partly constituted into a trust in the interest of his progeny and partly made into an endowment for the tomb of the founder. When Malik Nasir died, the inheritors who were highly influential people got it annulled in their interest and the endowment reverted to them as trustees. This incurred the indignation of some mystics who belonged to the college and they proved in the court, that the original founder had appointed katib-al-sir a state functionary as the trustee and the inheritors had no claim to the property. The matter came to a close when the management of the trust finally reverted to the State functionary, who had been entrusted with this duty according to the original deed.

Miqrizi, from whose book the account has been taken gives a detailed account of the proceedings of the case at its various stages. The whole episode throws light on the scrupulous care taken in preserving the form if not the, spirit of the educational and religious trusts and a genuine desire of the people to utilise the proceeds of a Waqf for the specific purposes for which it bad been made.

Bibliography

Abbas, Abdullah Nadwi : *Learn the Language of the Holy Quran,* Kitab Bhavan, New Delhi, 2002.

Abdali, M.R. : *Scientific Thought in Islam,* Pious Publications, Hyderabad, 2001.

Acquinas, St. Thomas : *The Political Ideas of Islam,* Hafner Publishing Company, New York, 1953.

Adams, C.C. : *Islam and Modernism in Egypt,* Oxford University Press, New York, 1953.

Aghanides, N.P. : *Mohammedan Theories of Finance,* Oxford, New York, 1916.

Ahmed, Hasanuddin : *Social Justice in Islam.* Goodword Books Pvt. Ltd., New Delhi, 1990.

Ahmad, Ilyas : *Social Contract and the Islamic State,* Urdu Publishing House, Allahabad, 1940.

Ahmad, Imtiaz : *Ritual and Religion among Muslims in India,* Manohar Publishers, New Delhi, 1984.

Ahmad, Moinuddin : *Religions of Mankind,* Kitab Bhavan, New Delhi, 1994.

Ahmad, Zubaid : *The Contribution of Indo-Pak to Arabi Literature,* Royal Pub., Lahore, 1968.

Antony, G.N. Flew : *Wants or Needs : Choices or Commands,* Allen & Co., Paris, 1953.

Anwarullah : *The Islamic Law of Evidence,* Kitab Bhavan, New Delhi, 2000.

Arnold, Thomas : *The Legacy of Islam,* Oxford University Press, New York, 2000.

Asad, Muhammad : *The Principles of State and Government in Islam,* University of California Press, California, 1961.

Athar, Ali : *Mughal Nobility under Aurangzeb*, Pupular Prakashan, Bombay, 1968.

Azad, G. Murtaza : *Judicial System of Islam*, Kitab Bhavan, New Delhi, 1994.

Aziz, Noomi Kurtha : *Prisoners of War and War Crimes*, Deep Publications, Lacknow, 1980.

Bagby, Philip : *Culture and History*, University of California Press, California, 1991.

Baksh, S. K. : *Politics in Islam*, Kitab Bhavan, New Delhi, 2003.

Beckett, Katharine Scarfe : *Perception of the Islamic Word*, Cambridge University Press, New Delhi, 1992.

Berkey, Jonothan P. : *The Formation of Islam : Religion and Society in the Near East*, Cambridge University Press, New Delhi, 1990.

Bhatia, H. S. : *Studies in Islamic Law, Religion and Society*, Deep & Deep Publications, New Delhi, 1997.

Brockelman, C. : *History of the Islamic People*, G.P. Putnam's Sons, New York, 1947.

Browne, G. Edward : *Islamic Medicine*, Goodword Books Pvt. Ltd., New Delhi, 1996.

Bucaille, Maurice : *The Bibal, Quran and Science*, Kitab Bhavan, New Delhi, 2004.

Chiragh, Ali : *The Proposed Political Legal and Social Reform under Muslim Rule*, Popular Prakashan, Bombay, 1883.

Cook, Michael : *Forbiding Wrong in Islam : An Introduction*, Cambridge University Press, New Delhi, 1985.

Daniel, N.A. : *Islam : Europe and Empire*, University Press, Edinburgh, 1966.

De, Laet : *Description of India and Fragment of Indian History*, Oxford, New York, 1963.

Dhagamwar, Vasudha : *Law, Power and Justice : Protection of Personal Rights under Islam*, Popular Prakashan, Bombay, 2001.

Durrani, F.K.K. : *Muhammad (PBUH) the Prophet*, Oxford, New York, 2001.

Elliot and Dowson : *History of India*, Ali & Co., Aligarh, 1952.

Fuller, J.F.C. : *Decisive Battles of the Western World,* Oxford, New York, 2000.

Gairdner, W.H. Temple : *Al-Ghazzali's Mishkatul-Anwar : the Niche for Lights,* Oxford, London, 1915.

Gellner, E. : *Doctor and Saint,* University of California Press, Berkeley, 1972.

Gibbon, Edward : *History of the Decline and Fall of Roman Empire,* Oxford, New York, 2000.

Gilsenam, Michael : *Recognizing Islam,* MacMillan, London, 2001.

Grunebaum, Gustave Edmund Von : *Unity and Variety in Muslim Civilization,* University of Chicago Press, Chicago, 1955.

Haqq, Enamul : *Muslim Bengali Literature*, Dar-ul Ishaat, Karachi, 1957.

Harun, Yahya : *Islam : the Religion of Ease,* Goodword Books Pvt. Ltd., New Delhi, 1993.

Hasan, Mushirul : *Islamic, Communities and the Nation : Muslim Identities in South Asia and Beyond,* Manohar Publishers , New Delhi, 1998.

Hasan, Ibn : *The Central Structure of the Mughal Empire*, Adam Pub., New Delhi, 1980.

Hasrat, B.J. : *Dara Shikoh: Life and Works*, Madan Lal & Co., New Delhi, 1982.

Heath, T. L. : *Aristarchus of Samos*, Oxford, New York, 1913.

Herbert, Friedman : *The Amazing Universe*, National Geographic Society, Washington D.C., 1980.

Hodgson, G.S : *The Order of Assassin*, Oxford, New York, 1955.

Huart, C. : *Histoire des Arabes*, Routledge & Kegal Paul Ltd., Paris, 1911.

Hurgronje, C. Snouck : *Selected Works,* Allen & Co., Leiden, 1957.

Husaini, H.A. : *The Religious thought of Mir Syed Ali Hamadani,* Al-Hamra Publishers, Srinagar, 1979.

Hussain, M. Hadi : *Imam Abu Hanifah : Life and Work,* Kitab Bhavan, New Delhi, 2001.

Imamuddin, S. M. : *Arab Muslim Administration,* Kitab Bhavan, New Delhi, 1984.

Iqbal, Muhammad : *The Reconstruction of Religious thought in Islam,* Oriental Publishers. Delhi, 1980.

Jabir, Ibn Hayyan : *Musannafat em-al-Kimiya,* A. B. C., & Co., Paris, 1928.

James, Conrnell and John Surowiecki : *The Pulse of the Planet,* Crown Publishers, U.S.A. 1972.

Jamila, Khatun : *The Face of God,* Adam Pub., New Delhi, 1996.

John, J. Hue and John L. Esposite : *Islam in Transition,* Oxford, New York, 1969.

Kalerji : *From War to Peace,* Oxford, New York, 1991.

Khaja, Khan : *Studies in Tasawwuf,* University of Madras, Madras, 1923.

Khan, Inayat : *Mysticism of Sound,* Pilgrims Book House, New Delhi, 1997.

Khan, N. M. Yamin : *God Soul and Universe in Science and Islam,* Kitab Bhavan, New Delhi, 1993.

Levonian, L. : *Studies in the Relationship between Islam and Christianity,* University Press, Millennium Pub., London, 1940.

Lewis, Bernard : *The Emergence of Modern World,* Millennium Pub., London, 1961.

Mac, Closky : *Pacts for Peace,* New Century Pub., London, 1980.

Maudoodi, S.A.A. : *Islami Education,* Islamic Book Foundation, New Delhi, 1999.

McIver, R.M. : *The Community,* Macmillan & Co., London, 1928.

Mohaghegh, Mahdi and Landolt, *Collected Papers on Islamic Philosophy and Mysticism,* Tehran, 1971.

Mommsen, T. : *Provinces of the Roman Empire,* MacMillan & Co., London, 1909.

Moreland, W.H. : *From Akbar to Aurangzeb,* MacMillan & Co., London, 1923.

Muir, William : *Early Caliphate,* Oxford, New York, 1970.

Murthy, T.S. : *Muslim : the Difficult Years,* Himalayan Books, Chandigarh, 1983.

Narayan : *Pan Islamism,* MacMillan, New York, 1953.

Nasr, Seyyed H. : *Sufi Essays,* MacMillan, London, 1972.

Nicholson, R.A. : *Tales of Mystic Meaning*, MacMillan, London, 1931.

Noorani, A.G. : *Islam and Jihad*, Manohar Publishers, New Delhi, 2002.

Palamer, E.H. : *The Quran*, Atlantic Publishers, New Delhi, 1996.

Philips, E.C. : *Politics and Society in India*, MacMillan & Co., London, 1963.

Qanungo, K.R. : *Dara Shikoh*, Modern Book Co., Calcutta, 1935.

Qureshi, I.H. : *The Administration of the Mughul Empire*, Feroz Pub., Karachi, 1966.

Rafiqi, A. Q. : *Sufism in Kashmir*, Ashish Pub., Delhi, 1977.

Raverty, H. G : *Selections from the Poetry of the Afghans*, MacMillan & Co., London, 1862.

Richard, Rowan : *The Story of Secret Service*, Oxford, New York, 1980.

Rizvi, S.A.A. : *Muslim Revivalist Movements in Northern India in the Sixteenth and Seventeenth Centuries*, Neeru Pub., Agra, 1965.

Rosenthal, E.I.J. : *Political Thought in Medieval Islam*, Cambridge, New York, 1962.

Sadiq, M. : *A History of Urdu Poetry*, MacMillan & Co., London, 1964.

Saksena, B.P. : *Educational Thought*, Vora Pub., Allahabad, 1958.

Saran, P. : *Provincial Government of the Mughals*, Deep & Deep Pub., Allahabad, 1941.

Saxena, V. K. : *Muslims and the Indian National Congress*, Discovery Publishing House, New Delhi, 1985.

Schacht, J. : *The Origins of Muhammadan Jurisprudence*, Clarendon Press, Oxford, 1953.

Schwartz, E. : *Science and Civilization in Islam*, Cambridge, London, 1966.

Shad, Abdur Rehman : *Muslim Etiquettes*, Idara Ishaat-e-Diniyat Pvt. Ltd, New Delhi, 1999.

Sharif, M.M. : *A History of Muslim Philosophy*, Feroz Pub., Lahore, 1993.

Sharma, S.R. : *Women's Education in Ancient and Muslim Period,* Discovery Publishing House, New Delhi, 1996.

Shemesh, A.B. : *Taxation in Islam,* MacMillan & Co., London, 1965.

Sherwani, H.K. : *Islamic Education,* Popular Prakashan, Bombay, 1968.

Siddiqi, M.Z. : *Hadith Literature,* Deepali Pub., Calcutta, 1961.

Sikandar, bin Manjhu : *Mirat-i Sikandari,* Department of History, Faculty of Arts, M. S. University, Baroda, 1961.

Smith, W. C. : *Modern Isiam in India : a Social Analysis,* Manohar Publishers, New Delhi, 1985.

Smith, M., Rabia : *The Mystic and her Fellow Saints in Islam,* Cambridge, London, 1929.

Smith, W. Cantwell : *The Cambridge History* of *Islam,* Cambridge University Press, New York, 1970.

Stanton : *Teaching of the Quran,* Discovery Publishing House, New Delhi, 1989.

Storey, C.A. : *Persian Literature* : *a Bibliographical Survey,* Lozac & Co., London, 1927.

Syed, Amir Ali : *The Spirit of Islam,* Royal Pub.,Lahore, 1979.

Syed, M. H. : *Human Rights in Islam,* Anmol Publications, New Delhi, 2004.

Syed, M. H. : *Impact of Islam,* Anmol Publications, New Delhi, 2003.

Syed, M. H. : *The Mysticism of Hazmali Fansuri,* A. Pub., Kuala Lumpur, 1970.

Tarn, W.W. : *The Greeks in Bactria and India,* Cambridge, London, 1938.

Temple, R.C. : *The Religious Policy of the Mughal Emperors,* MacMillan & Co., London, 1962.

Titus, M. : *Indian Islam,* Milford, New Delhi, 1979.

Tripathi, R.P. : *Some Aspects of Muslim Administration,* Vora Pub., Allahabad, 1959.

Ulama, Majlisul : *Islamic Hijaab,* Idara Ishaat-e-Diniyat Pvt. Ltd, New Delhi, 1997.

Underhill, E. : *Mysticism : a Study in the Nature and Development of Man's Spiritual Consciousness,* Oxford, New York, 1956.

Valliuddin, Mir : *The Quranic Sufism,* Motilal Banarsi Das Publishers, New Delhi, 1989.

Waheed, Akhtar : *Sufi Approach to the Problem of Alienation,* Wilson & Co., New Delhi, 1975.

Waines, Davids : *A Introduction to Islam,* Cambridge University Press, New Delhi, 1995.

Warmington, E.H. : *The Commerce between the Roman Empire and Arabs,* Faber & Faber Co., New York, 1939.

Watt, M. : *The Faith and Practice of Al-Ghazzali,* MacMillan & Co., London, 1953.

Watt, W.M. : *Muhammad at Mecca,* Oxford University Press, New York, 1953.

Wensick, A.E. : *A Handbook of Early Muhammadan Traditions,* Luzac & Co., Leiden, 1960.

Willoughby, W. : *Principles of the Constitutional Law of the United States,* Baker Voorthis & Company, New York, 1938.

Wolfson, H.A. : *The Philosophy of the Kalam,* Oxford, London, 1976.

Yusuf, Iblish and Peter Lambron Wilson : *Traditional Modes of Contemplation and Action,* University Press, Tehran, 1977.

Zafeeruddin, M.M. : *System of Modesty and Chastity in Islam,* Idara Ishaat-e-Diniyat Pvt. Ltd, New Delhi, 1995.

Zaydan, Jurji : *History of Islamic Civilization,* Kitab Bhavan, New Delhi, 1994.